Evolving Human Security Challenges
in the Atlantic Space

Nuno Severiano Teixeira and Daniel Marcos
Editors

Co-funded by the
Erasmus+ Programme
of the European Union

Nuno Severiano Teixeira and Daniel Marcos, eds., *Evolving Human Security Challenges in the Atlantic Space*

Jean Monnet Network on Atlantic Studies, 2019.

© Jean Monnet Network on Atlantic Studies, 2019

Distributed and available via Brookings Institution Press
https://www.brookings.edu/press/

ISBN 978-1-7337339-4-6

Cover Photograph: AKaiser, shutterstock.com

Contents

Part III—Forging Human Security Networks

Preface

We are pleased to present the book *Evolving Human Security Challenges in the Atlantic Space*, a collaboration among the institutions of the Jean Monnet Network on Atlantic Studies and the third text of this kind, resulting from the Network's research efforts.

The Jean Monnet Network on Atlantic Studies is an initiative across the four Atlantic continents by ten leading centres—many with Jean Monnet professorships and in countries identified by the EU as key strategic partners—aimed at the interdisciplinary exploration of three major Atlantic themes of particular relevance to the EU: energy, commercial interactions and challenges to human security.

The objective of the project is to create and develop a pan-Atlantic research network, to contribute to an emerging epistemic community on 'New Atlantic Studies', and to offer strategic perspectives for the design of energy, trade and security policies in the Atlantic world. The Jean Monnet Project is also supported and co-funded by the Erasmus+ Programme of the European Union.

The institutions involved in the Network or consortium are each vibrant centres of EU-related studies in their respective regions. Most have collaborated—recently as part of the FP 7 project "Atlantic Future"—on themes related to Atlantic issues and the role of the EU as a conspicuous actor in this space.

Fundação Getulio Vargas, through its International Intelligence Unit, FGV IIU, based in Rio de Janeiro, leads the consortium whose members are:

* Fundação Getulio Vargas, International Intelligence Unit – FGV IIU, Brazil

* Johns Hopkins University, School of Advanced International Studies - SAIS (Center for Transatlantic Relations, CTR), United States

* University of Pretoria, South Africa

- Universidade Nova de Lisboa, Instituto Português de Relações Internacionais – IPRI-NOVA, Portugal

- CIDE, Mexico

- Roskilde University, Denmark

- Orkestra - Basque Institute for Competitiveness, University of Deusto, Spain

- CIDOB, Barcelona, Spain

- Universidad Autónoma de Madrid, Spain

- Policy Center for the New South (former OCP Policy Center), Morocco

The Center for Transatlantic Relations of Johns Hopkins University SAIS led the first year's agenda on energy, focusing on the nexus between energy and transportation. The Fundação Getulio Vargas led the second year's agenda on trade and commercial issues. Instituto Português de Relações Internacionais (IPRI-NOVA) led the third year's agenda on human security issues.

As usual, the Project members wish to show their appreciation to the European Commission, that provided the funds which made this research and the related book publication possible. Though especially grateful to the team at the leading institution, in Lisbon, the Network partners have also participated, in a way or other, in the preparations and efforts that allowed the conference and the book come true.

It is our hope that the present work will continue to successfully propel this Jean Monnet Project, increasing its visibility and widespread impact.

The Network continues to pursue its goals to be a go-to resource on the contemporary role of the EU in the wider Atlantic space, advancing the comparative knowledge of integration processes in Europe and other Atlantic regions.

Nuno Severiano Teixeira and Daniel Marcos
in the name of all members of the Jean Monnet Atlantic Network

Contributors

Abdelhak Bassou is a Senior Fellow at the Policy Center for the New South, previously known as OCP Policy Center, who focuses on Security Studies and Strategies and Defense. He occupied several offices within the Directorate General of the Moroccan National Security where he was Borders' Division Chief from 1978 to 1993. He was the former Director of the Royal Institute of Police in 1998. He also served as the Chief of Regional Security (Errachidia 1999-2003, Sidi Kacem 2003-2005) and was also Head of the Central General Intelligence from 2006 to 2009.

Amal El Ouassif is a research assistant in International Relations and Geopolitics at the Policy Center for the New South in Rabat, Morocco. Prior to this, she worked as a programme coordinator at the Westminster Foundation for Democracy and served as a consultant in development policies with the office of the Deutsche Gesellschaft für Internationale Zusammenarbeit (GIZ) in Morocco.

Daniel Marcos holds a PhD in History of International Relations, Lisbon University Institute (2011). He is Researcher at IPRI-NOVA, where he works on Portuguese participation in NATO, from 1949 to 1976. He was Researcher at the Jean Monnet Network on Atlantic Studies, from 2016-2019. In 2008 he participated in the Decolonization Seminar, directed by William Roger Louis at the National History Center, Washington, DC.

Eloy Álvarez Pelegry is the Director of the Energy Chair at Orkestra, the Basque Institute of Competitiveness, located at Deusto University in Bilbao, Spain. Dr. Álvarez received his PhD in Mining from the Higher Technical School for Mining of Madrid (ETSIMM). He holds a bachelor's Degree in Economics and Business from the Complutense University of Madrid, and a Diploma in Business Studies from the London School of Economics. He has had a long executive career at the private sector as well as in the academic field as an Associate Professor at the Higher Technical School for Mining of Madrid (ETSIMM), the Complutense University of Madrid, and Deusto University.

Frank Mattheis is a researcher at the Institut d'études européennes (IEE), Université libre de Bruxelles (Belgium) and an associate researcher at the Centre for the Study of Governance Innovation, University of Pretoria (South Africa). He is trained in global studies (MA, PhD) and works on governance structures beyond the nation state in the fields of comparative regionalism and interregionalism. He has been involved in different books on the subject, such as *The New Politics of Regionalism* (Routledge, 2017) and *Fringe Regionalism* (Palgrave, 2018).

Gorm Rye Olsen is Dr. (pol.scien.) Professor in global politics, Institute of Social Sciences & Business, Roskilde University, Denmark. He has written widely on European Union-African relations, EU security politics and EU development aid policy. Recently he has also published on transatlantic relations and on the Africa policy of the United States. He has published on these themes in a range of international journals such as *European Security*, *Third World Quarterly*, *International Politics*, *Journal of European Integration*, *Cambridge Review of International Affairs* and *Journal of Contemporary African Studies*.

Jaime Menéndez Sánchez is a Mining Engineer (University of Oviedo) and a PhD Student at the Doctoral Programme in Business Management, Knowledge and Innovation at the University of the Basque Country (UPV/EHU). He is a researcher at the Orkestra-Basque Institute of Competitiveness since 2015, where he has been working on topics such as sustainable mobility, smart grids, air quality among other topics.

João Estevens holds a BA in Economics (NOVA SBE) and in Political Science and International Relations (FCSH/NOVA), postgraduate in Cultural Management and Programming (ECATI-ULHT) and in Intelligence Management and Security (NOVA IMS) and MA in Political Science and International Relations (FCSH/NOVA). PhD candidate in Global Studies at NOVA University (scholarship funded by FCT). His dissertation concerns the impact of democratization processes in state punitiveness. Currently he is a Researcher at IPRI-NOVA.

Joana Castro Pereira is a Junior Researcher at the Portuguese Institute of International Relations (IPRI-NOVA). Between January 2017 and April 2018, she was a Postdoctoral Fellow at the University of Brasília. She is the author of several publications on environmental politics and international relations, and co-editor of the book *Non-Human Nature in World Politics: Theory and Practice* (Springer, forthcoming).

Leonardo Paz Neves is a political scientist. He is International Intelligence Analyst at the International Intelligence Unit from the Fundação Getúlio Vargas and Lecturer at the Department of International Relations from the Ibmec College. He has a degree in social sciences from the Fluminense Federal University (UFF), a master's degree in political science, and a doctorate from the Institute of Economics of the Federal University of Rio de Janeiro (UFRJ).

Macarena Larrea Basterra is a senior researcher at Orkestra (the Basque Institute for Competitiveness) at Deusto University in Bilbao, Spain. She holds a Ph.D. in Business Advertising and Development from the University of the Basque Country. She has a Master's Degree in Management of Port and Maritime Businesses run by the University of Deusto in conjunction with the Basque Country School of Maritime Administration, and has a Degree in Business Administration and Management, specializing in Logistics and Technology.

Nuno Severiano Teixeira is Full Professor at NOVA University – Lisbon and Director of the Portuguese Institute of International Relations (IPRI-NOVA). He has been Visiting Professor at Georgetown University (2018-2019), Visiting Scholar at the Institute for European Studies, University of California, Berkeley (2004) and Senior Visiting Scholar at the Robert Schuman Centre for Advanced Studies, European University Institute – Florence (2006/2009). He served as Minister of Interior (2000/2002) and Minister of Defense (2006/2009) of the Portuguese Government.

Rafael de Arce is Professor of Econometrics at Universidade Autónoma de Madrid since 1994 and Professor Université Paris-Dauphine since 2004. He has been a visiting professor at various foreign universities such as Georgetown, Dresden, Southbank, Nancy and Florence.

Ramón Mahía is a Doctor in Applied Economics from the Autonomous University of Madrid. He is Professor of Multivariable Analysis in the Postgraduate of CIS. He is also a professor of Quantitative Methods for the analysis of information and Algorithms of information in various programs. With regard to academic research, his most relevant works are framed in the area of the study of migration and its economic significance.

Susana Ferreira holds a PhD in International Relations and International Security by the NOVA University of Lisbon and the UNED (Spain). Is a Research Fellow of the IPRI-NOVA and Research Associate of the IUM Research and Development Center (CIDIUM). Before that, she was a Visiting Scholar at the Institute for the Study of International Migration (University of Georgetown), and at the Instituto Universitario General Gutiérrez Mellado, with which she is closely involved.

Introduction

This is the third and final volume resulting from the Jean Monnet Network on Atlantic Studies, a project coordinated by the Fundação Getúlio Vargas and funded by the European Commission, under the Horizon 2020 research program. The project had three main clusters of research: energy, economy and human security. This volume addresses the human security dimension of the study on the Atlantic Basin.

The Atlantic Basin can be considered relatively peaceful in terms of military conflicts. The northern part of the region is politically stable and consolidated; the southern part is relatively more unstable with some military conflicts, especially in Africa. New political instability is emerging in the region, as the crisis of democracy is particularly felt in Venezuela, and in Southern Africa, with several moments of political transition, as in the case of Angola, Zimbabwe and South Africa. Broader challenges and issues that need to be addressed as matters of human security. The most pressing threats arising are political instability caused by fragile states, which increases also the humanitarian crisis and the multiplying of illicit trafficking (drugs, weapons, and human), as well as the flow of people, either legal or illegal.

This volume sheds new light in all these areas. The first part, "Human Security Threats in the Atlantic Basin", seeks to bring a new understanding on classical concepts and threats to human security. After a broader definition of the concept and the analysis of its evolution (Marcos and Teixeira), the chapters focus on the traditional challenges present in the Atlantic basin. From drug traffic to energy security, from the northern Mediterranean to the connection between fragile states and terrorism, we examine the different realities and answers across the Atlantic and its four continents. Bassou and Ouassif focus on assessing ways by which non-state actors, particularly terrorist networks, take advantage of the failure of states to proliferate and impose their own rules of the game. The developed countries' need for diversification of the energetic sources and its impact on the energy security is analyzed by Basterra, Pelegry and Sánchez.

However, there are new and intensive challenges to human security that could be left aside, and those are integrated on the second part of the volume. The most poignant are the migratory flows that course through this region, in several dimensions. Estevens and Ferreira both use comparative approaches in their chapters; Ferreira compares three migratory hotspots (the Central American caravans, the Venezuela humanitarian crisis and the so-called European migration crisis) to understand its impact in the region, whereas Estevens analyzes the strategic security documents of ten Atlantic countries to understand how they commit to the principles of human security. On another dimension of the migratory issue, Ramon Mahia and Rafael de Arce analyze the movement of people between urban centers, focusing on the metropolitan area of Mexico City. Leonardo Neves examines illicit flows of small arms and how they affect domestic and international politics. Then he investigates how the implementation of disruptive technologies can be used to support the fight against this threat.

In the final part of the volume, the authors focus on the possibility of "Forging Human Security Networks" within the Atlantic Basin. The main actors of the region have already developed several tools to deal with the threats and challenges concerning human security. However, do they or could they cooperate more and better? Is there an overlapping of the instruments at their disposal or, on the other hand, could they work together in order to maximize their results? These are the questions answered, in different regards, by the chapters in this third part. Mattheis focuses on the role of regional institutions as complements to other actors in the international system, which have a particular significance in the Southern Atlantic. On the other hand, Gorm Olsen focuses on US and EU policies towards Africa to conclude that there should much more cooperation between the two actors, but that is dependent on the evolution of the transatlantic relations, which have challenges of its own. Pereira shows the ways that the US, EU and Brazil have dealt with climate change governance, in particular with the policies that these actors have developed since 1992.

Most of the research that is now published in this volume was presented at the Human Security Workshop that took place in the end of 2018 in Lisbon. We wish to thank all the researchers present in the workshop, as well as to all the research centers who were part of the consortium.

Nuno Severiano Teixeira

Daniel Marcos

Part I

Human Security Threats in the Atlantic Basin

Chapter 1

From Security to Human Security:
The Evolution of the Concept and Current Perspectives
for the Atlantic Basin

Daniel Marcos and Nuno Severiano Teixeira

Security does not enjoy an established definition, and, as such, it is challenged from the academic point of view. This chapter seeks to understand, through the historical evolution of the concept of security, how it has evolved until the present day, in which the dynamics of human security play a fundamental role. As argued by Sakiko Fukuda-Parr and Carol Messineo, "human security is a concept that identifies the security of human lives as the central objective of national and international security policy." Actors other than states mark the pervasive dynamics of human vulnerability, which are increasingly present due to the new features of the conflicts. At the same time, new global threats such as poverty, disease, natural disasters and migrations demonstrate that state-centric security views do not meet the new security challenges of the contemporary world[1]. In the large basin of the Atlantic, the traditional security dynamics are not the main focus of instability. In fact, in this region, it is mostly the dynamics of human security that are present, carrying obvious risks to the stability of international security. In the final part of this chapter, we will address this issue with particular attention.

From Security to Human Security

The concept of security is an old one, and it has evolved over the past centuries. In a comprehensive way, we can define it as "protection from harm."[2] In the discipline of International Relations, the field of security studies began by focusing its analysis on two central dynamics: on the one hand, global security, which pertains to the protection and stability of the international system. On the other hand, national security, which addresses

---

1. Fukuda-Parr, Sakiko, & Messineo, Carol, "Human Security: a Critical review of the literature." In CRPD Working Paper no. 11, 2012, 2.
2. Andersen-Rodgers, David, & Crawford, Kerry, *Human Security. Theory and Action*. New York, Roman and Littlefield, 2018, 3.

3

the protection of individual states "from external harm and internal challenges or instability"[3].

In the theories of international relations, security studies began by associating security with 'national security', reflecting the close association with the realist school, for which the State was the main actor and referent for security—which means, "the protection of the state from external threats." Despite never losing its reference to the State, the term security is also connected to the idea of guaranteeing the safety of individuals against "violence or crimes, religious peace of mind, and financial measures to sustain a certain standard of living."[4] After the 1970s, and especially after the development of multilateral organizations, the traditional concept of security has also acquired a regional connotation. As Hideaki Shinoda puts it, "military measures and foreign policies to secure the independence of a state are not exclusive components of the term 'security.' The prevalence of national security discourses in the discipline of international relations ensues from the very modern recognition that the safety of a nation is the supreme mission for policy makers."[5]

These ideas developed from the moment when states became central to the architecture of the international system. In the late eighteenth and early nineteenth centuries, with the French Revolution and the Napoleonic Wars, threats to the state represented the most important security issues. This meant, according to MacFarlane and Khong, "the reification of the state—privileging state security over the security of individuals residing within it." Therefore, the centrality of the sate in terms of security "was the product of specific historical circumstances."[6]

With the emergence of the social contract, the state gradually took on the responsibility of protecting the fundamental rights of its citizens from external threats and internal instability, while maintaining its political and economic functions. In return, citizens would remain loyal to the state.[7]

---

3. Ibid.
4. Shinoda, Hideaki, "The Concept of Human Security: Historical and Theoretical Implications." In *Conflict and Human Security: A Search for new Approaches of Peace Building*. IPSHU English Research Report Series, 2004, 6.
5. Ibid.
6. MacFarlane, S. Neil, and Khong, Yuen Foong, *Human Security and the UN. A Critical History*, Indianapolis, Indianna University Press, 2006, 246. Emma Rotschild shows that, in reality, conceptions of security in Classical Antiquity combined a state perspective, but also individual. See more in Rotschild, Emma, "What is Security?." In *Daedalus*, 124:3, 1995, 61.
7. Andersen-Rodgers, David, & Crawford, Kerry, *Human Security. Theory and Action*. New York, Roman and Littlefield, 2018, 4-5.

Simultaneously, with the advent of nationalism, the 'nation' began to be understood as a living entity, and the dialectic between the nation and the individuals who compose it as something organic and the prime object of protection. However scarce its intervention in economic affairs might be, a state should never refuse to ensure the security of its nationals, from the military and political point of view.[8]

However, the very evolution of international historical circumstances has led to an influence of economic issues in the definition of the concept of security. The events of the first half of the 20th century are at the bottom of this. The liberal regimes felt gravely threatened both by the emergence of strong communist parties, especially after the Bolshevik Revolution, and by the social and political disbelief that followed the Great Depression of the 1930s. The answer was an increase in state intervention in the economy, with the implementation of policies such as the American 'New Deal', for example. Behind this notion was the premise that States were responsible not only for the political and military security of their citizens but also for their social wellbeing. Progressively, "economic and social security came to be recognized as an inalienable right of nationals," with states obliged to ensure it.[9]

Therefore, at the beginning of the twentieth century, the security paradigm once again changed. Until then, the balance of power was generally the guarantor of international stability, and this stability was achieved through adjustment between the great powers, which often played the destiny of small countries according to their interests. That is, national security was individual to each state and each state did what it felt necessary to guarantee it. However, after World War I, the idea of collective security emerged: the security of each state must be assured by the other states. Or put in another way: "national security of each state [was] a common goal that the entire international community ought to maintain."[10] This was the principle behind the League of Nations, which collapsed with World War II. However, the Cold War somewhat recovered the principle of collective security. Recognizing, on the one hand, the principle of the sovereign equality of nations, it ensured that "national security for each state should be respected." On the other hand, since only the superpowers could guar-

---

8. Shinoda, Hideaki, "The Concept of Human Security: Historical and Theoretical Implications." In *Conflict and Human Security: A Search for new Approaches of Peace Building*. IPSHU English Research Report Series, 2004, 7.
9. Ibid, 8.
10. Ibid, 8.

antee the national security of each state within its respective sphere of influence, it materialized the principle of collective security through a system of alliances, wherein NATO was the most successful example.[11]

At the same time, it was after the end of World War II that the internationalization of national security from an economic and social point of view became consolidated. The emergence of several international organizations after 1945 (such as UNICEF, WHO, World Food Program, etc.) signaled a widespread concern with people's economic and social wellbeing. According to Shinoda, "bilateral or multilateral aids between states expanded and created the notion that international agencies and industrial states are somehow responsible for economic and social security of developing states." The idea of public authorities responsible for political, economic and social security at national and international level was at the heart of the evolution of the concept of human security.[12]

Thus, since 1945, new attention has been given to economic and social aspects and the collective responsibility to protect the rights of individuals. This is the basis of the principles embodied in the Charter of the United Nations—"nations should act collectively to protect the freedom and dignity of individuals."[13] Despite this, the international Cold War system did not allow a *de facto* application of these principles, defended primarily by the United Nations. It is true that the concepts, norms, and foundational values of human security were already universalized. The emergence of human rights issues, as well as the emergence of new actors such as NGOs and groups of activists, continued throughout that period. Concerns about issues arising from globalization, including economic, technological and environmental development, have been the focus of international *think tanks*. However, bipolar competition did not allow changes in the centrality of the importance of states and national security—a matter of sovereignty and, therefore, protected from external interference in the internal affairs of states. It was the end of the Cold War and the emergence of various internal conflicts (Somalia, Bosnia, etc.) that paved the way for a genuine concern for the safety of individuals.[14]

---

11. Ibid, 9.
12. Ibid, 5-22.
13. Fukuda-Parr, Sakiko, & Messineo, Carol, "Human Security: a Critical review of the literature." In CRPD Working Paper no. 11, 2012, 4.
14. MacFarlane, S. Neil, & Khong, Yuen Foong, *Human Security and the UN. A Critical History*, Indianápolis, Indianna University Press, 2006, 138.

The theoretical formulations regarding the concept of security and security studies have followed this historical evolution. The concept of security has been used and defined in many different forms, which have evolved over the time. In the 1950s, in the height of the Cold War, security was regarded as something exclusive to the State—this was the perspective of the realist school—the referent of security was the State. In terms of International Relations, security meant studying State Security (National Security, in the case of the US, or National Defense, in the case of Europe). In this sense, security was related to "having": wealth, arms, power—economic power, political power, but mostly, military power. Security was seen as a commodity, and the more powerful you were, the more secure you would be.[15]

Following the spirit of the liberal school, authors such as Keohane and Nye introduced in the 1970s a different approach to security studies: they broadened the traditional concept to include non-state actors, thus shifting the paradigm of security from inter-state to transnational, where they identify interdependency as the main element to consider when analyzing the international system.[16] Departing from Karl Deutsch's concept of security communities, the liberal school argues that, through the communities of shared values, networks and multilateralism, it is possible to keep the peace. Deutsch contended that there were pluralist security communities with shared values that could contribute to achieve peace, even amidst international anarchy—the region of the North Atlantic and NATO[17] being the prime example of such communities. Deutsch's work is innovative not only because it contested the realist state-centric approach to international relations, but also and especially, because he introduces the regional dimension in security studies, replacing national security with regional security—and even cooperative security, which would be used only after the end of cold war. As a matter of fact, it was only after the end of the bipolar conflict that these concepts had the chance to emerge in the theory of security studies and become virtually overriding in the 1990s.

Indeed, the post-Cold War period brought an intense paradigm shift in terms of the conceptual definition of security, from being centered in the state to being focused on the individual and even on universal values.

---

15. David, Charles Philippe, *A Guerra e a Paz:. Abordagens contemporâneas da segurança e da estratégia*. Lisboa: Instituto Piaget, 2001, 32-35.
16. Keohane, Robert, & Nye, Joseph, *Power and Interdependence: World Politics in Transition*. London: TBS The Book Service, 1977.
17. Battistella, D., "L'apport de Karl Deutsch à la théorie des relations internationales." In *Revue internationale de politique comparée*, vol. 10(4), 2003.

Moreover, this paradigm shift will follow closely the evolution of the practices in this area of studies, analyzed later on in this chapter.

The Copenhagen School, centered on the works of Buzan, Weaver and de Wilde, further contributed to this paradigm shift.[18] These authors introduced two new concepts that would simultaneously broaden and deepen the concept of security. First, Buzan and other authors adopt a multisectoral approach to the concept of security, which included five sectors as referents to security: military security, political security, economic security, societal security and environmental security. Four of five of these sectors are non-military, i.e., they are not exclusively depending on the state to implement and ensure their security. In order to deepen the concept, they also include non-state actors as possible securitizing actors. Buzan and Weaver concur that the state plays a role in terms of security, but they shed the assumption that it stands as the only referent in terms of security studies.[19] In this same work, they present a new conceptual tool that would open the way to the development of an "analytical framework to study security": the concept of securitization.[20] This concept draws from the constructivist approach to international relations and identifies security as "a speech act: a concrete action that is performed by virtue of its being said."[21] In Weaver's own words, an issue can be securitized "not necessarily because a real existential threat exists but because the issue is presented as such a threat."[22] This shows that the perception of threat derives from a subjective dimension of that threat and that it is a social construction.

The importance of the historical context of the post-Cold War world should not be ignored. The theoretical considerations and its evolution are closely related to the events and scenarios of the 1990s. Therefore, the following paragraphs focus on that historical context and reality, in order to understand how the term security evolved until reaching "Human Security."

---

18. Buzan, B., Weaver, O., & Wilde, Jaap de, *Security: A New Framework for Analysis.* Boulder, Colorado: Lynne Rienner Publishers, 1998.
19. Ibid, 7-8.
20. Emmers, Ralf, "Securitization." In Collins, Alan, *Contemporary Security Studies.* Oxford: Oxford University Press, 2010, 136-151.
21. Mutimer, David, "Critical Security Studies: a Schismatic History." In Collins, Alan, *Contemporary Security Studies.* Oxford: Oxford University Press, 2010, 84-105.
22. Buzan, B., Weaver, O., & Wilde, Jaap de, *Security: A New Framework for Analysis.* Boulder, Colorado: Lynne Rienner Publishers, 1998, 24.

A historical evolution of the human security concept

With the end of the Cold War, the concept of human security begins to take root. Historically, the concept of human security has been associated with the 1994 Human Development Report on Human Security, drafted by Mahbub ul Hak under the UN auspices. The report argued that, over the previous decades, the concept of security had been interpreted narrowly, emphasizing the security of the territories from external aggressions, or as protection of the national interests and the external policies of the states, on the one hand, or against the nuclear threat, on the other. In this sense, it was focused more on the state than on the individuals. This report sought to build a bridge to the United Nations Charter, written in 1945, wherein the question of security rested on the dynamic between "freedom from want and freedom from fear." In other words, ensuring that individuals were free from violence and poverty.

As the report argued, human security was understood as a concern for human life and dignity, not the threat of weapons. It was also a universal concept, relevant to all people, whether from wealthy nations or poor states. It was focused on people, as the concern was about how they live in the societies they belong to, how they express their political and social choices, the freedom to access the market economy and what social opportunities they have, whether they live in peace or in conflict. In this sense, the report identified seven core elements that together developed the concept of human security: economic security, food security, health security, environmental security, personal security, community security, and political security. Once the bipolar conflict was over, it was now time to bring forth human development as the main concern for the international community.[23]

However, the comprehensiveness of the definition of human security embodied in the report generated deep criticism. As Sabine Akire points out, the main assessment was that, because of the unclear interconnection between human development and security, the report had, for many, an "idealistic" component and "naïve" recommendations. These criticisms helped to substantiate the concept of human security in two dimensions: a broad and a narrow one.

In relation to the first, starting with the 1994 Human Development Report, it argues that human security is "concerned with human vulnerability

---

23. Kaldor, Mary, "Human Security in Complex Operations." In PRISM, Vol. 2 (2), 2011, 2.

overall, and therefore encompasses all forms of threats from all sources." In other words, it includes, in addition to organized political violence, other forms of violence or threats such as natural disasters, diseases, climate change, hunger and economic problems[24]. This approach was embodied in the Commission on Human Security report in 2003. Building upon the definition presented in 1994, the report of this independent commission set up in 2000 sought to bridge the 'narrow' and 'broad' definitions of the concept. Refraining from listing all the threats to human security, it advanced with a set of elementary rights and freedoms that every human being should enjoy—as a "vital core." However, its main contribution was the emphasis on the need to involve multiple actors who went beyond the state, such as NGOs, regional organizations and civil society, in managing human security. In this sense, it has clearly shown that "the empowerment of people" was seen as "an important condition of human security," emphasizing that "security and human security are mutually reinforcing and dependent on each other."[25]

By contrast, the 'narrow' formulation advocates a less holistic view of human security. Assuming that the 'broad' version is too comprehensive to be useful, critics consider that human security focuses primarily on protecting the individual against political violence, on the one hand, and on the ability to intervene to obviate threats at the expense of long-term strategies and planning on issues of sustainability and human development, on the other. As a result, the threats to be addressed turn out to be relatively traditional, such as armed conflicts, human rights abuse, insecurity and the fight against organized crime. Contrary to the broad view, proponents of this approach seek to prevent the concept of human security from becoming a useless shopping mall of threats. Countries such as Canada have defended this position and contributed to the debate on Responsibility to Protect (R2P), which advocated the right of the international community to intervene in the internal affairs of states in the event of attempts against human security. To some extent, and in the light of the international context of the late twentieth century, when the intervention in Kosovo marked the international scene, this approach ended up guaranteeing a certain prevalence of the state in the protection of human life.

The main resistance to the adoption of these definitions came from states, fearing that such a broad definition of threats could create legitima-

---

24. Fukuda-Parr, Sakiko, & Messineo, Carol, "Human Security: a Critical review of the literature." In CRPD Working Paper no. 11, 2012, 5.
25. Ibid, 6.

cy for interventions that go beyond and override their national sovereignty. One of the initial premises of the concept of human security, as embodied in the 1994 Human Development Report, is the principle that "human security is easier to ensure through early prevention than later intervention." That is, it is less expensive and more efficient to try to prevent threats to human security from establishing risks and consolidating instruments for support, than to later try to nullify these threats. On the other hand, the various measures that have been implemented reflect a narrower or broader approach to the concept of human security. Interestingly, proponents of a more limited approach to the concept of human security, which refers merely to threats of violence, repression and human rights abuses, tend to point to responses around global policy initiatives. On the contrary, those who have a broader view of the concept of human security advocate a set of responses at the regional or even national level in the context of development aid cooperation.[26]

The case of Japan, which even had the initiative to create, along with the UN Secretariat, the United Nations Trust Fund for Human Security (UNTFHS), is a clear example of a broad approach to the concept of human security and type of threats it encompasses. Nowadays, Japan remains the champion of a broad approach to the concept and its officers are a top-level presence with the United Nations General Secretariat.[27] By contrast, Norway (besides the abovementioned Canada) has adopted narrower perspectives of the concept and has also included them in their foreign policy guidelines.[28]

The broader concept of human security is thus subject to a number of criticisms, namely that it is too vague and ambiguous, making it more difficult to operate. There is also a risk that such a broad definition might encourage "the application of military solutions or the illegitimate use of political, social and economic problems."[29] And this could lead to a culture of intervention on the grounds that the prevention of possible threats would justify any external intervention.[30]

---

26. Ibid, 11.
27. See, for example, the UNTFHS website: https://www.un.org/humansecurity/ [Consulted at 16 April 2019].
28. Alkire, Sabine, "A conceptual Framework for Human Security. Working Paper 2." Centre for Research on Inequality, Human Security and Ethnicity, CRISE, Queen Elizabeth House, University of Oxford, 2003, 20-21.
29. Fukuda-Parr, Sakiko, & Messineo, Carol, "Human Security: a Critical review of the literature." In CRPD Working Paper no. 11, 2012, 13.
30. Ibid, 11.

However, there are also those who find advantages in such a broad definition: it becomes easily adaptable to national or regional realities, a sort of adaptation to the national context where it is directly related to the local specificity of the population that it is supposed to protect. In addition, its methodology, dependent on the causality of the processes, allows the "policy makers to establish linkages between traditional military threats, non-traditional human security threats and human development and to create coherent policy responses that simultaneously mitigate insecurity and promote sustainable development."[31]

In sum, the emergence of concerns over human security in the post-Cold War era marked the end of the state's natural privilege over individuals—human beings are now at the center of security concerns—and the securitization of issues such as health and climate change naturally increased the concern and attention given to these topics as well as facilitated the distribution of resources for their protection. On the other hand, we see an incorporation of the concepts, both from the point of view of vocabulary, and from the point of view of local/regional application of its principles.[32]

Security threats in the Atlantic Basin

As we have seen above, the concept of security has evolved from pertaining exclusively to states, to a notion that addresses all that may threat individuals, including threats posed by states. In this sense, security has become transnational, as it encompasses previously disconnected areas such as economy, environment, health and food security. However, the type of answers demanded are also more expensive: there is a need for "complex, coordinated and costly approaches that often cannot be afforded" by individual countries or even regional organizations.[33]

The Atlantic basin can be seen as a highly cohesive region, with several elements of "shared culture and values," such as religion, language and human rights visions, which "have the potential to facilitate coalition building, or bilateral and multilateral security cooperation." Additionally, there is also space for an "urban and demographic revolution," as the Afri-

31. Ibid, 13.
32. Ibid, 14.
33. Kotsopolos, John, "The Atlantic as a new Security area? Current engagements and prospects for security cooperation between Africa and its Atlantic counterparts," *Atlantic Future Project*, 2014, p. 4. Available at http://www.atlanticfuture.eu/contents/view/the-atlantic-as-a-new-security-area [consulted in 22 April 2019]

can and Latin American societies are booming and expecting to double in size by 2050. It is also a region with high military capacities, as NATO remains at the "epicenter of security architecture with global reach." Finally, one cannot forget the importance of the Atlantic's economic and energetic dynamics[34]. In sum, one can say, "there are concrete elements of globalization, with people, commodities, technologies of transportation and communication creating specific interdependence links between the four shores of the Atlantic Space."[35]

Consequently, there are also common threats and security challenges within the region. The most wide-ranging are piracy, trafficking (whether of drugs, humans or arms), terrorism and political instability.

Piracy is often associated "with other organized criminal activities," and it turned out to be more important "as it became more violent and organized in the Gulf of Guinea (…), as pirates take advantage of poor maritime surveillance and still-incipient regional cooperation" in this area. At the same time, transatlantic drug trafficking flows also remain relevant security threats to both sides of the Atlantic. Exploiting "local weaknesses as deficient controls at ports and poor inspection equipment, South American drug cartels have targeted Atlantic waters as preferable transit routes for European markets."[36]

It is in West Africa where piracy is mostly felt. In 2014, piracy and armed robbery in the Gulf of Guinea represented a quarter of worldwide reported attacks. Maritime insecurity in this region affects more than a third of oil shipment of Africa per day, destined mostly to Europe and the United States. Thus, the major target in Gulf of Guinea Piracy is related to oil trafficking, whereas there are also some small theft episodes on the north coast of the Americas and in the Caribbean. Combating piracy has become more complex due to the increasing cooperation between criminal trafficking organizations and violent or extremist groups. "In order for governments to this cross-regional challenge, they will need to be able to monitor what is happening on the seas, detect illegal activities, and develop legal and

---

34. Lété, Bruno, "Addressing the Atlantic's Emerging Security Challenges." *Atlantic Future Project*, 2015, p. 3. Available at http://www.atlanticfuture.eu/contents/view/atlantics-emerging-security-challenges [consulted at 22 April 2019].
35. Teixeira, Nuno Severiano, & Marcos, Daniel, "A Historical Perspective of the Atlantic's Evolution." In Bacaria, Jordi and Tarragona, Laia (eds.), *Atlantic Future. Shaping a New Hemisphere for the 21st century: Africa, Europe and the Americas*. CIDOB, Barcelona, 2016, 10.
36. Seabra, Pedro, "Stretching the Limits? Strengths and Pitfalls of South Atlantic Security Regionalism." In *Contexto Internacional*, vol. 39(2) May/Aug 2017, 316.

administrative frameworks, as well as adequate coastguard capacities."[37] This is increasingly harder as some of the main countries affected by this piracy have political rivalries going on between them—there is mistrust among them because ongoing border disputes (in the case of West Africa countries) and states disagree on how to share the financial burden of the shared responsibilities.[38]

Another major threat to security in the Atlantic is the interconnection between organized crime, trafficking and terrorism. These features bring political instability to the region. As Daniel Hamilton puts it, currently, "flows of drugs, arms and cash flow across the full Atlantic space."[39] The flexibility and the ability to move quickly make these networks of organized crime relevant sources in the "increase in money laundry, corruption, which in turn erodes state authority and creates areas of unsecured, ungoverned or under-governed territory."[40] Arms trafficking, light weapons in particular, is on the rise in the region. On the one hand, this is in itself a problem (particularly felt in Mexico or Nicaragua, for example);[41] on the other, light weapons are traded/exchanged for drugs and natural resources (oil, precious stones, metals, timber), which is present, for example, in Central and West Africa.[42]

Drug trafficking remains a major threat to security in the Atlantic. The US and Europe continue to be the major consumers of cocaine, while three

37. Lété, Bruno, "Addressing the Atlantic's Emerging Security Challenges." *Atlantic Future Project*, 2015, 4. Available at http://www.atlanticfuture.eu/contents/view/atlantics-emerging-security-challenges [consulted at 22 April 2019].

38. IBID, 4-5. On the broader issue of piracy in Africa, see Sergi, Bruno S. & Morabito, Giacomo, "The Pirates' Curse: Economic Impacts of the Maritime Piracy." In *Studies in Conflict & Terrorism*, 39:10, 2005, pp. 935-952; Bueger, Christian, "Learning from piracy: future challenges of maritime security governance." In *Global Affairs*, 1:1, 2015, 33-42.

39. Hamilton, Daniel, "Promoting Human Security and Effective Security Governance in the Atlantic Hemisphere." In Hamilton, D. (ed.), *Dark Networks in the Atlantic Basin. Emerging trends and Implications for Human Security*. Center for Transatlantic Relations, Johns Hopkins University, Washington, 2015, p. ix.

40. Lété, Bruno, "Addressing the Atlantic's Emerging Security Challenges." *Atlantic Future Project*, 2015, 5. Available at http://www.atlanticfuture.eu/contents/view/atlantics-emerging-security-challenges [consulted at 22 April 2019].

41. Both Mexico and Nicaragua are profiled as moderate cases of threat (Tier II) by the Council on Foreign Relations' Center for Preventive Action. See *Preventive Priorities Survey 2019*. Available at https://www.cfr.org/report/preventive-priorities-survey-2019 [consulted at 22 April 2019].

42. Lété, Bruno, "Addressing the Atlantic's Emerging Security Challenges." *Atlantic Future Project*, 2015, 6. Available at http://www.atlanticfuture.eu/contents/view/atlantics-emerging-security-challenges [consulted at 22 April 2019].

southern American countries remain the world's producers: Columbia, Peru and Bolivia. There are two main routes for supplying US and Europe. Mexico and Caribbean Sea are the routes to the US. For Europe, there are two points of shipment: through Guinea-Bissau and Guinea, and other through the Benin. Besides this, there is an important circulation of cannabis in North Africa.[43]

However, more recently, we have assisted to a change in the consumption and trafficking routes, with African countries gradually becoming consumers, in addition to being part of the drug trafficking routes. Having in mind the particular characteristics of African societies, one might expect that "increased drug trafficking in Africa will lead to similar effects as seen in some Latin American communities."[44]

This upsurge in criminal activities has led to an increase in money laundering, which can have disastrous consequences in terms of the economic stability in the region. This has direct interaction with the global financial system and economic crises are increasingly endangering global economic stability. The International Monetary Fund (IMF) links these activities to the financial instability of national institutions (putting corruption in the center of the political frailty of certain states) and these problems can easily spread to other countries in the region or other parts of the world.[45]

In fact, political instability is also spreading in the Atlantic Basin. In the abovementioned *Preventive Priorities Survey 2019*, the Council of Foreign Relations attaches particular relevance to the high level of risk that the Venezuelan crisis represents. Civil unrest in Brazil (the survey was collected in November 2018) is also something that might be expected to spill over to neighboring countries. As noted by the report, for the first time since 2008, three Central and South America contingencies have been assessed. Besides Venezuela, also Mexico and Nicaragua were identified as posing

---

43. Ibid, 7. See also Hesterman, Jennifer, "Transnational Crime and Terror in the Pan-Atlantic: Understanding and Addressing the Growing Threat." In Hamilton, D. (ed.), *Dark Networks in the Atlantic Basin. Emerging trends and Implications for Human Security.* Center for Transatlantic Relations, Johns Hopkins University, Washington, 2015, 35-56.
44. Mouzouni, Mustapha, "Cooperation Against Transnational Crime: The Case of the Zone of Peace and Cooperation of the South Atlantic." In *Atlantic Currents: An Annual Report on Wider Atlantic Perspectives and Patterns*, German Marshall Fund and OCP Policy Center, 2016, 45 (42-56). Available at http://www.policycenter.ma/publications/atlantic-currents-annual-report-wider-atlantic-perspectives-and-patterns-1 [consulted at 22 April 2019].
45. Lété, Bruno, "Addressing the Atlantic's Emerging Security Challenges." *Atlantic Future Project*, 2015, 7. Available at http://www.atlanticfuture.eu/contents/view/atlantics-emerging-security-challenges [consulted at 22 April 2019].

moderate level threats due to "intensification of organized crime-related violence" (Mexico) and to the "consequences to the migration crisis in Central America" that the political violence and instability in Nicaragua might bring. Indeed, three Central and South American countries lead the rank of worsened countries in the Fragile States Index (FSI) 2019, produced by the Fund for Peace: Venezuela, Brazil and Nicaragua.[46] Venezuela faces a critical combination of "widespread human flight, a public health catastrophe, economic collapse, and significant crime and violence" that explains the rise in the FSI. On the other hand, Brazil is feeling the spillover effects of neighboring Venezuela, which add to the country's most recent political developments. Nevertheless, Brazil's score in the FSI has been worsening since 2013, which is explained as "far more deeply-rooted in a general economic malaise, rampant corruption, and crumbling public services that have seen Brazil's FSI score worsen for six straight years." Nicaragua was a case for some stability, but the events in 2018, when "hundreds were killed and thousands more disappeared" in clashes with the government forces in protests against Ortega's cuts in social security programs brought the country to a high level of frailty.[47]

The problem of fragile states, in terms of a broader security perspective in the Atlantic Basin, is that they have greater difficulty to "achieve and consolidate" any security or development gains, "further increasing these countries' vulnerability to shocks (whether financial, natural disasters, social unrest, political instability or violent conflict)."[48]

However, the possibility of political instability in the European Union is also envisaged in the Preventive Priorities Survey 2019, due to, "among other things, continuing populist and anti-immigrant sentiments as well as a disruptive exit by the United Kingdom" from the EU.[49]. The same can be said of the emerging populist regimes that are gaining more relevance in Europe, such as those in Poland and in Hungary.

---

46. Followed by United Kingdom, and other Atlantic countries like Togo, Cameroon, Honduras and Mali. See Fragile State Index 2019 Report, Avaliable at https://fragilestatesindex.org/wp-content/uploads/2019/03/9511904-fragilestatesindex.pdf [consulted at 22 April 2019].
47. Fragile State Index 2019 Report, Avaliable at https://fragilestatesindex.org/wp-content/uploads/2019/03/9511904-fragilestatesindex.pdf [consulted at 22 April 2019].
48. Faria, Fernanda, "Fragile States: Challenges and Opportunities for Atlantic Relations." *Atlantic Future*, 2014. Available at http://www.atlanticfuture.eu/contents/view/fragile-states-in-the-atlantic [consulted at 22 April 2019].
49. Council on Foreign Relations Center for Preventive Action, *Preventive Priorities Survey 2019*. Available at https://www.cfr.org/report/preventive-priorities-survey-2019 [consulted at 22 April 2019].

In fact, some analysts refer that the Venezuelan crisis illustrates some of the difficulties that the European Union faces in what regards its role as a global actor. The struggle to find a common position which would allow a commitment by the EU to the crisis was echoed by EU High Representative Federica Mogherini's declaration on minimum terms, underlining the EU's agreement "on one crucial point: 'the presidential elections that were held in (sic) last May in Venezuela were lacking democratic legitimacy'." If it could have a stronger position, Europe would "make a difference in a world in which the US, China, Russia, and other states are increasingly committed to the politics of raw power," according to ECFR's Pawel Zerka.[50]

Another security challenge faced by Atlantic concerns its energy infrastructures. In recent years, the Atlantic basin has become an important energy provider, both in terms of oil and hydrocarbons. A significant contingent of Atlantic nations has been relying on the trade of these products for their economic development. The main holders of oil reserves were Venezuela and Canada (having become 1st and 3rd worldwide producers), but countries such as Nigeria, Angola, Equatorial Guinea, the US, Brazil and Mexico should also be considered.[51] China is becoming a major net importer and aggressively seeks to secure oil supplies to from Africa and South America, although without any concerns regarding the "environmental impacts, revenue transparency and good governance."[52]

However, as the energy sector is becoming very important in economic and development terms, and countries are investing in infrastructure development plans, concerns with security are also rising. One of the most important issues for both governments, as well as for private companies, is "managing the security, safety and external threats that can affect the infrastructure." Attacks in the oil sector have cost billions of dollars in lost revenue, destabilized global energy prices and led to many environmental disasters along the West and Central coast of Africa[53].

---

50. Zerka, Pawel, *Europe should do better in Venezuela*. European Council for Foreign Relations (ECFR), 22.02.2019, available at https://www.ecfr.eu/article/commentary_europe_should_do_better_on_venezuela [consulted at 22 April 2019].
51. Kraemer, Andreas and Stefes, Christoph, "The changing energy landscape in the Atlantic Space." In Bacaria, Jordi and Tarragona, Laia (eds.), *Atlantic Future. Shaping a New Hemisphere for the 21st century: Africa, Europe and the Americas*. CIDOB, Barcelona, 2016, 87-102.
52. Lété, Bruno, "Addressing the Atlantic's Emerging Security Challenges." *Atlantic Future Project*, 2015, 8. Available at http://www.atlanticfuture.eu/contents/view/atlantics-emerging-security-challenges [consulted at 22 April 2019].
53. Ibid.

The energy sector is fundamental for the Atlantic Basin and its security is interconnected in many ways to the security of the whole region. An attack to any critical energy infrastructure would have a general impact on several security interests. In the first place, on the national security of the targeted country; secondly, on regional security and stability; thirdly, on the investment security of multinational oil companies; and lastly, on global energy security.[54] Therefore, these matters cannot be left to private companies' security systems, as it is usually done, as the threat at hand jeopardizes national and regional economic interests and human security in general.[55]

As such, and keeping in mind these different security threats, what are the existing security structures that could deal with them?

The integration of the South Atlantic is more difficult because the region is marked by a higher degree of fragmentation compared to the north—and NATO's continuity after the Cold War highlights this stability. But still, there are several initiatives that reflect certain security policy alignments and even institutional arrangements at the regional and sub-regional levels. According to Seabra, the prevalence of multilateral institutions in the security framework in South Atlantic can "prove to be problematic," as one tends to focus excessively on them—which adds to the fact that there are several of such bodies and institutions that "co-exist (…) without taking the next step of either additional institutionalization or shared sovereignty."[56]

Brazil and South Africa see their ever-increasing role in Latin America and Africa as a way to gain global influence. ZOPACAS (South Atlantic Peace and Cooperation Zone, created 1986, last meeting in Montevideo in 2013) is the main initiative so far bridging the gap in the South Atlantic security framework. This brings African and South American states together. Brazil is particularly interested in ZOPACAS since its new defense policy makes the South Atlantic one of its top priorities. Currently it has an action plan that boosts cooperation along nuclear non-proliferation, development and economic relations. Coordination among member-states is still incipient and there is wide variability in the capacity and political willingness of those states to make ZOPACAS the focal hub of the South Atlantic. There

---

54. Lété, Bruno, "Addressing the Atlantic's Emerging Security Challenges." *Atlantic Future Project*, 2015, 9. Available at http://www.atlanticfuture.eu/contents/view/atlantics-emerging-security-challenges [consulted at 22 April 2019].
55. Ibid.
56. Seabra, Pedro, "Stretching the Limits? Strengths and Pitfalls of South Atlantic Security Regionalism." In *Contexto Internacional*, vol. 39(2) May/Aug 2017, 306.

are other initiatives in the region, but they are often characterized by low degrees of institutionalization and weaker results.

The other regional institutions, such as African Union, ECOWAS or the Organization of American States, are interesting because they already work as *fora* for political coordination and consultation and have proven to be able to prevent and solve conflicts in the region. Additionally, they have all established extra-regional dialogues with the EU, the US or the UN.

Concluding remarks

As we have seen, the concept of security has evolved and changed over the time. It was deepened and broadened in its definition through the evolution of its practices, but also thanks to the development of different approaches and theories. From a state-centered approach, which characterized the realist theory, to the inclusion of societal and economic dynamics concerning non-state and global actors, we have now reached a broader concept of security: Human Security. This is a more comprehensive concept, which on occasion entails a military capacity, but which mostly concerns non-conventional responses. It is based on the belief that prevention is the best solution to fight possible threats and that states must work together with multilateral, non-governmental and regional organizations to prevent these threats (which very often come from non-state actors). As Dan Hamilton puts it, "[Governments] …must protect their society's critical functions, the networks that sustain them, and the connections those networks bring with other societies. These developments call for private-public partnerships and close interactions among governments, the private sector, the scientific community and non-governmental organizations."[57]

The Atlantic basin is an excellent example of how security issues have evolved to become full human security concerns. Although it is a very uneventful region in terms of inter-state conflicts, intra-state or transnational conflicts, however, are abundant, as are the threats posed by health epidemics, natural resources scarcity and migrations. The development of international and regional organizations, the cooperation between state and non-state organizations and the prevalence of cooperation in the Atlantic

---

57. Hamilton, Daniel, "Promoting Human Security and Effective Security Governance in the Atlantic Hemisphere." In Hamilton, D. (ed.), *Dark Networks in the Atlantic Basin. Emerging trends and Implications for Human Security*. Center for Transatlantic Relations, Johns Hopkins University, Washington, 2015, xii.

basin have been used to counter and, mainly, to attempt to prevent the threats posed by these challenges.

References

Alkire, Sabine, "A conceptual Framework for Human Security. Working Paper 2." Centre for Research on Inequality, Human Security and Ethnicity, CRISE, Queen Elizabeth House, University of Oxford, 2003.

Andersen-Rodgers, David, & Crawford, Kerry, *Human Security. Theory and Action*. New York, Roman and Littlefield, 2018.

Battistella, D., "L'apport de Karl Deutsch à la théorie des relations internationales." In *Revue internationale de politique comparée*, vol. 10(4), 2003, 567-585.

Bueger, Christian, "Learning from piracy: future challenges of maritime security governance." In *Global Affairs*, 1:1, 2015, 33-42.

Buzan, B., Weaver, O. and Wilde, Jaap de, *Security: A New Framework for Analysis*. Boulder, Colorado: Lynne Rienner Publishers, 1998.

Council on Foreign Relations' Center for Preventive Action, *Preventive Priorities Survey 2019*. Available at https://www.cfr.org/report/preventive-priorities-survey-2019 [consulted at 22 April 2019].

David, Charles Philippe, *A Guerra e a Paz:. Abordagens contemporâneas da segurança e da estratégia*. Lisboa: Instituto Piaget, 2001.

Emmers, Ralf, "Securitization." In Collins, Alan, *Contemporary Security Studies*. Oxford: Oxford University Press, 2010, 136-151.

Faria, Fernanda, "Fragile States: Challenges and Opportunities for Atlantic Relations." *Atlantic Future*, 2014. Available at http://www.atlanticfuture.eu/contents/view/fragile-states-in-the-atlantic [consulted at 22 April 2019].

Fukuda-Parr, Sakiko, & Messineo, Carol, "Human Security: a Critical review of the literature." In CRPD Working Paper no. 11, 2012.

Hamilton, Daniel, "Promoting Human Security and Effective Security Governance in the Atlantic Hemisphere." In Hamilton, D. (ed.), *Dark Networks in the Atlantic Basin. Emerging trends and Implications for Human Security*. Center for Transatlantic Relations, Johns Hopkins University, Washington, 2015, p. ix.

Hesterman, Jennifer, "Transnational Crime and Terror in the Pan-Atlantic: Understanding and Addressing the Growing Threat." In HAMILTON, D. (ed.), *Dark Networks in the Atlantic Basin. Emerging trends and Implications for Human Security*. Center for Transatlantic Relations, Johns Hopkins University, Washington, 2015, 35-56.

Kaldor, Mary, "Human Security in Complex Operations." In PRISM, Vol. 2 (2), 2011, 2.

Keohane, Robert and NYE, Joseph, *Power and Interdependence: World Politics in Transition*. London: TBS The Book Service, 1977.

Kotsopolos, John, "The Atlantic as a new Security area? Current engagements and prospects for security cooperation between Africa and its Atlantic counterparts," *Atlantic Future Project*, 2014, 4. Available at http://www.atlanticfuture.eu/contents/view/the-atlantic-as-a-new-security-area [consulted at 22 April 2019].

Kraemer, Andreas and Stefes, Christoph, "The changing energy landscape in the Atlantic Space." In Bacaria, Jordi and Tarragona, Laia (eds.), *Atlantic Future. Shaping a New Hemisphere for the 21st century: Africa, Europe and the Americas*. CIDOB, Barcelona, 2016, 87-102.

Lété, Bruno, "Addressing the Atlantic's Emerging Security Challenges." *Atlantic Future Project*, 2015. Available at http://www.atlanticfuture.eu/contents/view/atlantics-emerging-security-challenges [consulted at 22 April 2019].

MacFarlane, S. Neil, & Khong, Yuen Foong, *Human Security and the UN. A Critical History*, Indianápolis, Indianna University Press, 2006.

Mouzouni, Mustapha, "Cooperation Against Transnational Crime: The Case of the Zone of Peace and Cooperation of the South Atlantic." In *Atlantic Currents: An Annual Report on Wider Atlantic Perspectives and Patterns*, German Marshall Fund and OCP Policy Center, 2016, 42-56. Available at http://www.policycenter.ma/publications/atlantic-currents-annual-report- wider-atlantic-perspectives-and-patterns-1 [consulted at 22 April 2019].

Mutimer, David, "Critical Security Studies: a Schismatic History." In Collins, Alan, *Contemporary Security Studies*. Oxford: Oxford University Press, 2010, 84-105.

Rotschild, Emma, "What is Security?." In *Deadalus*, 124:3, 1995.

Seabra, Pedro, "Stretching the Limits? Strengths and Pitfalls of South Atlantic Security Regionalism." In *Contexto Internacional*, vol. 39(2) May/Aug 2017.

Sergi, Bruno S., & Morabito, Giacomo, "The Pirates' Curse: Economic Impacts of the Maritime Piracy." In *Studies in Conflict & Terrorism*, 39:10, 2005, 935-952

Shinoda, Hideaki, "The Concept of Human Security: Historical and Theoretical Implications." In *Conflict and Human Security: A Search for new Approaches of Peace Building*. IPSHU English Research Report Series, 2004.

State Index 2019 Report, Avaliable at https://fragilestatesindex.org/wp-content/uploads/2019/03/9511904-fragilestatesindex.pdf [consulted at 22 April 2019].

Teixeira, Nuno Severiano and Marcos, Daniel, "A Historical Perspective of the Atlantic's Evolution." In Bacaria, Jordi and Tarragona, Laia (eds.), *Atlantic Future. Shaping a New Hemisphere for the 21st century: Africa, Europe and the Americas*. CIDOB, Barcelona, 2016.

UNTFHS website: https://www.un.org/humansecurity/ (Consulted in 16 de April 2019).

Zerka, Pawel, Europe should do better in Venezuela. European Council for Foreign Relations (ECFR), 2019, available at https://www.ecfr.eu/article/commentary_europe_should_do_better_on_venezuela [consulted at 22 April 2019].

Chapter 2

Understanding Terrorism and Organized Crime in Light of Fragile States: Case Study on Niger, Mali and Chad

Abdelhak Bassou and Amal el Ouassif

The definition of a "failed state" has never been a subject of genius consensus between the scholars of International Relations. In addition to the classic limitations of subjectivity, there is one other important criticism that[1] have explicitly addressed which is the fact that the use of the term "failing state" is predominantly western, and hence reflects western judgment of security and stability. Particularly after the events of 11 September, where states with similar patterns were perceived and treated differently, because of their interactions with the security interests of the US. While this interpretation is not widely approved, it has the benefit of highlighting the need to bring the notion of "failing" states to an objective unbiased framework of analysis. For the purpose of this chapter, we seek to address the limitation of subjectivity by evaluating states' resilience by the ability of the state to perform a certain set of functions. The latter are the provision of basic public goods and military control over its territory.

This chapter aims at assessing ways by which non-state actors, particularly the ones involved in criminal and terrorist acts, take advantage of the failure of states in this region to proliferate and impose their own rules of the game, in the gray zones left out of the state control.

The authors sought to introduce by this paper a new evaluation of states' resilience, by looking at the "functional legitimacy of states" in opposition to political or historical legitimacy. In other words, what constitutes the basis of the assessment of a state's performance is its ability to provide two basic functions: First, provide basic services for its population, like education, health and safety. Second, ability to exercise control and ensure the safety of the totality of its territory.

---

1. Bøås, Morten and Jennings, Kathleen. "'Failed States' and 'State Failure': Threats or Opportunities?". In *Beyond International Development-Towards Recognition and Redistribution in Global Politics*. Vol. 4, 2007.

The suggested approach captures the new orientation in the literature on state fragility that is no more limited to the post-cold war perspectives, linking states' fragility or failure to merely security considerations, like the struggle with armed groups, ethnic conflicts and collapse of state institutions. While these aspects undoubtedly say lot on states' resilience, there are other important aspects to consider. These are the ability of the state to fulfill basic functions that widely affect the life and wellbeing of citizens, like access to public goods.

The following chart suggests ways by which criminal and terrorist actors are both a cause and a consequence of state fragility and failure. The proliferation of troubling non-state actors can occur in two cases. First, when due to limited capacity a state in unable to provide basic needs and safety in some of its regions, which leads to the creation of "gray zones" that become later refuge for terrorists and criminal groups. The second case is where, due to external influences, non-state actors enter a country and destabilize its institutional system, to the point that it becomes unable to perform its basic functions, which leads to the emergence of gray zones. In this paper, both cases are illustrated through the cases of Mali and Chad (see Figure 1).

Theoretical framework

The selected evaluation criteria find origin in the work of two well-recognized scholars: Jean Jack Rousseau, "The Social Contract", in which the ability of states to protect its citizens' safety is key to state's legitimacy and Max Weber, for which the state is defined, above all, by its ability to exercise the "legitimate physical violence in a given territory".

The legitimacy of the state in The Social Contract doctrine

Central to the work of the three founders of the Social Contract theory (T. Hobbes, J. Locke and J. J. Rousseau) is the idea that individuals, by virtue of a social contract, agree to make a concession on a part of their freedom to the government, in exchange for provision of a set of rights like safety and basic services. By this, the Social Contract doctrine states clearly that the motivation of people to give away a part of their freedom to a ruling entity, is above all the willingness to be protected from anarchy that prevails in the state of nature. Hence, failure of the government/state to provide this protection affects it legitimacy and questions the whole validity of the social contract.

Figure 1. States' fragility both a cause and consequence of criminal non-state actors

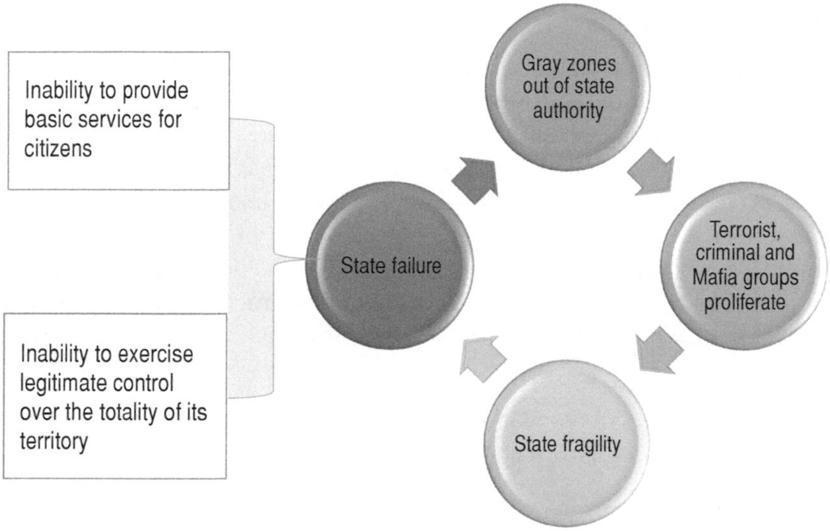

Max Weber's Theory of the Modern State

Weber identifies two main characteristics for the modern state. First, its ability to rule as an independent legal entity over a given territory, and second, its monopoly over the use of *legitimate* physical violence, to impose the respect of the community rules.

The Sovereign functions of the state

The sovereign functions of the state is an additional set of principles that complement the two doctrines mentioned above. It refines the legitimacy of states, by directly linking it to its ability to provide a certain set of functions, over which, states are supposed to have complete monopoly. These functions are generally identified as internal security (police and justice), External security (army) and Currency. The recent point is not of a consensus between the absolutists, who are the initiators of this doctrine,[2] and the liberalists, who think that currency is not necessary among the "marks of States' sovereignty". For the purpose of this chapter, such divergence is

2. Bodin, Jean & Douglas McRae, Kenneth. "The Six Bookes of a Commonweale". In *Harvard Political Classics*. Cambridge: Harvard University Press; Reprint 2014. DOI: ISBN-10: 0674733142.

not of a key interest. The focus is on the two first functions, which are the ability of the state to ensure internal and external security.

Sources of empirical data

The literature of "failing states" also commonly called "fragile states" has lot of indicators and instruments that international institutions like the World Bank use to measure the resilience of states for development aid purposes. For this paper, we sought to use the data available on recognized resources like: The World Bank's Country Policy and Institutional Assessment: which measures the resilience of a country in terms of institutional and political structures, and its ability to act on the determinants of development like poverty reduction. The second instrument is The Failed State Index (FSI), which looks at aspects like security, human rights and external intervention.

Other sources of secondary data like the UNHCR, International Monetary Fund are mobilized to enrich the analysis.

Scope of the study

For comparison purposes, we sought to select three countries of West Africa that are also members of the G5 Sahel group (Mali, Niger, and Chad). We selected them because of their comparable economic and social indicators, and because they are all subject to the threat of terrorist and criminal groups.

The causes of state failure from a governance, territorial, and state regime perspective

Mali

Between 30% and 35% of the 17 million people in Mali, live with less than 1.9 dollar per day (the world bank poverty line).[3] In the recent years, Mali's economy has been growing at rates that pass 5%, particularly driven by the performance of the Agricultural sector. However, uneven distribution of wealth has led to important disparities between the rural and urban areas, and the country faces the threat of food insecurity. Wealth is highly

---

3. Garba, Abdoulahi. "Macroeconomic Management for Poverty Reduction: Chad, Mali, Niger". In *World Bank Group*. Vol. Spring, 2016.

concentrated in the region of Bamako, in the hands of actors, like executives in the agricultural, mining and energy sectors.

A survey conducted by *Afro Barometer* on a sample of 600 rural residents, prior and after the crisis of 2012 suggests that the main preoccupation of the rural population is access to basic needs like health, education and infrastructures, rather than the political crisis and territorial breakdown that the country was going through. "Villagers felt disconnected from and "abandoned" by the state. These sentiments were only compounded by the crisis."

These findings are not surprising, since the main argument used by the rebellion groups, in all insurrections is that populations of the North are neglected by the south centric state.

Contrary to the common perception, the territories of North Mali were not ungoverned,[4] but due to poor governance and the inability of the Malian state to fulfill basic functions, non-state actors flourished in those territories.

Interestingly, an important part of the Malian population saw in the insurrections led by Junta, despite their violence, a necessary shock to the ruling elite. Therefore, what initially started as Junta's call for support for its uprising project converted to a general demand for better public services' provision and infrastructures.

The aforementioned survey had as a target the residents in the rural regions between the territories under the Malian ruling and those under the rebellion authority. Hence, the researchers expected that those populations are more concerned about the political crisis, but the following figures highlight a different reality (see Figures 2 and 3).

Through history, violent conflicts characterized the Northern region of Mali, between the Tamasheq also referred to as Tuareg and the Arab communities located in the Sahel region. The reason of these conflicts is the willingness of the North communities to be autonomous from the rest of Mali. The initiators of the rebellion movements accuse the central government of financial and social neglect.

---

4. Dowd and Raleigh argue that poor policy rather than ungoverned spaces led to non-state actors flourishing (often in cooperation with government actors). Dowd, C., & Raleigh. The myth of global Islamic terrorism and local conflict in Mali and the Sahel.

**Figure 2. Citizens' policy priorities before and after the crisis
of 2012 in the regions in frontier between territories under the
Malian government's authority and territories under the rebel's
authority.**

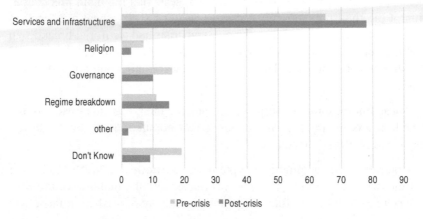

Source: Bleck, Jaimie & Michelitch, Kristin. "On the primacy of weak public service provision in rural Africa: Malians redefine 'state breakdown' amidst 2012 political crisis". In *Afrobarometer*. No. 155, 2015, p. 7.

Despite its efforts to contain conflicts in the central region of Mali, the government seems unsuccessful in dealing with the inter-community violence in this region. One of the main problems the Malian security services are facing is the lack of capacities. The government forces are only able to cover the urban centers and hence, neglect the small rural areas, which create a vacuum for extremists and criminal actors to fill.

Taking advantage of the vulnerable situation of the Malian government, following the coup of 2012, extremist groups comprised of Malian and neighboring countries fighters flourished in some regions of Mali. Few days after the political uprisings, the alliance of Ansar Edine, with Al Qaeda in West Africa and the secular movement of MNLA (Azawad National Liberation Movement) occupied the northern parts of Timbuktu, Kidal, and Gao up to the Mopti region in which they claimed the independent state of Azawad.

In order to face the rebellions in the Northern regions, the Malian government called for international support, which came under the format of French and international coalition military interventions.

Figure 3. Citizens' prefered news subject before and after the crisis of 2012 in the regions in frontier between territories under the Malian government authority and territories under the rebels authority.

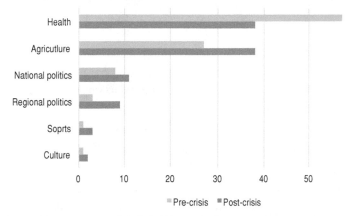

Source: Bleck, Jaimie & Michelitch, Kristin. "On the primacy of weak public service provision in rural Africa: Malians redefine 'state breakdown' amidst 2012 political crisis". In *Afrobarometer*. No. 155, 2015, p. 8.

In 2015, a peace agreement was concluded between the government and Armed groups. However, the agreements blocked, because of allegations of government's disengagement and continuous violence of the armed groups.

In the regions that were under rebellion ruling, the situation is mitigated. In Gao for example, the presence of the government is limited to towns and the provision of public services is merely symbolic. In other regions like Kidal, the government is absent, and the local populations are deprived of basic needs.[5]

Niger

Niger is a country with important resources that range from Oil, gas to uranium and gold. In 2017, Niger had a growth rate of 5.2%, driven by the performance of the oil and agricultural sectors.[6] The government is mak-

---

5. C. N. There is a crisis overlap in northern Mali (Rep.). Mali: Voices from the Field
6. Diallo, Kalidou. "Perspectives Économiques en Afrique 2018, Niger," [Consulted at: 8 November 2018]. Available at: https://www.afdb.org/fileadmin/uploads/afdb/Documents/Generic-Documents/country_notes/Niger_note_pays.pdf

ing important efforts to scale up its investments in infrastructures, but the financial system remains limited.

Overall, the poverty rate in Niger has witnessed a significant drop from 2005 to 2011.[7] However, this was not reflected in all the parts of the country. Because of an underdeveloped agricultural sector, the rural population in Niger is highly dependent on basic farming production.

Corruption is another challenge facing the Nigerien economy and administration, in particular the judicial system. In the recent report of Business Anti-Corruption Portal, corruption was identified as one of the highest risks facing the business sector in Niger.

The provision of public services is insufficient with high disparities between the urban and rural areas. 70% of the population of Niger does not have access to electricity, particularly in the rural regions.[8]

Niger is hit by armed conflict with extremist groups, which has led to important numbers of refugees and internally displaced persons. The country is directly affected by the consequences of the Malian and Libyan crisis, which puts extra pressure on the social and economic resilience of this country. Such pressures are translated in insufficient provision of basic needs, like health, education and food necessities. The high demographic growth (approximatively 3.9% per year) is an additional element of concern is this regard.

Like neighboring countries, Niger is suffering from the attacks of Boko Haram. In 2015, Boko Haram made its first attack in Niger. As consequences, a deep crisis in the Diffa region emerged, with 129.000 internally displaced persons in addition to the already existing 108.000 refugees that fled the atrocities of Boko Haram in Nigeria.

In 2017, the Nigerian government spent as much as 7.4% of the GDP on security expenses to combat Boko Haram[9]. Such important spending has led to deepening the budget deficit of the country.

---

7.   World Bank Group. "Trends In Poverty, Inequality and Growth". In *Poverty Reduction and Economic Management*. Vol. 89837-NE, 4, 2014.

8.   Logan, Carolyn. "Developing Africa's infrastructure: The rough road to better services" [Consulted at: 18 November 2018]. Available at http://afrobarometer.org/fr/publications/ad3-developing-africas-infrastructure-rough-road-better-services

9.   Diallo, Kalidou. "Perspectives Économiques en Afrique 2018, Niger » [Consulted at: 08 November 2018]. Available at https://www.afdb.org/fileadmin/uploads/afdb/Documents/Generic-Documents/country_notes/Niger_note_pays.pdf

The direct confrontation of the Nigerian government with Boko Haram caused instability in the southeast and exacerbated the conflicts over access to resources in this region. However, despite its multiple attempts, Boko Haram was unsuccessful in spreading influence beyond the Diffa region, which has historical and cultural ties with Nigeria.

Although joining the Multinational Joint Task Force (MNJTF), was costly for the Nigerien government, the latter managed to disturb the insurrection of Boko Haram in the Diffa region, mainly through military operations and the state of emergency that blocked the access of extremists to commercial services necessary to their survival in the region.

In fact, in Niger also, insurgents exploited the existence of inter communal tensions, which has led to bloody conflicts in the region. The Nigerien government attempted to limit this by ensuring mediation between the communities of the region. The concerned communities welcomed the initiative of the government, although lot is yet to be done to dissipate all tensions.

Chad

In 2015, the growth rate in Chad was estimated at 1.8%, in comparison to 6.2% in 2014[10]. This decline is particularly the result of the slowdown of investments, in oil and constructions sectors, in addition to the considerable cuts in public expenditures.

In Chad, poverty is an important challenge to development. It is mainly a rural phenomenon. The most recent Household Consumption and informal sector Survey, conducted in 2011, shows that the recent monetary crisis' effects were twice higher in rural than in urban areas.[11] Knowing that 82% of Chadians live in rural areas, poverty is a structural challenge to social and economic development.

The government made significant efforts to reduce poverty, but the fall in the national poverty headcount (55% in 2003 to 47% in 2011) is quickly mitigated by the demographic growth. Hence, over the years the numbers of Chadian under the poverty line raises. In Chad, about half of the population is aged under 14, which creates high demand for primary educa-

---

10. Diabaté, Alassane. "Perspectives Économiques en Afrique 2018, République Chad". [Consulted at: 08 November 2018]. Available at https://www.afdb.org/fileadmin/uploads/afdb/Documents/Publications/African_Economic_Outlook_2018_-_FR.pdf
11. World Bank Group. "Dynamics of Poverty and Inequality following the Rise of the Oil Sector." In *Poverty Reduction and Economic Management*. Volume 4, 2013.

tion and health.[12] Conjugated to the limited capacity of the government to collect taxes and revenues, because of the important share of the informal sector, the provision of public services is insufficient.

In 2016, following the elections, wide public protests emerged because of corruption, austerity and the cost of living.[13]

Originally, the magnitude of Boko Haram's attacks in Chad was limited. However, in 2015 the violence escalated in response to the military involvement of Chad in fighting Boko Haram in neighboring countries. Particularly under the framework of the Lake Chad Basin Multinational Joint Task Force (MNJTF). Terrorist acts of Boko Harma mainly consisted of explosive attacks targeting civilians in the towns of Guite and Miterine.

In 2016 thanks to the international and regional support, the Chadian government managed to limit the attacks of Boko Haram, taking advantage of the internal tensions that emerged within this movement.

On the legislative level, the Chadian government passed a counterterrorism law on August 2015 (Law 034/PR/2015) that criminalizes the terrorist acts and punishes to death penalty and life imprisonment individuals involved in funding or recruiting for terrorist activities. Although, unclear if there have been prosecutions under this law, the latter constitutes a strong statement by the Chadian government in favor of counter-terrorism.

Overall, Chad has been to a certain extent effective in restricting the activities of Boko Haram on its territory. Anti-terrorism measures are a priority area for the government and the national forces has displayed a certain level of command through improved screening in borders, to prevent the crossing of Boko Haram fighters and other militias from central Africa.[14] Nevertheless, the war on Boko Haram is very costly for the Chadian government who has been involved in counterterrorism assistance to neighboring countries, like Cameroon and Niger. According to the last Country Report on Terrorism 2016, by the US Department of State, the Chadian government is facing challenges to meet its basic financial commitments like paying the police and military salaries.

---

12. Garba, Abdoulahi. "Macroeconomic Management for Poverty Reduction: Chad, Mali, Niger". In World Bank Group. Vol. Spring, 2016.
13. Overview. (n.d.). Retrieved from https://www.worldbank.org/en/country/chad/overview
14. United States Department of State. "Country Reports on Terrorism" [Consulted at: 15 October 2018]. Available at https://www.state.gov/documents/organization/272488.pdf

Drug trafficking and human smuggling, other ways of states' fragility

The challenges of Mali, Niger and Chad are not limited to their vulnerability to terrorism alone. Transnational Organized Crime finds also in the weakness and bankruptcy of these states an opportunity to flourish. Networks and cartels of transnational criminality settle and use the territory. Their influence goes even to certain levels of government and administrative hierarchy, from which they get support for their activities.

The weaknesses of governance and lack of means of control combined to the immensity of territories of (More than one million km^2 per country for Chad, Mali and Niger) reinforce the vulnerability of these countries, which are physically unable to protect thousands of km of borders. These hence become traffic areas of all kinds of criminal activities.

The vastness of the territories and the immense distances of frontiers to be covered in addition to the geographical specificity of the Sahel all hamper these states' ability to provide a satisfactory level of territorial protection.

Criminal networks use the Sahel as a crossing point or a storage area for prohibited goods intended for criminal activity. The routes of the Sahel are connected to the Atlantic Ocean, the Mediterranean Sea and the Red Sea. It is precisely for this particular geographic position that criminal networks flourish in the desert roads of the region.

The proliferation of traffic in the Sahel and the use of the territory of these States and their borders by cartels and mafia groups add another important element to the definition of fragile/failed states. In fact, a failed state is not only a government that is unable to provide vital needs of its population, or one that cannot monitor and secure its borders. It is also a state with weak institutional structures, that are porous to the temptations of corruption and criminal networks that get power through the corruptibility of the administration.

The "Air Cocaine" case in Mali[15]; had revealed to the world the role played by the territory of Mali in the international cocaine traffic. It opened eyes on the massive arrival of Colombian cocaine to West Africa. The multinational character of this case demonstrates the extra-territorial dimension of criminal groups, which took advantage of the weakness of the Ma-

---

15. In November 2009 a plane, carrying 5 tons of cocaine, crashed in Mali, in the Gao region.

Figure 4. Trafficking in West Africa.

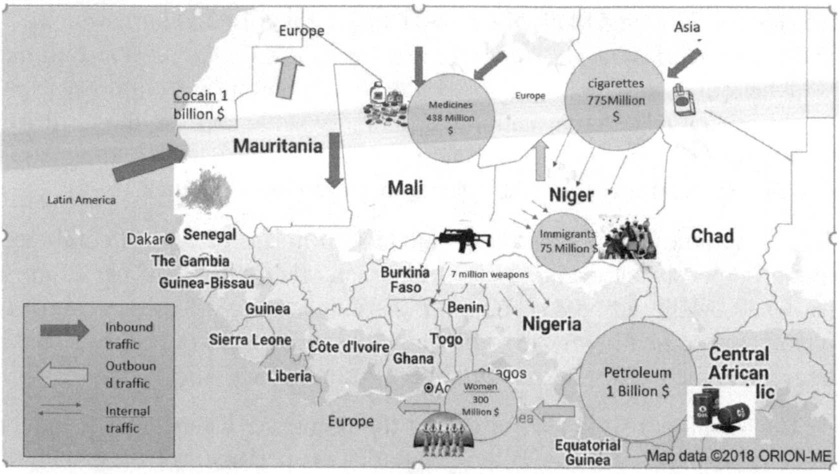

Source: The authors, Data: *Les Trafics dans l'Afrique de l'Ouest*

lian State to use, as it sees, the territory of this country in the largest drug traffic in the world. The question that rises: Is the massive traffic at hands, a cause of Mali's inability to manage the security of its territory; or is it a more structured crime, at the level of some of the state's administration officials who made it possible for a plane full of cocaine to land on the Malian territory?

Several media and observers had, at that time, invoked the weakness of the Malian state, but several other journalists and investigators did not reject the hypothesis of complicity of the Malian administration in this wide scale traffic scandal.

In fact, it is clear that the bankruptcy of the state and the installation of transnational organized crime networks is a vicious circle. As soon as there is a slight breach in the governance of a state, criminal networks encrust themselves to enlarge it. These networks have both the means and power to buy officials, interfere in the electoral processes to elect people who can support their activities, and consolidate their hand-put on the wheels of the state. The latter becomes weaker which leaves space to criminal actors, and the circle continues until a radical change occurs, or the state eventually collapse.

Networks of clandestine migration and human trafficking in the Sahel

Illegal migration and its criminal corollary and trafficking in human beings is another cause and consequence of states' fragility in the Sahel. The city of Agadez in Niger is considered the hub and obligatory route of clandestine migration In the Sahel (see Figure 5A).

It is from the bus station of Agadez that trucks leave loaded with candidates for illegal migration, taken care of by travel agencies sometimes legally registered with the authorities, but used by mafia networks. The majority of the candidates for illegal migration are not nationals of Niger, but the traffickers present them as Africans who have the right to transit through Niger to travel elsewhere. The question is: Why Niger authorities did not strengthen the control on Agadez, which is now worldwide known to be the city of human smuggling? Is it because of the lack of means, or is that pertaining to the power of the criminal mafia that prevent the state from fulfilling its sovereign prerogatives? Besides, is the geographical position of Agadez, an important determinant of the poor performance of the government of Niger?

We are inclined to think that that all the above factors combined has led to the situation at hand (see Figure 5B). The situation in Agadez is similar to the one in Gao, Mali, where illegal migrants are also supported by criminal networks that are sent to neighbouring Niger with impunity. This traffic flourished in Gao well before 2012 when terrorist groups took control of the city. They colluded with organized transnational crime groups who became a source of income to finance their terrorist activities.

Drug trafficking: the failed states of the Sahel

Africa has become an area of choice for cocaine from Latin America to cross to Europe and Asia.

According to Samuel Benshimon, editor of the site "Sahel Intelligence", boats arrive from Latin America and transit the Gulf of Guinea especially in Guinea Bissau, Cape Verde and Senegal. The goods "are then transported by land to Togo through two routes: the first from Mali, Burkina Faso and Benin, while the second transit through Mali, Burkina Faso and Ghana. Then the merchandises leave from Togo by planes to Europe. However, the most popular routes are those on land, across the Sahel, especially countries led by almost bankrupt states such as Niger or Mali.

Figure 5A. Networks of clandestine migration and human trafficking in the Sahel.

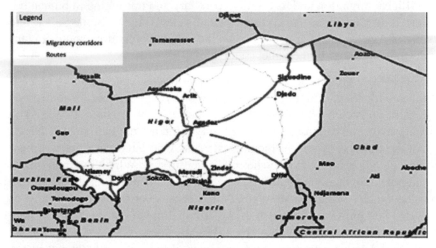

Source: IOM Niger.

Figure 5B. Cocaine traffic in West Africa.

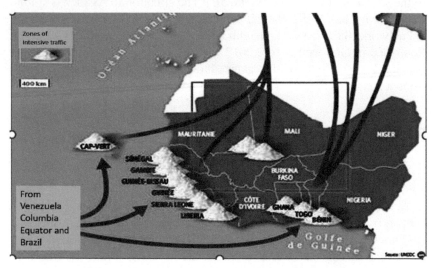

Drug trafficking, particularly cocaine, in the Sahel, generated $ 900 million in profits between 2013 and 2014 according to the United Nations Office on Drugs and Crime (UNODC). Some 21 tonnes passed through the Sahel desert, which became the preferred route to Europe. A colossal windfall that traffickers reinject into the local economy.

Figure 5B shows that the majority of the states in which the storage and departure of cocaine trafficking occur are states with weak governance/failed states; Niger and mainly Mali are, like in the case of human smuggling, among the favourite spots of mafia and criminal actors.

The examination of the maps of other traffics highlight the consequences of weak states, on the proliferation of cross-border criminal organizations that undermine institutions and lead to states' bankruptcy. A major threat to report is that transnational organized crime and terrorist groups join efforts to eliminate any possibility for these states to restore authority over their territory. The whole region can thus become destabilized by a contamination effect.

Wrap up analyses and conclusions

From the exposed country profiles, we conclude that the three countries in the study display certain similarities. First, they are all countries will vulnerable economic and social indicators: high poverty and unemployment rates, in addition to important inequalities between the urban and rural areas. Second, this sample of countries is characterized by inter-community conflicts that were exploited by terrorist groups, in order to destabilize the system. In the case of Mali, Ansar Edine, Al Qaeda in West Africa and the secular movement of MNLA (Azawad National Liberation Movement) were only able to occupy the North of Mali, when the central government was fully mobilized in the aftermath of the 2012 political coup. Moreover, these movements were implemented in the Northern region of Mali that historically witnessed important ethnic and communal conflicts, and more important; where a general feeling of state neglect is strongly present. Niger is a slightly different case, in the sense that it suffered from its geographic position, in the frontiers with Nigeria the cradle of Boko Haram. The latter, again, chose to settle in the Diffa region, historically known to be conflictual, because of communal tensions, which Boko Haram attempted to play against the government. However, the Niger state, has managed to certain extent to disturb the presence of Boko Haram in this region. Chad is a similar case to Niger, in the sense that it was affected by the spill-

Figure 6. Public Health and Education in percentage of total expenditures from 2013 to 2015 in Mali, Niger and Chad.

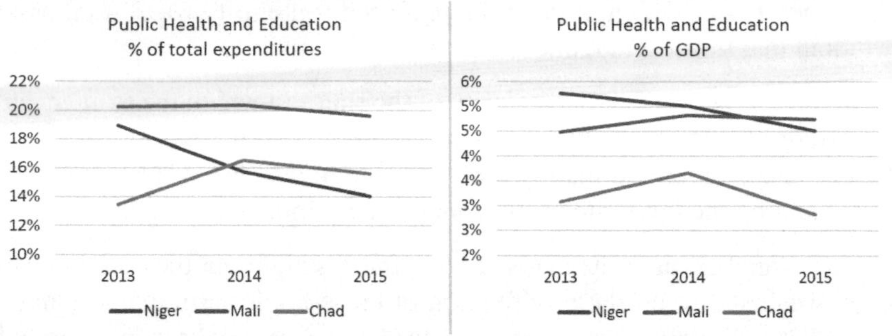

Source: World Bank Group. "Dynamics of Poverty and Inequality following the Rise of the Oil Sector". In *Poverty Reduction and Economic Management.* Volume 4, 2013.

over effects of the Boko Haram activities in the region and became itself a target of the terrorist groups, because of its military support to the Lake Chad Basin Multinational Joint Task Force (MNJTF). The main difference is that in Chad, Boko Haram did not manage to occupy a whole region, but rather targeted the centre of the country through repetitive bombing attacks in towns and villages.

One other important observation in the three cases is that, the activities of the terrorist groups aggravated the fragility of the economic and social tissues. Figure 6 represents the share of public spending on health and education from 2013 to 2015, according to the World Bank.

In Niger, 2015, which is the year in which Boko Haram, made the most violent attacks in the country, the government's investment in health and education witnessed a sharp decline, undoubtedly in favour of security spending. Chad is a similar case, starting from 2014 the government spending on public services declined and reached its lowest levels in 2015, the year that corresponds to the peak of the security crisis in Chad. Mali is a different figure, where public investments in health and education followed the same tendency since 2013, which is the year that followed the political coup and insurrections in the North of Mali.

Figure 7 compares the share of health and education in the GDP of the three countries, with the share of public spending on security.

Figure 7. Comparison between public spending on education and Health vs. Security in Chad, Mali and Niger (2013–2015).

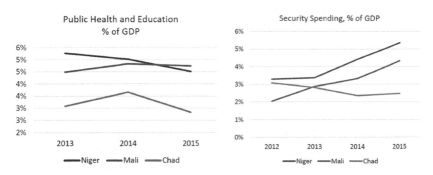

Source World Bank, *Macroeconomic Management for Poverty Reduction: Chad, Mali, Niger,* 2016.

The above figure clarifies that in parallel to the decline observed in public spending on health and education on the observed period, there is a net increase in security expenses. Except for the case of Chad, which has committed from the beginning important financial resources to security and was later forced to review its budget allocations.

All these figures tell us about the mechanisms by which states fragility is at the same time a cause and consequence for the proliferation of terrorist and criminal groups. Back to the model in the introduction section, we can conclude that terrorist groups, mafias and cartels need a set of conditions to flourish, among which the inability of states to provide quality public services. However, by a dual mechanism, these actors, once established in a country hinder a lot its development and the ability of the state to perform its basic functions, which leads to a vicious circle.

To link these findings to the main argument of the paper, we conclude that assessing the resilience of a state is not a scientific process, particularly in the case of West African states, in the sense that each country represents a different case study. Mali was at a certain time, a failed state, when it lost control over its Northern region, because it failed the criteria to exercising control in the totality of its territory. Niger and Chad and to a certain extent Mali today exhibit the symptoms of fragile states that have lot of internal development challenges, which conjugated to the regional context made of them a target of terrorist groups.

References

Bleck, Jaimie & Michelitch, Kristin. "On the primacy of weak public service provision in rural Africa: Malians redefine 'state breakdown' amidst 2012 political crisis". In *Afrobarometer*. No. 155, 2015.

Bøås, Morten and Jennings, Kathleen. *ernational Development-Towards Recognition and Redistribution in Global Politics*. Vol. 4, 2007.

Bodin, Jean & Douglas Mcrae, Kenneth. "The Six Bookes of a Commonweale". In *Harvard Political Classics*. Cambridge: Harvard University Press; Reprint 2014. DOI: ISBN-10: 0674733142.

Diabaté, Alassane. "Perspectives Économiques en Afrique 2018, République Chad". [Consulted at: 08 November 2018]. Available at https://www.afdb. org/fileadmin/uploads/afdb/Documents/Publications/African_Economic_ Outlook_2018_-_FR.pdf

Diallo, Kalidou. "Perspectives Économiques en Afrique 2018, Niger » [Consulted at: 08 November 2018]. Available at https://www.afdb.org/fileadmin/uploads/ afdb/Documents/Generic-Documents/country_notes/Niger_note_pays.pdf

Dowd, Catriona and Raleigh, Clionadh. "The myth of global Islamic terrorism and local conflict in Mali and the Sahel". In *African Affairs*. University of Sussex, 2013, 498-509.

Garba, Abdoulahi. "Macroeconomic Management for Poverty Reduction: Chad, Mali, Niger". In *World Bank Group*. Vol. SPRING, 2016.

Logan, Carolyn. "Developing Africa's infrastructure: The rough road to better services" [Consulted at: 18 November 2018]. Available at http://afrobarometer. org/fr/publications/ad3-developing-africas-infrastructure-rough-road-better-services

Pozo Marín, Alejandro. "Perilous terrain: Humanitarian action at risk in Mali" [Consulted at: 10 November 2018]. Available at https://arhp.msf.es/emergency-gap-case-studies/perilous-terrain-humanitarian-action-risk-mali

United States Department of State. "Country Reports on Terrorism" [Consulted at: 15 October 2018]. Available at https://www.state.gov/documents/organization/272488.pdf

World Bank Group. "Dynamics of Poverty and Inequality following the Rise of the Oil Sector". In *Poverty Reduction and Economic Management*. Volume 4, 2013.

World Bank Group. "Trends in Poverty, Inequality and Growth". In *Poverty Reduction and Economic Management*. Vol. 89837-NE, 4, 2014.

Chapter 3

Energy Security in the Framework of Human Security, Oil, and Gas in the North Atlantic Basin

*Macarena Larrea Basterra, Eloy Álvarez Pelegry,
and Jaime Menéndez Sánchez*

Since the energy crises of the 1970s, the management by government authorities of the relation between energy needs and economic growth has been a priority.[1] During the last century, the energy system has relied on fossil fuels. Today fossil fuels still represent more than 80% of total energy demand. Furthermore, their geographical distribution implies that the principal oil and gas production fields are not located in the same areas as the largest energy consumers.[2] Therefore, developed countries (mainly located in the Atlantic Basin) have suffered from a lack of energy sources, so energy security has become a priority for them. However, this has changed recently as a result of the 'Atlantic energy renaissance'. While import dependency continues to be a driver for energy security concerns in Europe, the rest of the basin is increasingly self-sufficient and more and more a net exporter.[3]

Growing energy demand (both in developed and developing countries), which is shown in next table, has heightened concern about energy security, a concept that has broadened to include different elements of sustainability.[4] In this regard, however, between 1990 and 2015 more than 80% of the increase in global energy consumption occured in developing nations.[5]

---

1. Sodupe, K., & Molina, G. "Gobernanza, seguridad energética y sostenibilidad". In *Gobernanza para un sistema energético sostenible*. Universidad del País Vasco, 2018, 31.
2. Ibid.
3. Isbell, P. and Álvarez Pelegry, E. (Eds.) *Energy and transportation in the Atlantic Basin*. Center for Transatlantic Relations, Johns Hopkins University SAIS, with Brookings Press, in conjunction with the Jean Monnet Network Project on Atlantic Studies, co-financed by the Erasmus+ Programme of the European Union, Washington D.C. 2017. Available at: https://www.orkestra.deusto.es/es/investigacion/publicaciones/libros-informes/otras-colecciones/1244-energy-transportation-atlantic-basin
4. Keiji, K. "Energy security and human insecurity". In *Poole Gakuin University* (Ed.). (n.d.). Available at: https://ci.nii.ac.jp/els/contentscinii_20180330134441.pdf?id=ART0010407155
5. Sodupe, K., & Molina, G. Op. cit..

Table 1.Total primary energy demand by region in the New Policies Scenario (Mtoe) (2017-2040)

	2000	2017	2025	2030	2035	2040	Change	CAAGR
North America	2,678	2,624	2,675	2,667	2,661	2,693	69	0.10%
USA	2,271	2,148	2,185	2,162	2,139	2,149	1	0.00%
Central and South America	449	667	730	784	847	916	249	1.40%
Brazil	184	285	315	338	363	391	106	1.40%
Europe	2,028	2,008	1,934	1,845	1,779	1,752	-256	-0.60%
EU	1,693	1,621	1,512	1,404	1,321	1,274	-347	-1.00%
Africa	490	829	980	1,086	1,192	1,299	470	2.00%
South Africa	103	131	133	132	135	138	7	0.20%
Middle East	353	740	846	957	1,085	1,200	460	2.10%
Eurasia	742	911	943	960	986	1,019	108	0.50%
Russia	621	730	745	744	754	769	39	0.20%
Asia Pacific	3,012	5,789	6,803	7,344	7,798	8,201	2,412	1.50%
China	1,143	3,051	3,509	3,684	3,787	3,858	807	1.00%
India	441	898	1,238	1,465	1,683	1,880	982	3.30%
Japan	518	428	415	403	390	379	-48	-0.50%
Southeast Asia	383	664	826	923	1,018	1,110	446	2.30%
International bunkers	274	404	476	525	578	635	231	2.00%
Total	10,026	13,972	15,387	16,168	16,926	17,715	743	1.00%
Current policies			15,782	16,943	18,125	19,328	5,356	1.40%
Sustainable development			14,146	13,820	13,688	13,175	-257	-0.10%

Note: CAAGR = Compound average annual growth rate.
Source: IEA, "How does the IEA respond to major disruptions in oil supply?". 2011b. [Consulted at 25th November 2018]. Available at: https://www.iea.org/newsroom/news/2011/march/how-does-the-iea-re-spond-to-major--disruptions-in-the-supply-of-oil-2011-03-10-.html

Today, the principal energy demand dynamics have turned to Asia and, as a consequence, the Atlantic Basin has lost some of its tradicional demand relevance.

This chapter focuses on energy security: it includes, first, a conceptual framework for the term and its relationship with human security. Given that, traditionally, the principal global energy flows have taken place within the North Atlantic Basin (NAB), there is then an analysis of energy security context across this territorial and maritime space, including the main policies adopted by the EU and the USA, both key players. The chapter ends with some considerations about energy security in the North Atlantic Basin.

Energy security within the framework of human security

Today energy is one of the major inputs for industry, transportation and social welfare. In this regard, according to E.F. Schumacher, energy is "not just another commodity, but the precondition of all commodities, a basic factor equal with air, water, and earth." Therefore, energy security can be considered a public good.[6] Some authors believe that public intervention in energy could be justified. Indeed, energy security has been synonymous with national security during times of war over the last 100 years.[7]

Energy security has gained influence within human security, at least since the 1970s—when many countries nationalized their fossil fuel reserves and developed national oil companies and the two oil crises occurred (in 1973-74 and 1979-80). Fuel importing nations began to consider energy supply disruptions as questions of national security to be addressed with military strategies[8.] Additionally, economic stability and growth became essential concerns of national security[9]. This catalyzed, in 1974, the

6. Sovacool, B. K., & Mukherjee, I. "Conceptualizing and measuring energy security: A synthesized approach". In *Energy. The International Journal*. Vol. 36, 2011, 5343-5355.
7. Energy Charter Secretariat "International energy security. Common convept for energy producing, consuming and transit countries". 2015. Available at: https://energycharter.org/what-we-do/trade-and-transit/trade-and-transit-thematic-reports/international-energy-security-common-concept-for-energy-producing-consuming-and-transit-countries-2015/
8. Karlsson-Vinkhuyzen, S. I., & Jollands, N. "Human security and energy security: A sustainable energy system as apublic good". In *International handbook of energy security*. Cheltenham: UK, Edward Elgar, (n.d.). 507-525. Available at: https://papers.ssrn.com/sol3/papers.cfm?abstract_id=2562594
9. Graf, R. "Between national and human security: Energy security in the United States and Western Europe in the 1970s". In *Historical Social Research*. Vol. *35*, No. *4*, (n.d.),

creation of the International Energy Agency (IEA) which historically associated energy security principally with oil supply.[10]

It is true that energy supply interruptions at that time did not pose the severe limitations to people's freedoms as do wars or ecological disasters (which are also related to the concept of human security explained next). However, during the 1980s, when oil supply expansion and lower oil demand led to a loss of control by OPEC (the Organization of Petroleum Exporting Countries), the 1987 Brundtland Report that established the concept of sustainable growth argued that "the traditional concept of security which concerned political and military threats to national sovereignty had to be extended because of the increasing influence of environmental pollution on a local, national, regional and global level."[11]

The 1990s opened with the Gulf War and the fall of the Soviet Union and continued to unfold with a trend towards privatization and liberalization of energy industries and markets.[12]

In 1994, the United Nations Development Programme (UNDP) prepared the Human Development Report which identified seven types of security beyond physical violence: economic (related to income), food, health, environmental, personal, community and political. Later, in 2003, the Ogata-Sen Commission developed a definition of human security as "to protect the vital core of all human lives in ways that enhance human freedoms and human fulfilment." In 2004, the EU developed the Human Security Doctrine for Europe. In general, 'human security' is mainly used to describe the security of people's livelihoods which may be threatened by civil wars, natural disasters, or failing states.

Energy was not mentioned in either of the UNDP or Ogata-Sen Commission reports. Nevertheless, some authors[13] claim that energy security participates in at least four of the seven security dimensions previously mentioned, including economic, food, health and environmental security.

Therefore, human insecurity can be caused by energy insecurity. To confront this challenge, the UN decided that 2014 would mark the start of the United Nations Decade of Sustainable Energy for All and called on inter-

329-348. Available at: https://doi.org/10.12759/hsr.35.2010.4.329-348
10. IEA "Energy supply security 2014". Paris. 2015. Available at: www.iea.org
11. Graf, R. Op. cit.
12. Energy Charter Secretariat. Op. cit.
13. Karlsson-Vinkhuyzen, S. I., & Jollands, N. Op. cit.

national agents to bring modern and sustainable energy to everyone on the planet.[14]

Compared with developed nations, most developing countries find themselves in a more difficult situation due to the lack of any meaningful political, economic and military power to influence the stability of energy supply. As a result, there are still two main positions in relation to energy security: that of the developed consumer countries and that of those nations where a considerable part of society still does not have access to modern energy supply. In this regard, the NAB is located among the first group and the South Atlantic Basin (SAB) in the second one.

About the energy security concept

There are 45 distinct definitions of the energy security concept, with similarities among them. Some consider this concept from the point of view of the countries of the Organization for Economic Cooperation and Development (OECD). Some are centered on aspects such as electricity supply, so they are not fully applicable to the least developed countries that had incomplete electricity networks, limited access to electricity (as next table shows) or nuclear power units, and non-motorized forms of transport,[15] and therefore such definitions do not cover the entire Atlantic Basin, specially the SAB.

In the past, combining "energy" and "security" in a straightforward sense meant stable energy flow, but today there should be references to other questions.[16] In this regard, the IEA defines energy security simply as "the uninterrupted availability of energy sources at an affordable price,"[17] a definition that does not include any environmental or social notions.

Thus, there is a need for a "holistic" energy security definition which could reveal and reflect the complexity of the concept. It could be the continuous availability of sustainable energy in varied forms, in sufficient quantities, at affordable prices. Furthermore, some authors feel that this definition should include two more dimensions: technology and regulation.

---

14. Keiji, K. "Energy security and human insecurity". In *Poole Gakuin University* (Ed.). (n.d.). Available at: https://ci.nii.ac.jp/els/contentscinii_20180330134441.pdf?id=ART0010407155
15. Sovacool, B. K., & Mukherjee, I. "Conceptualizing and measuring energy security: A synthesized approach". In *Energy. The International Journal*. Vol. 36, 2011, 5343-5355.
16. Energy Charter Secretariat Op. Cit.
17. IEA "Energy supply security 2014". Paris. 2015. Available at: www.iea.org

Table 2. Access to electricity (% of population)

Country	1990	2015
USA	100	100
Mexico	94.3	100
Honduras	54.7	87.6
Brazil	87.5	100
UK	100	100
Spain	100	100
Morocco	48.1	100
Nigeria	27.3	59.3
South Africa	59.3	84.2

Source: Own elaboration from The World Bank Data - "Access to electricity (% of population)". 2018. [Consulted at 25th November 2018]. Available at: https://data.worldbank.org/indicator/EG.ELC.ACCS.ZS

According to the IEA there are still two further dimensions of energy security: long-term and short-term energy security. In addition, during the negotiations for the "International Energy Charter" in 2014, an attempt was made to develop a common concept of energy security for both developing and developed economies, due to the fact that an integrating concept of energy security would lie precisely at the nexus of interdependence between all the actors involved.[18]

Theoretical approaches

It is important to know and understand the main actors and principal factors that influence energy security.

International relations theories

There are three international relations theories that are key to understanding energy security: realism, liberalism and radicalism.[19]

The liberalism approach argues that instead of a simple inter state system, the world is more complex, pluralistic and interdependent; as there are multiple actors, such as companies, regional and international bodies and the variety of local and international NGOs and civil society groups.

18. Escribano-Francés, G. *Políticas energéticas: geopolítica y seguridad energética en el sistema internacional*. Unpublished manuscript. 2018.
19. Dannreuther, R. *Energy security*. Cambridge: Polity, 2017. doi: ISBN: 978-0-745-66191-9.

Table 3. Energy security and theoretical frameworks

Theoretical	Global energy framework	Conflict vs. cooperation	Key values
Realism	States as dominant actors	Anarchical system tends towards inter-state conflicto	Security
Liberalism	Multiple actors, including companies, NGOs as well as states	Potential for cooperation through interdependence	Economic prosperity
Radicalism	Structures of domination: North-South	Resistance and revolution	Justice Sustainability

Source: Dannreuther, R., *Energy security*. Cambridge: Polity, 2017. doi: ISBN: 978-0-745-66191-9.

The realism approach may also be seen within the context of an anarchical international system lacking an overaching global sovereign authority and the primacy of sovereign States as actors in the international system. In the radicalism the fight and the domination structure North-South are key to understand energy security.

Table 3 summarizes each of these theoretical perspectives regarding the global energy framework, conflict and cooperation, and their key values.

In the NAB the influence of markets and institutions, as well as States, plays a key role in energy security, but it is also important to attend to the dynamics between North and South to understand energy security as a whole.

Energy security from the point of view of countries

Some authors consider that the three main dangers to energy security are: disruptions in energy flows with a political origin, the devastating effects of natural disasters and deficiencies in planning.[20] Consumer countries are principally concerned with the first risk, while the other two questions mainly affect supplier countries.

From the point of view of importing countries this concept covers energy supply availability, reliability, affordability, and geopolitical considerations. Europe and the USA are major energy importing regions in the

---

20. Sodupe, K., & Molina, G. "Gobernanza, seguridad energética y sostenibilidad". In *Gobernanza para un sistema energético sostenible*. Universidad del País Vasco, 2018, 31; Sodupe, K. "Gobernanza en situaciones de emergencia energética". In *Gobernanza para un sistema energético sostenible*. Universidad del País Vasco, 2018, 17.

Atlantic Basin. "While Europe generally shares American concerns over rising energy imports, the EU does not necessarily seek to maximise energy self-sufficiency and rather stresses supply source diversification."[21] In this regard the development of renewable energy sources in Europe is not observed from the point of view of increasing security of supply, but from the perspective of meeting international environmental compromises. This trend is in line with the challenge of achieving a more resilient energy infrastructure to face climate change, which could add threats to security of energy supply.

For many energy exporting countries international energy security means the possibility to export its energy at a "reasonable" price that will assure new investments in energy. This point of view was developed after the oil price collapse of 1986, when oil exporting countries faced a reduction of oil export revenues.

There is an additional point of view, that from transit countries for whom energy security could be defined as "the attainment of a technically reliable, stable, competitive and environmentally sound supply of energy resources for the economy and social sphere of the country."[22]

The four As and vital energy systems

It is relatively common to refer to energy security issues as the four As: availability, affordability, accesibility, and acceptability. The first two remain at the heart of the above-mentioned IEA definition. The two other As were linked to energy security in 2007 in the Asia Pacific Energy Research Center (APERC) report.[23]

The four As can be analysed in relation to three key questions: "security for whom?", "security for which values?", and "security from what threats?"

The classic energy security studies proceeded from the strong connection between national values such as political independence, territorial integrity and a particular energy system. Therefore, a central question for contemporary energy security studies is to identify and explore connections between energy systems and important social values. As such, human security should be considered.

---

21. Energy Charter Secretariat Op. cit.
22. Ibid.
23. Cherp, A., & Jewell, J. "The concept of energy security: Beyond the four As". In *Energy Policy*. Vol. 75, No. 415, 2014. Available at: https://www.sciencedirect.com/science/article/pii/S0301421514004960

Table 4. Different interpretations of affordability—the importance of asking: 'Security for whom?'

Affordability for whom?	Energy prices should be…
Households and private consumers	Low compared to competitors' prices
Industry and businesses	Low compared to household income
Nations	Low enough to ensure the energy import bill is small compared to export earnings
Energy companies and investors	High enough to ensure sufficient profitability for energy companies and investors

Source: Cherp, A., & Jewell, J., "The concept of energy security: Beyond the four As". In *Energy Policy*. Vol. 75, No. 415, 2014. Available at: https://www.sciencedirect.com/science/article/pii/S0301421514004960

Figure 1. Energy security concept

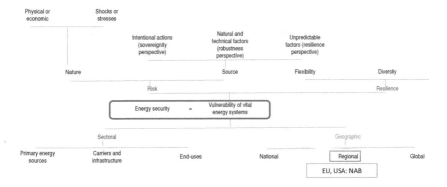

Source: Modified from Cherp, A., & Jewell, J., "The concept of energy security: Beyond the four as". In *Energy Policy*. Vol. 75, No. 415, 2014. Available at: https://www.sciencedirect.com/science/article/pii/S0301421514004960

Figure 1 summarises the vision of the concept of energy security as "low vulnerability of vital energy system." This vision differentiates between risks and resilience concepts and can be applied in two ways to energy: sectorally or geographically.

Quantitative framework

The energy situation varies between countries and among regions within countries. The actual policy instruments, which ensure energy security are wide-ranging as next table shows. As important as having emergency response mechanisms is the capability to use them at short notice and to

Table 5. Policy instruments for energy security

Instrument	Characteristics
Diversification	Look for new energy origins, sources and technologies.
Supply expansion	Domestic resource development vs. foreign resources. Production surge is a short-term measure to increase indigenous oil production within a very short period of time. The measure is limited to member countries with significant levels of production.
Security enhancement	Oil and gas production, refining, treatment, storage and distribution by pipelines; electricity generation and transmission, production and storage/processing of nuclear fuel
Stockpiling/Stockdraw	Nowadays IEA countries are required to hold oil stocks equivalent to at least 90 days of net oil imports. Significant regional differences in stockholdings are also evident. It is the most commonly used measure and the most effective, providing additional oil to an undersupplied market. Stocks are generally held either by industry or a combination of industry and a public entity. During an oil supply disruption, member countries can release stocks.
Energy efficiency	It minimises the impact of an energy supply cut. In the case of an emergency the supply to interruptible consumers, and especially to large scale industry users or power plants, would be cut to keep non-interruptible consumers (typically household users) supplied.
Demand restraint	One of the key goals of demand restraint measures is to free up oil in an under-supplied market. Such measures are not restricted to one particular sector of consumption. Because of the high and increasing proportion of oil used for transportation, most demand restraint policies focus on this sector.
Energy subsidies	Energy subsidies are intended either to make energy products affordable or to make energy production economically feasible. They are employed to fight against energy poverty
Energy trade and pricing	Energy trade let energy consumers to secure supplies and producers to gain revenues.
	The price level should be considered as "fair" and "reasonable" when it is equal to the cost of a marginal supplier. Spot trading volumes at hubs in Europe have been increasing rapidly.
Fuel switching	It is a short-term measure that encourages the use of other energy sources as alternatives to oil such as coal or natural gas. The actual potential to use fuel switching in a crisis has declined significantly in member countries since the 1970s.
Production surge	It is a short-term measure to increase indigenous oil production within a very short period of time. The measure is limited to member countries with significant levels of production.

Source: Own elaboration from Energy Charter Secretariat, "International energy security. Common convept for energy producing, consuming and transit countries". 2015. Available at: https://energycharter. org/what-we-do/trade-and-transit/trade-and-transit-thematic-reports/international-energy-security-common-concept-for-energy-producing-consuming-and-transit-countries-2015/; IEA, "Energy supply security 2014". Paris. 2015. Available at: www.iea.org

Table 6. MOSES and USA Chamber of Commerce approaches vs. the international relations framework and the Four A's point of view

	Risks	Resilience
External	External risks: risks associated with potential disruptions of energy imports	External resilience: ability to respond to disruptions of energy imports by substituting with other suppliers or supply routes.
Domestic	Domestic risks: risks arising in connection with domestic production and transformation of energy	Domestic resilience: domestic ability to respond to disruptions in energy supply such as fuel stocks.

Source: own elaboration.

understand the variety of threats. Most of these instruments are employed by countries in the NAB.

There are no standard metrics to evaluate energy security. Including more perspectives (i.e., as in the four As, with environment[24] and society, etc.) has made this task even more complicated. According to the literature, energy security could be categorized within 320 simple indicators and 52 complex indicators.[25] The next two approaches are applied to the NAB and are presented below. The first is from the International Energy Agency (IEA) and the second (more complete, as will be seen) is from the USA. They consider all international relations approaches and the four As.

The IEA approach of short-term energy security

Founded in response to the oil crisis of 1973, the IEA initially focused on oil supply security with a rather traditional view of security of supply, which considered only accessibility and availability.[26]

The IEA has developed the Model of Short-Term Energy Security (MOSES), a tool based on a set of quantitative indicators that measures two aspects of energy security in IEA contries: risks of energy supply disruptions; and resilience of a national energy system to cope with such disruptions.[27]

---

24. For instance, in those countries with a quite developed energy infrastructure there is an increasing need to undertake studies on the resilience of the energy infrastructure to climate change (i.e. the RESET project by Tecnalia and Orkestra addresses this topic for the energy infrastructure of the Basque Country-Spain).
25. Sovacool, B. K., & Mukherjee, I. "Conceptualizing and measuring energy security: A synthesized approach". In *Energy. The International Journal*. Vol. 36, 2011, 5343-5355.
26. IEA. "Measuring short-term energy security". Paris. 2011a. Available at: www.iea.org
27. Ibid.

Table 7. Dimensions of energy security as measured by MOSES

	IEA (MOSES)	USA Chamber of Commerce
Acceptability	—	✓
Affordability	—	✓
Accessibility	✓	✓
Availability	✓	✓
Realism	✓	✓
Liberalism	—	✓
Radicalism	—	✓

Source: IEA, "Measuring short-term energy security". Paris. 2011a. Available at: www.iea.org.

MOSES integrates approximately 30 indicators, analyzes vulnerabilities of primary energy sources and how these affect the security of secondary fuels. It includes external factors related to imported energy, as well as domestic factors related to domestic production, transformation and distribution of energy.

Figure 2 includes the results of some of the IEA methodology indicators calculated by employing different databases for a selection of countries in the NAB region, as well as for some non-IEA countries from the South Atlantic (i.e., Brazil and South Africa). The indicators for some of the parameters remain the same as the IEA estimates from 2011 (particularly for diversity of suppliers for the different primary energy sources).[28]

The US Chamber of Commerce approach to global energy security

One of the main attempts to provide a confident measure of energy security in the USA is the *US Energy Security Index* elaborated by the US Chamber of Commerce.

The design of this index is based on 37 indicators related to energy security risk, based on nine categories including global fuels, environment and R&D among others. The index creates four subindexes—geopolitical, economic, reliability and environmental—which are then combined into a full index and indicate an overall evaluation of energy security.

Policies must pursue the lowest indexes. The basis of the index is 100 for the year 1980. So every measured risk which scores above 100 is considered bad. In this regard, 1992 can be considered a good year (74.8). The

---

28. Since 2011 there has been no publically-available updated version of energy security using this methodology.

Figure 2. Indicators for countries in the Atlantic Basin

Energy source	Indicator	Mexico	Netherlands	Germany	Canada	UK	USA	Spain	Belgium	France	Brazil	South Africa	Morocco
Crude oil	Net-import dependence												
	Entry points (ports)												
	Pipelines												
	Diversity of suppliers												
	Proportion of offshore production												
	Stock level IEA												
	Diversity of suppliers												
Oil products	Diversity of suppliers												
	Entry points (ports)												
	Pipelines												
	Number of refineries IEA												
Natural gas	Net-import dependence												
	Entry points (LNG ports)												
	Pipelines												
	Diversity of suppliers												
	Proportion of offshore production												
	Daily send-out capacity from underground and LNG storage (%capacity over consumption)												
Coal	Entry points (ports)												
	Diversity of suppliers IEA (those that represent more than the average)												
	Proportion of mining that is underground												
Hydropower	Annual volatility of production												
Nuclear	Average age of nuclear power plants												
	Diversity of reactor models												
	Number of nuclear power plants												

Best position ██████ ░░░░░ ░░░░░ ██████ Worst position

Note: red shades indicate a negative situation with respect to the indicator in question (the darkest red means the worst position). Yellow signifies that the situation may be qualified as intermediate. Finally, green shades indicate good, positive indicators in terms of energy security (the darkest green means the best position). Source: Own elaboration.

Figure 3. Development of energy security index and subindexes for the US in the 21st Century

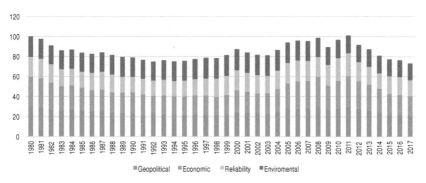

■ Geopolitical ■ Economic ■ Reliability ■ Enviromental

Source: Own elaboration from Global Energy Institute, "Energy Security Risk Index". 2018. [Consulted at 3rd December 2019]. Available at: https://www.globalenergyinstitute.org/energy-security-risk-index

Figure 4. Energy security risk comparison for selected countries (North America, European Union, EFTA and NATO) in 2018

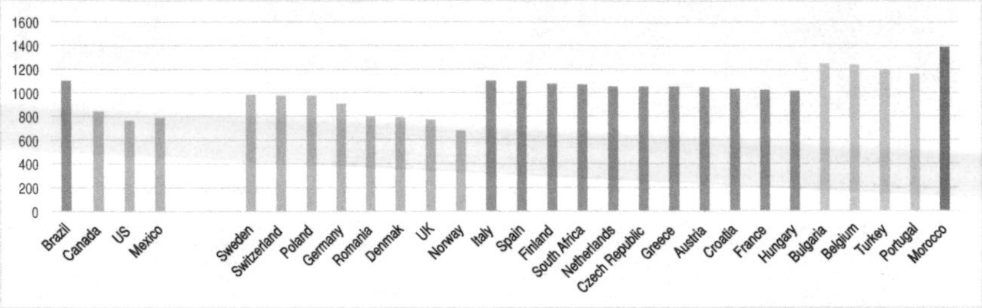

Source: Own elaboration from Global Energy Institute, "Energy Security Risk Index". 2018. [Consulted at 3rd December 2019]. Available at: https://www.globalenergyinstitute.org/energy-security-risk-index

evolution of the full index for the USA (including its four subindexes) can be seen in the following graph.

As far as subindexes are concerned, the highest values during this period can be found for the reliability factor, so a strong focus of policies on this may be pursued. Oppositely, lowest values during this period are performed by the economic factor, which have increased and have shown ample variations in the last ten years, probably due to financial crisis. It is interesting to highlight the evolution of the environmental subindex that remains the highest together with reliability. The tendency clearly shows a coupling of geopolitical events.

These results should be considered in context of other countries of the Atlantic Basin, especially Canada and Mexico. In the following graph, those countries in green and blue are those, on both sides of the Atlantic Basin, that exhibit the lowest energy security risk indexes. Nevertheless, an important number of countries from the European Union and some from the NATO (like Turkey) are not in the same high performing group (indicated by yellow and red).

Other countries considered include Morocco, South Africa and Brazil. Among these, South Africa and Brazil show the second lowest risk group of the 75 top consuming countries. On the other hand, Morocco is located in the highest risk group, although all three of these countries share a deteriorating evolution of their indexes when compared with OECD countries since the 2000s.

It could be concluded, that in the NAB, where the principal energy security frameworks were developed, the nexus between energy security and human security has little to do with the level of demand insecurity and supply inaccessibility among poor consumers suffering from energy poverty, and a lack of energy infrastructures of all types as it happens in the SAB.

However, in spite of the above mentioned conclusion, in the NAB climate change is today a relevant hazard to security of energy supply and will continue to exert a damaging influence on energy infrastructure, which should be made more resilient in the near future. Furthermore there are other threats that could probably affect reducing energy security level in the NAB inducing higher human insecurity (for example, growing domestic energy prices due to energy transitions that may increase energy poverty level [29] or cyber attacks that could affect the energy infrastructure leaving at all consumers with no energy access). Therefore, next section deals with energy security policies in this territory.

Energy security in the Atlantic Basin
Data on oil reserves, trade, and refining capacity in the NAB

As in this document energy security is mainly related to oil and gas,[30] it is convenient to have an overview on reserves, trade and refining capacity, which influence, among others, the energy politics. Next there are some notes about these elements.

Venezuela and Canada hold the first and the third largest proven oil reserves in the world (estimated at 297 billion barrels and 167 billion barrels respectively including the sand oil in Canada). Other Atlantic countries are also developing and exporting their oil reserves too. In Africa, Nigeria is the continent's biggest oil producer, followed by Angola with (with oil reserves of 13 billion barrels), and Equatorial Guinea. In the Americas, other large oil nations are the USA (with 30.5 billion barrels of proven reserves), followed by Brazil (13.3 billion barrels) and Mexico (12.7 billion barrels of oil).[31]

---

29. For more information, see Álvarez et al., 2016; Álvarez and Álvaro, 2017; and Álvaro and Larrea, 2018.
30. For gas infrastructures there is a description focused on the Atlantic Basin in Álvarez Pelegry & Larrea Basterra, 2019.
31. Lété, B. Op. cit.

Figure 5. Major gasoline and diesel/gas oil trade movements. Flows from the EU (2015)

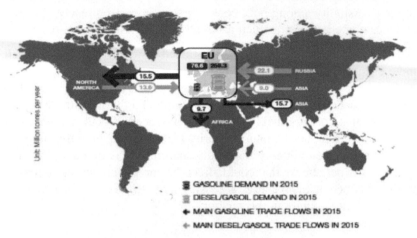

Source: BP Statistical Review of World Energy 2017 in FUELS EUROPE. – "Statistical report". Belgium. 2018. Available at: https://www.fuelseurope.eu/publication/statistical-report-2018/

In 2002, trade movement was mainly north-north. However, from 2002 to 2017 it has increased in the Atlantic Basin and especially north-south according to recent data from BP.[32]

Refining is spread around the world and is a truly global business. Most of the regions are dependent on imports to meet market demand. Europe has lost 29 refineries during the last five years. 40% of total refining capacity is in the NAB.[33] By 2023, 10.1% (777 thousand barrels per day) of new refining capacity will be developed in the NAB. 20.3% in the whole Atlantic Basin. The NAB will loose relevance in terms of refining capacity.

The main trade flows to and from the EU have been the result of the gasoline/diesel imbalance demand. The EU also suffers also from shortage of jet production. NAB oil products trade is within a framework of very diverse and complex flows worldwide.

---

32. BP. "BP statistical review 2002 of world energy". 2003. Available at: https://www.gri-equity.com/resources/industryandissues/Energy/bp2002statisticalreview.pdf ; BP. "BP statistical review 2018". 2018. Available at: https://www.bp.com/content/dam/bp/en/corporate/pdf/energy-economics/statistical-review/bp-stats-review-2018-full-report.pdf

33. FUELS EUROPE. "Statistical report". Belgium. 2018. Available at: https://www.fuelseurope.eu/publication/statistical-report-2018/

Current situation and perspectives

Several geostrategic events during the last two decades have shaped the current situation. These events include: 9/11, the wars in Afghanistan and Iraq, the Fukushima accident, the Arab Spring, the rise of the Islamic State and Russia's affair with Ukraine. Nevertheless, the Atlantic remains a relatively stable geopolitical space, in contrast to the territorial disputes and military tensions of the Pacific Rim. This is largely due to the lack of great power conflict.[34] However, the prominence of the region in security and military considerations is rising, especially with the aim of combating illegal activities.[35]

There are growing trade flows of, and new maritime transportation routes for, raw materials and final products within the Atlantic Basin (driven by emerging economies like Brazil and South Africa). These new trade flows and their maritime transportation routes require surveillance and security. In this regard, the port-cities of the NAB could contribute.[36]

Piracy is the biggest threat against open and secure maritime transportation routes in South Atlantic Basin, especially in the Gulf of Guinea, where it affects among others Nigeria, Togo, and Cote d'Ivoire. In 2013, for example, out of 47 cases of piracy 29 took place in the coast of Nigeria.[37] This country lost around 2.8 billion dollars in revenues in 2018, mainly related to oil and maritime crime and piracy. [38] Such security threats may affect change across the Atlantic energy landscape as new energy production is developed in the USA, Canada, Brazil, Angola and Nigeria and as Europe continues to pursue diversification of its import sources.

Given the well-advanced level of NAB integration, Europe and the USA have a direct mutual interest in contributing their resources and experience to assist in the securitization of the entire Atlantic Basin,[39] so its maritime network and infrastructure enjoy shared protection against piracy, organized crime, terrorism and sabotage. Such Atlantic cooperation should also

---

34. For more information see (Hamilton, 2014).
35. Lété, B. Op cit.
36. For more information see (Fonseca Ribeiro, 2017).
37. UNOWA "Maritime security in the Gulf of Guinea". 2019. [Consulted at 29th January 2019]. Available at: https://unowa.unmissions.org/maritime-security-gulf-guinea
38. Times Premium "Nigeria lost $2.8 billion to 'oil-related crimes' in 2018 UN". 2019. [Consulted at 30th January 2019]. Available at: https://www.premiumtimesng.com/news/headlines/304717-nigeria-lost-2-8-billion-to-oil-related-crimes-in-2018-un.html
39. Lété, B. Op. cit.

include cybersecurity, as organizations like NATO have underlined, following some known attacks to cyber-infrastructures in places like Ukraine.[40]

Politics

Energy is a key element in terms of economic competitiveness and social welfare. In order to guarantee energy security, nations develop policies that must be put into practice, as will be demonstrated below.

Europe

The EU imports more than half of all the energy it consumes, especially crude oil (90%) and natural gas (69%). Many countries are heavily reliant on a single supplier (e.g., Russia), so they are highly vulnerable to supply disruptions.[41]

Traditionally, measures to face these problems were in the hands of each member state. However, the EU has become increasingly involved in energy security, even if individual national initiatives still remain relevant.[42]

The EU has pursued the creation of a European energy space, but the efforts to promote convergence faced serious obstacles due to Member States' reluctance to transfer sovereignty in the energy security realm.[43] However, as the next table shows, several milestones towards a European energy security concept have been achieved.

A few years later, in May 2014, the European Commission released its Energy Security Strategy, which is an integral part of the 2030 policy framework on climate change. It is also fully consistent with their competitiveness and industrial policy objectives. Short-term measures were developed together with long-term ones that address challenges to security of supply.[44]

---

40. NATO "What happens when a power plant comes under cyber attack?" 2016. [Consulted at 20th December 2018]. Available at: https://www.youtube.com/watch?v=bV47gBsrDkc

41. European Commission "Energy Security Strategy". 2018. Available at: https://ec.europa.eu/energy/en/topics/energy-strategy-and-energy-union/energy-security-strategy

42. Energy Charter Secretariat Op. cit.

43. Escribano-Francés, G. "Risk of energy availability: common corridors for Europe supply security". Madrid, 2009.

44. European Commission "Energy Security Strategy." Op. cit.

Table 8. Relevant EU documents related to energy security

Document	Observations
European Energy Charter (1991)	The Charter's general objectives are quite wide. Among the most important: increase security of supply; abstention by signatory countries to impose discriminatory measures concerning access to energy resources; easing the obstacles to freer energy trade, including energy equipment and services; promotion and protection of investments in the energy sector; and technological cooperation.
White Paper on EU's energy policy (1995)	The European Commission explicitly rejects the fragmentation of EU's energy markets, proposing the integration of domestic markets and its liberalization.
Green Paper on the security of energy supply (2000)	Vulnerability from energy dependency and its relation with markets and renewables
Green Paper on a European strategy for sustainable, competitive and secure energy (2006)	The European energy security vision had an external and an internal dimension. The external dimension included energy dialogues with Russia and OPEC, and the more ambitious proposal for the creation of a "wider-Europe Energy Community". The internal dimension of EU's energy security was identified in terms of institutions but it implicitly pointed to physical infrastructures and the achievement of the internal market.
Energy package (2007)	Agrees on a two-year action plan towards a common European energy policy. It includes a common external energy policy and the need to link energy issues to EU's external relations in general.
Green Paper "Towards a Secure, Sustainable and Competitive European Energy Network", and the Second Strategic Energy Review: "EU Energy Security and Solidarity Action Plan" (2008)	The Second Strategic Energy Review insists on the focal points already raised by former EU documents: diversifying energy sources and origins, ensuring effective competition and competitiveness, achieving the internal market, enhancing energy efficiency, fostering interconnections, increasing the share of renewables, solidarity mechanisms, the role of stocks and crisis response procedures, storage and LNG capacities, and a greater focus on energy in EU's foreign policy.

Source: Own elaboration from Escribano-Francés, G. – "Risk of energy availability: common corridors for Europe supply security". Madrid, 2009.

One key aspect of the strategy is to promote closer competition while respecting national energy choices.[45] The following points indicate the policies/objectives of the strategy.

Strengthening emergency/solidarity mechanisms including the coordination of risk assessments and contingency and protecting strategic infrastructure.

- Moderating energy demand.

- Building a well-funcioning and fully-integrated internal market.

- Increasing energy production in the EU.

- Further developing of energy technologies.

- Diversifying external supplies and related infrastructure,

- Improving coordination of national energy policies and one voice in the external energy policy.

These pillars may be considered respectively in relation to the liberal and realist theoretical perspectives mentioned above as the reader may notice. For instance, the first, third, sixth and seventh points could be studied under the perspective of the liberalism approach. In the meanwhile, the second, fourth and fifth points are mainly related to the realism.

2016 is another relevant year in relation to energy security, when the European Commission presented the Winter Package with special emphasis on energy efficiency, claiming that it would reduce European dependency on energy imports. It included measures to keep the EU competitive while the clean energy transition transforms global energy markets. The final objective of this package in general terms was to give consumers across the EU a better choice of supply, access to reliable energy prices comparison tools and the possibility to produce and sell their own electricity.[46]

---

45. European Commission "EU energy security strategy. Communication from the commission to the european parliament and the council. COM (2014)330 final". 2014. Available at: https://www.eesc.europa.eu/resources/docs/european-energy-security-strategy.pdf
46. European Commission. "Putting energy efficiency first: Consuming better, getting cleaner". Brussels. 2016a. Available at: www.europa.eu/rapid/press-release_MEMO-16-3986_en.pdf

In this package, energy efficiency appears as "one of the most cost-effective ways to ensure energy security" and is presented as an instrument for resolving social issues like energy poverty,[47] mentioned before.[48]

The importance of gas imports, instruments of risks assessments and collective response was shown by the 2017/1938 Regulation, which covered the issues of gas infrastructure coordination and the guarantee of gas supply to "protected clients" against risk.[49]

In the most recent European Commission documents, the strategy proposes: (1) a space for common regulation within the EU and its neighborhoods; (2) reinforcement of agreements with third countries (e.g., energy exporters or transit countries, see map below); and (3) clarification that strategic energy partnerships with producer countries should be based on the rules and principles of the community's energy policy.[50]

In this regard, one important aspect of energy security is the promotion of energy corridors (where transit countries point of view is suitable). The EU has developed, particularly in gas, several access routes to gas imports, shown in Figure 6.

The next few years will be crucial for European energy policy. The basis of the Energy Union that will articulate a single market and a common external energy policy must be established. Some of these foundations are related to investments in energy infrastructure and others to the catalyzing of the coordination of external energy policies. Furthermore, the EU must decide on how to cooperate with the United Kingdom and how to articulate foreign energy policy to fight against climate change in its relationships with the Middle East, the Mediterranean, Russia, Central Asia and the Atlantic Basin.[51]

---

47. For more information see Larrea Basterra, M. "La pobreza energética en la Unión Europea y el Reino Unido. El caso de Inglaterra". In *Revista ICADE*, No. 102, 2017. ISSN 1889-7045.
48. European Commission "Putting energy efficiency first: Consuming better, getting cleaner". Brussels. 2016a. Available at: www.europa.eu/rapid/press-release_MEMO-16-3986_en.pdf
49. European Parliament, E. C. "Regulation (EU) 2017/1938 of the European Parliament and of the Council of 25 October 2017 concerning measures to safeguard the security of gas supply and repealing regulation (EU) no 994/2010". 2017. Available at: https://eur-lex.europa.eu/legal-content/EN/TXT/PDF/?uri=OJ:L:2017:280:FULL&from=ES
50. Escribano-Francés, G. *Políticas energéticas: geopolítica y seguridad energética en el sistema internacional.* Unpublished manuscript. 2018.
51. Ibid.

Figure 6. Main energy corridors of the EU

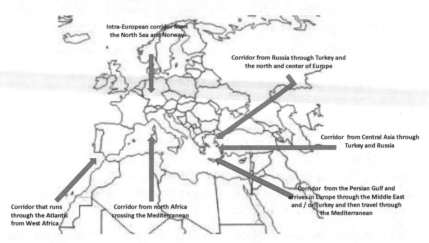

Source: Own elaboration from Escribano-Francés, G., Políticas energéticas: geopolítica y seguridad energética en el sistema internacional. Unpublished manuscript. 2018.

North America's energy security integration

When describing energy security interactions in North America, the USA becomes the central actor because of its geographic and economic position between Canada and Mexico. Furthermore, recent interactions between the US and Europe may produce changes in relationships across the Atlantic Basin. As a consequence, the analysis below will delve into US energy security policy in depth.

Geopolitical events during the last decades of 20th Century induced the USA (first, and the later all of North America) to make energy supply the top priority of energy policy.[52]

First, the North American Energy Working Group (NAEWG) was established in 2001 with the purpose of improving communication and cooperation regarding energy matters of common interest.[53] Subsequently, the

---

52. CEA "Engineering a Collaborative & Clean Energy Future". 29th Mexican National Congress of Engineering. 2018a. Available at: https://electricity.ca/wp-content/uploads/2018/03/Remarks-at-Mexican-National-Congress-of-Civil-Engineering-Final.pdf

53. DOE "North American Energy Work Group Releases Updated Trilateral Energy Report". 2006. [Consulted at 10th December 2019]. Available at: https://www.energy.gov/articles/north-american-energy-work-group-releases-updated-trilateral-energy-report

NAEWG was incorporated into a trilateral Security and Prosperity Partnership (SPP) in 2005 to improve security cooperation in broader areas.

Despite these preliminary efforts, the initiative to foster energy security cooperation suffered from a lack of resources. North America therefore entered into a seven-year period during which no relevant steps were taken.[54]

In December 2014, an inflection point in North American energy cooperation was reached with the signing of a Memorandum of Understanding (MOU) between the responsible agencies of the three countries. This provided an institutional framework for consultation and sharing publicly available information among the participants. As a result, the North American Cooperation on Energy Information common initiative was created.

Today, North America is a semi-integrated energy market in which internal commodity flows, on the one hand, and common external interactions with rest of the world, on the other hand, can be identified.[55] It is a highly interdependent and multidirectional market that includes trade, innovation and investment by the private sectors.[56]

Recently the three governments decided that the NAFTA (North American Free Trade Agreement) should be replaced. As a result, in October 2018 the USMCA (United States-Mexico-Canada Agreement) was concluded. This could lead to a potential change in North American energy market integration with benefits for the US,[57] although there was already an

---

54. Wood, D. "Integrating North America's Energy Markets: A Call for Action". In Wilson Center, Mexico Institute. 2014. Available at: https://www.wilsoncenter.org/sites/default/files/Integrating%20North%20America%27s%20Energy%20Markets.pdf
55. NACEI "North American Cooperation on Energy Information". 2018. [Consulted at 30th November 2018]. Available at: http://nacei.org/#!/overview
56. Cattaneo, C. "Shooting themselves in the foot': How NAFTA's collapse could disrupt U.S.-Canada energy trade". In *Financial Post*. 2018. [Consulted at: 1st December 2018]. Available at: https://business.financialpost.com/commodities/energy/shooting-themselves-in-the-foot-how-naftas-collapse-could-disrupt-u-s-canada-energy-trade; Wayne, E. A. "The Economic Relationship Between the United States, Canada, and Mexico': Earl Anthony Wayne Testifies before the US Senate Committee on Foreign Relations". Mexico Institute, Wilson Center. 2018. Available at: https://www.wilsoncenter.org/article/the-economic-relationship-between-the-united-states-canada-and-mexico-earl-anthony-wayne
57. Wayne, E. A. and Shedd, D. R. "Assuring Energy Security with a Modern NAFTA". In *Forbes*. 2018. [Consulted at 10th December 2018). Available at: https://www.forbes.com/sites/themexicoinstitute/2018/05/09/assuring-energy-security-with-a-modern-nafta/#35f3e5983019

attempt to reach a common framework under the so-called "North American Energy Strategy."[58]

Nevertheless, both Canada and Mexico have developed a framework for bilateral cooperation. In October 2004, the Canada-Mexico Partnership (CMP) was launched,[59] which included issues like indigenous consultations for the development of energy projects. Another point was subnational cooperation as, in fact, some Canadian provinces and territories are interested in the expansion and modernization of the Mexican energy sector.[60]

North American cooperation has also experienced a progressive shift towards protecting energy infrastructures against external attacks. For instance, due to a wave of cyber attacks both in Canada and the US, both countries established in 2012 a Cybersecurity Action Plan. Mexico has also included international cooperation on cybersecurity as one of the main actions in its National Security Program 2014-2018[61], although differences between cybersecurity capabilities between Mexico and US can be viewed as risks emanation from the former to the latter.[62]

US energy security in the 21st Century

Three administrations (two republicans and one democratic) have governed the US during this 21st century whose positioning on energy security is explained next.

---

58. CEA "Engineering a Collaborative & Clean Energy Future". 29th Mexican National Congress of Engineering. 2018a. Available at: https://electricity.ca/wp-content/uploads/2018/03/Remarks-at-Mexican-National-Congress-of-Civil-Engineering-Final.pdf; US Mission To Mexico "Secretary Perry Remarks at Press Event with SENER". 2017. [Consulted at 10th December 2018]. Available at: https://mx.usembassy.gov/secretary-perry-remarks-press-event-sener/

59. Government Of Canada "The Canada-Mexico Partnership". 2018. Available at: https://www.canadainternational.gc.ca/mexico-mexique/cmp-pcm.aspx?lang=eng

60. Government Of Alberta "Mexico Alberta Relations". 2011. Available at: https://open.alberta.ca/dataset/911b2ffd-0990-43c3-85ab-b0b1e0b3833f/resource/3a672bb8-f75d-4d14-ba29-78191f6bf020/download/mexico-ab.pdf

61. Kobek, L. P. "The State of Cybersecurity in Mexico: An Overview". 2017. Available at: https://www.wilsoncenter.org/sites/default/files/cybersecurity_in_mexico_an_overview.pdf

62. Lee, S. "Cybersecurity Strategy Advice for the Trump Administration: US-Mexico Relations". In *The Henry M. Jackson School of International Studies*. University of Washington. 2017. [Consulted at 20th December 2018]. Available at: https://jsis.washington.edu/news/cybersecurity-strategy-advice-trump-administration-us-mexico-relations/#_ftn21

The Bush Administration (2001-2009)

George W. Bush Administration considered energy security as a key element since the presidential campaign, when he argued that "America, more than ever, is at the mercy of foreign governments and cartels."[63] Also, during his second mandate Bush continued to underline this by affirming that "America is addicted to oil."[64]

Several initiatives were developed including the Royalties Conservation Fund, implemented to support new drilling and oil and gas production in Alaska's Artic Refuge, ANWR [65], and the National Energy Policy (NEP) in search of strong relationships with energy-producing nations within global alliances. [66]

The US decision to not sign the Kyoto protocol became a factor of geopolitical tension between the EU and the US,[67] contributing to shifts which European diplomats described as marking a "significant divergence" between both regions.[68]

An inflection point occurred when Hurricanes Katrina and Rita made land in 2005. These meteorological events represented a political crisis, particularly with respect to energy security issue: oil production and refinery facilities in the Gulf of Mexico were seriously damaged (next table shows the main energy infrastructure in the US related to oil and gas). Given, on the one hand, the serious impact on infrastructures[69] and, on

---

63. Allen, M. "Bush Supports Oil Exploration. In Arctic Refuge". In *The Washington Post*. 2000. [Consulted at: 25th November 2018]. Available at: https://www.washingtonpost.com/archive/politics/2000/09/30/bush-supports-oil-exploration-in-arctic-refuge/33563dc1-5c66-4afa-8f5e-cb135f3defb9/?utm_term=.a040d57b0055
64. Bumiller, E. & Nagourney, A. "Bush: 'America is addicted to oil". In *The New York Times*, Archives. 2006. [Consulted at: 25th December 2018]. Available at: https://www.nytimes.com/2006/02/01/world/americas/01iht-state.html
65. The White House "The President's Energy Legislative Agenda". 2001. [Conulted at 5th December 2018.] Available at: https://georgewbush-whitehouse.archives.gov/news/releases/2001/06/energyinit.html
66. Presidency of US "Reliable, Affordable, and Environmentally Sound Energy for America's Future". 2001. Available at: https://www.wtrg.com/EnergyReport/National-Energy-Policy.pdf
67. Kahn, G. "The Fate of the Kyoto Protocol under the Bush Administration". In *Berkeley Journal of International Law*. Vol. 21, No. 3, Article 5. 2003. Available at: https://scholarship.law.berkeley.edu/cgi/viewcontent.cgi?article=1248&context=bjil
68. Borger, J. "Bush kills global warming treaty". In *The Guardian*. 2001. [Consulted at: 28th November 2018]. Available at: https://www.theguardian.com/environment/2001/mar/29/globalwarming.usnews
69. More than 100 oil and gas production platforms were destroyed and nearly 20% of US daily refining capacity went off-line from late August to October. See Chow, E. & Elkind, J. "Hurricane Katrina and US Energy Security". In *Survival*. Vol. 47, No. 4, 145-

Asia' on this part of the Obama Administration's foreign policy. In any event, none of this means that the USA has disengaged from the Middle East.[77]

The Trump Administration (2017-Present)

A key document for understanding the main philosophy of Donald Trump Administration is the new National Security Strategy (NSS), which appeared in December of 2017 to replace the last NSS of the Obama Administration.[78] The purpose of the new NSS is to reveal the primary national security concerns of the country and the related plans that the administration proposes to follow. According to García,[79] energy infrastructure is one of the main targets of the new NSS strategy.

The new NSS includes the objective to "embrace energy dominance," implying that the US will hold a central leadership position in the global energy system for first time in generations as producer, consumer and innovator. This drive to dominance is intended to lead to resilient and secure US energy infrastructure, along with diversified access to energy. In this sense, the NSS underlines the need to unleash domestic resources (from coal to renewables) and includes a call to continue the integration of the North American energy system along with others for new initiatives to unlock shared potential.[80]

Such energy dominance implies a strategy based on diversification of supply. The US would wield its intended role as energy, technology, and services exporter around the world as a mechanism to help the country's allies and partners to improve their resilience in the face of those suppliers who use energy as a tool for "coercion." This posture is consistent with the potential of US economy to use and offer as wide a variety of energy forms and services as possible. To a certain degree, Trump's energy dominance strategy implies somehow taking the "all of the above" philosophy of the Obama Administration, but promoting those sources that the previ-

---

77. Woertz, E. "Has the Shale Revolution Really Led to US Disengagement from the Middle East?". In *CIDOB*. 2016. Available at: https://www.cidob.org/en/articulos/monografias/elecciones_presidenciales_en_estados_unidos/has_the_shale_revolution_really_led_to_us_disengagement_from_the_middle_east
78. NSSA "National Security Strategy Archive". 2018. [Consulted at 19th December 2018]. Available at: http://nssarchive.us/
79. García, C. G. Op. cit.
80. NSSA. "National Security Strategy Archive". 2018. [Consulted at 19th December 2018]. Available at: http://nssarchive.us/

ous administration attempted to either regulate or to reduce their share in the energy mix.[81]

This new strategy is in line with the requests of the energy industry. Only a few days after Donald Trump won presidential election in November 2016, the American Petroleum Institute [API]) called for Trump's strategy to include all forms of energy.[82] In this way, a comprehensive vision of energy resources has been translated into renewed federal support to industries (such as coal[83]) whose relevance during former administration was thought to be on the decline.

The energy and environmental policy changes of the first year of the Trump Administration were among the most visible and effective decisions taken by the administration to date.[84] In this regard, the June 2017 decision to withdraw from the Paris Agreement constitutes the cornerstone of Trump's energy policy—including energy security issues, given that climate change actions appear to be viewed with skepticism by this administration. Moreover, the 2017 NSS does not include any references to "climate change" (even if there are several references to clean energy).

Concerns regarding energy security have changed somewhat in the last few years, as the focus has shifted from the traditional attempt to guarantee supply to a new perspective in which integrity of energy infrastructures must be assured.[85] In February 2018 US Department of Energy (DOE) was assigned the creation of the Office of Cybersecurity, Energy Security, and Emergency Response (CESER) with cybersecurity and energy security as main areas and with a multiyear Plan for Energy Sector Cybersecurity.[86] At

---

81. House Committee On Natural Resources "All-of-the-Above Energy Approach". 2014. Available at: https://naturalresources.house.gov/energy/

82. Green, M. J. "The Legacy of Obama's "Pivot" to Asia". In *Foreing Policy*, 2016. [Consulted at 10th December 2018]. Available at: https://foreignpolicy.com/2016/09/03/the-legacy-of-obamas-pivot-to-asia/

83. Nevertheless, current trends have driven to a major number of coal plants closed during first two years of Trump Adinistration's than during Obama's first term: see EIA, 2018; Weir, 2019; or Jones, 2019..

84. Friedman, L. and Mufson, S. "Energy & Environment in Trump's First Year". Podcast, 2018. Columbia | SIPA Center on Global Energy Policy. 2018. [Consulted at 5th December 2018]. Available at: https://energypolicy.columbia.edu/energy-environment-trumps-first-year

85. CEA "Engineering a Collaborative & Clean Energy Future". 29th Mexican National Congress of Engineering. 2018a. Available at: https://electricity.ca/wp-content/uploads/2018/03/Remarks-at-Mexican-National-Congress-of-Civil-Engineering-Final.pdf

86. DOE "Secretary of Energy Rick Perry Forms New Office of Cybersecurity, Energy Security, and Emergency Response". 2018a. Available at: https://www.energy.gov/

Table 10. Comparison of last three US administrations on key energy security issues

	George W. Bush (2001-2009)	Barack Obama (2009-2017)	Donald Trump (2017-present)
Main driver	Global alliances	Shale revolution	Energy dominance
External supply	Diversification of imports from production countries	Reduction of dependence through domestic production	US allies and partners to diversify their energy sources through promotion of US energy exports
Domestic energy sources	Royalties Conservation Fund	Coal regulation	Encourage of coal and nuclear industry
	Critical infrastructures improvement and modernisation	POWER+ Plan for affected coal communities	Support to oil industry
	Renewable energy incentives	Nuclear plants security	Completion of critical infrastructures (Dakota Access and Keystone XL oil pipelines)
		"All of the above" but shift from oil to gas in transport	Inclusion of renewable sources in universal access to domestic resources
		Some restrictions on drilling permits (Alaska and outer continental shelf)	
		Renewable energy incentives	
R&D	First encourage for smart grids	New transport fuels and technologies	Cybesecurity
	Coal plants	Energy efficiency	Nuclear industry
	Energy efficiency	Carbon Capture and Sequestration Technologies	Petroleum reserves and fossil fuels R&D
Climate and environment	Air quality protection	Clean Power Plan for air quality and GHG	Withdrawal from Paris Agreement

Table 10. Comparison of last three US administrations on key energy security issues

	George W. Bush (2001-2009)	Barack Obama (2009-2017)	Donald Trump (2017-present)
	Refusal to join Kyoto Protocol	Climate change as global goal and active participation in climate initiatives. Joined Paris Agreement (COP21)	Amendment to CPP
	National goals to reduce GHG emissions intensity		
North American cooperation	North American Energy Working Group (NAEWG)	Memorandum of Understanding (MoU)	Replacement of North American trade agreement: NAFTA by USMCA
Focus on Asia/Atlantic relationships	Close transatlantic relationships with some crisis and restorations	Alignment on climate goals with Europe	Search for new share of efforts within NATO and Europe's dependence
	First initiatives toward Asia	Announced pivot toward Asia	Withdrawal from TPP (Pacific trade)
Energy security programs	Energy for America´s Future	New energy for America?	NSS (2017)
	National energy future	ACES (2009)	
	NSS (2002)	ARRA (2009)	
	Energy Policy Act (2005)	NSS (2010)	
	Advanced energy initiative	CPP (2014)	
	NSS (2006)	Energy security Trust	
	EISA (2007)	FAST Act	
	Food and energy security act (2008)	NSS (2015)	
	Energy improvement and extension act (2008)		
Main events related to energy security	11-S	Deepwater Horizon oil rig explodes off Louisiana	Paris Climate Agreement withdrawal

Table 10. Comparison of last three US administrations on key energy security issues

	George W. Bush (2001-2009)	Barack Obama (2009-2017)	Donald Trump (2017-present)
	Iraq War	Arab Spring	Iran Nuclear Deal abandonment
	Hurricane Katrina	Libya attack	
	Financial crisis of 2000	Iraq war over	
	First BRIC´s formal summit	First federal government shutdown in two decades	
		Crimea crisis	
		Back to Iraq	
		Syria airstrikes	
		End of Afganistan	
		Paris Climate Agreement	
		Iran Nuclear Deal	
		Sacred Native American sites	
		Sanctions against Russia	

the same time, the National Cyber Strategy of September 2018 identifies energy and power as one of its seven key areas.[87]

The second half of Trump's first term has begun with a change of majority in the House of Representatives and a government shutdown. If the proposed budget for a fiscal year is not approved by the Congress, the non-essential functions of US government cease to function until an agreement is reached. This could have partially affected energy security, although

articles/secretary-energy-rick-perry-forms-new-office-cybersecurity-energy-security-and-emergency; DOE "Multiyear plan for energy sector cybersecurity". 2018b. Available at: https://www.energy.gov/sites/prod/files/2018/05/f51/DOE%20Multiyear%20Plan%20for%20Energy%20Sector%20Cybersecurity%20_0.pdf

87. Presidency of the Us "National Cyber Staretgy of the United States of America". 2018. Available at: https://www.whitehouse.gov/wp-content/uploads/2018/09/National-Cyber-Strategy.pdf

the corresponding energy and water budget was assigned before the shutdown.[88]

Recent events regarding the political crisis in Venezuela, are also expected to induce changes in the US energy security policies, due to oil implications. In fact the US has been the main importer of oil from the Caribbean country, and it is supposed that oil from Canada and Mexico may gain importance for the US.[89]

As a summary, there have been changes through every legislative period. The context has led to some remarkable differences between each administration views that are analysed in Table 10.

Final remarks and conclusions

Energy security and economic growth have played a key role since the 1970s, when an important global energy crisis occurred. Energy security — the definitional complexity of which has increased over the last decade as it has incorporated more elements (such as technology and sustainability) — can be analyzed from different points of view.

The realist, liberal and radical approaches to international relations can be brought to bear upon energy security issues in the NAB, as the states, the institutions, the markets and the value of sustainability are very relevant across the basin and its surrounding territories. Moreover, given the clear difference between the North Atlantic (particularly the US and Europe) in their energy export/import profiles with respect to different energy regions, it is clear that views on energy security are influenced by the differing points of view of exporting, importing and transit countries.

Energy security has traditionally been understood as security of supply for energy buyers; however, it could also be analysed from the point of view of the security of demand. The traditional concepts of energy securi-

---

88. Morello, L. "US science agencies hit by government shutdown". In *Nature*. 2018. [Consulted at 15th January 2019]. Available at: https://www.nature.com/articles/d41586-018-07836-6; Wasson, E., Litvan, L. and Flavelle, C. "Here's What Would Happen If There's a Government Shutdown in December". In *Bloomberg*. 2018. [Consulted at 10th January 2019]. Available at: https://www.bloomberg.com/news/articles/2018-12-11/shutdown-impact-would-be-limited-as-only-some-agencies-unfunded

89. Kumar, D. K. and Eaton, C. "Venezuelan oil exports to U.S. still a primary source of cash". In *Reuters*, 2019. [Consulted at 27th January 2019]. Available at: https://www.reuters.com/article/us-venezuela-politics-usa-oil-graphic/venezuelan-oil-exports-to-u-s-still-a-primary-source-of-cash-idUSKCN1PJ2CT

ty, availability, affordability, accessibility and acceptability have to merge with a broader approach of "energy security as low vulnerability of vital energy systems".

Countries have developed different indicators and metrics that have become key for a better understanding energy security issues. This chapter has dealt mainly with the quantitative approaches of the IEA and the US Chamber of Commerce. This second approach (more complete and updated yearly) includes other increasingly relevant elements such as R&D and the environment. For instance, currently the reduction of greenhouse gases and other pollutant emissions, along with the improvement of energy efficiency, are at the focus of most national and international regulations and commitments. However, the IEA approach does not include them. This approach should be updated, incorporate new parameters, and consider other countries in order to have a tool with which to make comparisons. In any case, the results obtained, show that nowadays the situation is relatively similar in terms of energy security as at the beginning of this decade.

Energy security should also be framed within the human security concept as it impacts at least four dimensions of human security: economic, food, health and environment. Even if today the nexus between energy security and human security could seems stronger in the SAB, climate change and other elements as energy transitions or cyber attacks could cause different types of supply problems in the NAB as it happened when hurricane Katrina for instance.

In order to face the problems of energy insecurity and to provide adequate responses, NAB countries adopt different measures. The abundant tools to ensure security of supply include trade, diversification, supply expansion, security enhancement, stockpiling, and demand control, and, to some extent, energy subsidies.

The politics and objectives of energy security can differ between the USA (energy dominance, competitiveness and job creation) and the EU (decarbonization of the economy, RES and energy efficiency). These policy divergences are accentuated by the currently diverging trends in domestic production and exports/imports of oil and gas, and in renewable energy development.

In the EU member states have evolved from taking national measures to face the main challenges on energy security to developing some European rules that can be implemented by the EU itself. In part this shift has been provoked by oil and gas issues. Currently the European Commission encourages the consumer to be more active in both offering their opinion and taking decisions, and even to play a role as both consumer and producer (prosumers), a role that could become a reality through use of certain renewable energy technologies. Such energies could play a relevant role in reducing energy insecurity in the EU. Likewise, these energies could also facilitate and promote the access to energy in the SAB where energy infrastructure is not so developed.

In the USA, common energy security rhetoric can be found over the three last administrations. Climate issues have progressively moved from being considered solely as an environmental concern to gaining importance within energy security, even if support for new energy sources has been varying. Furthermore, the USA's perspective began from a vision of its dangerous reliance on oil. This changed with the "shale" revolution and pivoted to an emphasis on fossil fuel exports for the first time in decades, creating a new situation.

Energy security is therefore important in the NAB, and future developments will need to address this security across the entire Atlantic Basin (including the South Atlantic Basin) by developing rules and encouraging actors to take relevant measures.

References

Allen, M. "Bush Supports Oil Exploration. In Arctic Refuge". In *The Washington Post*. 2000. [Consulted at: 25th November 2018]. Available at: https://www.washingtonpost.com/archive/politics/2000/09/30/bush-supports-oil-exploration-in-arctic-refuge/33563dc1-5c66-4afa-8f5e-cb135f3defb9/?utm_term=.a040d57b0055

ÁLVAREZ Pelegry, E.; Ortiz Martínez, I.; Menéndez Sánchez, J. "The German energy transition (Energiewende). Policy, Energy Transformation and Industrial Development". 2016. Available at: https://www.orkestra.deusto.es/es/investigacion/publicaciones/cuadernos-orkestra/1156-german-energy-transition-energiewende

Álvarez Pelegry, E.; Álvaro Hermana, R. "Implications of the Energiewende for the Power Sector". 2017. Available at: https://www.orkestra.deusto.es/en/research/publications/cuadernos-orkestra/1598-implications-energiewende-power-sector

Álvarez Pelegry, E.; Larrea Basterra, M. "LNG trade in the Atlantic Basin. Situation and perspectives". In Conjunction with the Jean Monnet Network Project on Atlantic Studies, co-financed by the Erasmus+ Programme of the European

Union, Washington D.C. 2018. Available at: http://jeanmonnetnetwork.com.br/lng-trade-atlantic-basin/

Álvaro Hermana, R.; Larrea Basterra, M. "La transición energética en Francia". 2018. Available at: https://www.orkestra.deusto.es/images/investigacion/publicaciones/cuadernos/transicion-energetica-francia.pdf

Borger, J. "Bush kills global warming treaty". In *The Guardian*. 2001. [Consulted at: 28th November 2018]. Available at: https://www.theguardian.com/environment/2001/mar/29/globalwarming.usnews

BP. "BP statistical review 2002 of world energy". 2003. Available at: https://www.grieequity.com/resources/industryandissues/Energy/bp2002statisticalreview.pdf

BP. "BP statistical review 2018". 2018. Available at: https://www.bp.com/content/dam/bp/en/corporate/pdf/energy-economics/statistical-review/bp-stats-review-2018-full-report.pdf

Bumiller, E. & Nagourney, A. "Bush: 'America is addicted to oil". In *The New York Times*, Archives. 2006. [Consulted at: 25th December 2018]. Available at: https://www.nytimes.com/2006/02/01/world/americas/01iht-state.html

Cattaneo, C. "Shooting themselves in the foot': How NAFTA's collapse could disrupt U.S.-Canada energy trade". In *Financial Post*. 2018. [Consulted at: 1st December 2018]. Available at: https://business.financialpost.com/commodities/energy/shooting-themselves-in-the-foot-how-naftas-collapse-could-disrupt-u-s-canada-energy-trade

CEA. "Engineering a Collaborative & Clean Energy Future". 29th Mexican National Congress of Engineering. 2018a. Available at: https://electricity.ca/wp-content/uploads/2018/03/Remarks-at-Mexican-National-Congress-of-Civil-Engineering-Final.pdf

CEA. "Remarks by the Honourable Sergio Marchi, President and CEO of the Canadian Electricity Association". Washington: Canadian Embassy and annual CEA Washington Board Forum Dinner. 2018b. Available at: https://electricity.ca/wp-content/uploads/2018/04/Remarks-by-Sergio-at-Washington-Dinner-Distribution.pdf

Cherp, A., & Jewell, J. "The concept of energy security: Beyond the four as". In *Energy Policy*. Vol. 75, No. 415, 2014. Available at: https://www.sciencedirect.com/science/article/pii/S0301421514004960

Chow, E. & Elkind, J. "Hurricane Katrina and US Energy Security". In *Survival*. Vol. 47, No. 4, 145-160, 2005. Available at: https://www.tandfonline.com/doi/full/10.1080/00396330500433449?scroll=top&needAccess=true

Dannreuther, R. *Energy security*. Cambridge: Polity, 2017. doi: ISBN: 978-0-745-66191-9.

DOE. "North American Energy Work Group Releases Updated Trilateral Energy Report". 2006. [Consulted at 10th December 2019]. Available at: https://www.energy.gov/articles/north-american-energy-work-group-releases-updated-trilateral-energy-report

EIA. "U.S. coal consumption in 2018 expected to be the lowest in 39 years". 2018. [Consulted at 15th January 2019]. Available at: https://www.eia.gov/todayinenergy/detail.php?id=37817

DOE. "Secretary of Energy Rick Perry Forms New Office of Cybersecurity, Energy Security, and Emergency Response". 2018a. Available at: https://www.energy.gov/articles/secretary-energy-rick-perry-forms-new-office-cybersecurity-energy-security-and-emergency

DOE. "Multiyear plan for energy sector cybersecurity". 2018b. Available at: https://www.energy.gov/sites/prod/files/2018/05/f51/DOE%20Multiyear%20Plan%20for%20Energy%20Sector%20Cybersecurity%20_0.pdf

Energy Charter Secretariat. "International energy security. Common convept for energy producing, consuming and transit countries". 2015. Available at: https://energycharter.org/what-we-do/trade-and-transit/trade-and-transit-thematic-reports/international-energy-security-common-concept-for-energy-producing-consuming-and-transit-countries-2015/

EOPUS. "All-of-the-Above Energy Strategy as a Path to Sustainable Economic Growth". Executive Office of the President of the United States. 2014. Available at: https://obamawhitehouse.archives.gov/sites/default/files/docs/aota_energy_strategy_as_a_path_to_sustainable_economic_growth.pdf

Escribano-Francés, G. "Risk of energy availability: common corridors for Europe supply security". Madrid, 2009.

Escribano-Francés, G. *Políticas energéticas: geopolítica y seguridad energética en el sistema internacional*. Unpublished manuscript. 2018.

European Commission. "EU energy security strategy. Communication from the commission to the european parliament and the council. COM (2014)330 final". 2014. Available at: https://www.eesc.europa.eu/resources/docs/european-energy-security-strategy.pdf

European Commission. "Putting energy efficiency first: Consuming better, getting cleaner". Brussels. 2016a. Available at: www.europa.eu/rapid/press-release_MEMO-16-3986_en.pdf

European Commission. "Commission proposes new rules for consumer centred clean energy transition". 2016b. [Consulted at 7th December 2018]. Available at: https://ec.europa.eu/energy/en/news/commission-proposes-new-rules-consumer-centred-clean-energy-transition

European Commission. "Energy Security Strategy". 2018. Available at: https://ec.europa.eu/energy/en/topics/energy-strategy-and-energy-union/energy-security-strategy

European Parliament, E. C. "Regulation (EU) 2017/1938 of the European Parliament and of the Council of 25 October 2017 concerning measures to safeguard the security of gas supply and repealing regulation (EU) no 994/2010". 2017. Available at: https://eur-lex.europa.eu/legal-content/EN/TXT/PDF/?uri=OJ:L:2017:280:FULL&from=ES

Friedman, L. and Mufson, S. "Energy & Environment in Trump's First Year". Podcast, 2018. Columbia | SIPA Center on Global Energy Policy. 2018. [Consulted at 5th December 2018]. Available at: https://energypolicy.columbia.edu/energy-environment-trumps-first-year

Fonseca Ribeiro, J. "The Greening of Maritime Transportation, Energy and Climate Infrastructures in the Atlantic Basin: The Role of Atlantic Port-Cities and Maritime Policy". In Conjunction with the Jean Monnet Network Project on Atlantic Studies, co-financed by the Erasmus+ Programme of the European Union, Washington D.C. 2017. Available at: http://jeanmonnetnetwork.com.br/lng-trade-atlantic-basin/

Fuels Europe. "Statistical report". Belgium. 2018. Available at: https://www.fuelseurope.eu/publication/statistical-report-2018/

García, C. G. "The Trump Administration's National Security Strategy". In *Royal Institute Elcano*. Working Paper 14/2018, 2018. Available at: http://www.realinstitutoelcano.org/wps/wcm/connect/25d788de-9e45-4c6d-acb6-d4e98f89845c/WP14-2018-GarciaEncina-Trump-Administration-National-Security-Strategy.pdf?MOD=AJPERES&CACHEID=25d788de-9e45-4c6d-acb6-d4e98f89845c

Global Energy Institute. "Energy Security Risk Index". 2018. [Consulted at 3rd December 2019]. Available at: https://www.globalenergyinstitute.org/energy-security-risk-index

Goering, L. "Climate change an 'imminent' security threat, risk experts say". World Economic Forum, 26th February. 2019. [Consulted at 2nd March 2019]. Available at: https://www.weforum.org/agenda/2019/02/climate-change-an-imminent-security-threat-risk-experts-say

Government Of Alberta. "Mexico. Alberta Relations". 2011. Available at: https://open.alberta.ca/dataset/911b2ffd-0990-43c3-85ab-b0b1e0b3833f/resource/3a672bb8-f75d-4d14-ba29-78191f6bf020/download/mexico-ab.pdf

Government Of Canada. "The Canada-Mexico Partnership". 2018. Available at: https://www.canadainternational.gc.ca/mexico-mexique/cmp-pcm.aspx?lang=eng

Graf, R. "Between national and human security: Energy security in the United States and Western Europe in the 1970s". In *Historical Social Research*. Vol. *35*, No. *4*, (n.d.), 329-348. Available at: https://doi.org/10.12759/hsr.35.2010.4.329-348

Green, M. J. "The Legacy of Obama's "Pivot" to Asia". In *Foreing Policy*, 2016. [Consulted at 10th December 2018]. Available at: https://foreignpolicy.com/2016/09/03/the-legacy-of-obamas-pivot-to-asia/

Hamilton, D. *A New Atlantic Community: Generating Growth, Human Development and Security in the Atlantic Hemisphere*. Center for Transatlantic Relations, The Paul H. Nitze School of Advanced International Studies: The Johns Hopkins University. 2014. Available at: https://jmaznar.es/file_upload/news/pdfs/20140312190406_94.pdf

House Committee On Natural Resources. "All-of-the-Above Energy Approach". 2014. Available at: https://naturalresources.house.gov/energy/

IEA. "Measuring short-term energy security". Paris. 2011a. Available at: www.iea.org

IEA. "How does the IEA respond to major disruptions in oil supply?". 2011b. [Consulted at 25th November 2018]. Available at: https://www.iea.org/newsroom/news/2011/march/how-does-the-iea-respond-to-major--disruptions-in-the-supply-of-oil-2011-03-10-.html

IEA. "Energy supply security 2014". Paris. 2015. Available at: www.iea.org

IEA. "World energy outlook 2018". Paris. 2018. Available at: www.iea.org/weo

Irie, K. "The Evolution of the Energy Security Concept and APEX Energy Cooperation". In *International Association for Energy Economics*. Singapore Issue 2017. Available at: https://www.iaee.org/en/publications/newsletterdl.aspx?id=429

Isbell, P. and Álvarez Pelegry, E. (Eds.). *Energy and transportation in the Atlantic Basin*. Center for Transatlantic Relations, Johns Hopkins University SAIS, with Brookings Press, in conjunction with the Jean Monnet Network Project on Atlantic Studies, co-financed by the Erasmus+ Programme of the European Union, Washington D.C. 2017. Available at: https://www.orkestra.deusto.es/es/investigacion/publicaciones/libros-informes/otras-colecciones/1244-energy-transportation-atlantic-basin

Jones, C. "Trump's U.S. Coal Consumption Is Less Than Obama's". In *Forbes*. 2019. [Consulted at 20th January 2019]. Available at: https://www.forbes.com/sites/chuckjones/2019/01/01/trumps-u-s-coal-consumption-is-less-than-obamas/#2a3a88e5fa85

Kahn, G. "The Fate of the Kyoto Protocol under the Bush Administration". In *Berkeley Journal of International Law*. Vol. 21, No. 3, Article 5. 2003. Available at: https://scholarship.law.berkeley.edu/cgi/viewcontent.cgi?article=1248&context=bjil

Karlsson-Vinkhuyzen, S. I., & Jollands, N. "Human security and energy security: A sustainable energy system as apublic good". In *International handbook of energy security*. Cheltenham: UK, Edward Elgar, (n.d.). 507-525. Available at: https://papers.ssrn.com/sol3/papers.cfm?abstract_id=2562594

Keiji, K. "Energy security and human insecurity". In *Poole Gakuin University* (Ed.). (n.d.). Available at: https://ci.nii.ac.jp/els/contentscinii_20180330134441.pdf?id=ART0010407155

Kobek, L. P. "The State of Cybersecurity in Mexico: An Overview". 2017. Available at: https://www.wilsoncenter.org/sites/default/files/cybersecurity_in_mexico_an_overview.pdf

Koranyi, D. "A US Strategy for Sustainable Energy Security". Atlantic Council Strategic Papers. 2016. Available at: https://www.atlanticcouncil.org/images/publications/AC_SP_Energy.pdf

Kumar, D. K. and Eaton, C. "Venezuelan oil exports to U.S. still a primary source of cash". In *Reuters*, 2019. [Consulted at 27th January 2019]. Available at: https://www.reuters.com/article/us-venezuela-politics-usa-oil-graphic/venezuelan-oil-exports-to-u-s-still-a-primary-source-of-cash-idUSKCN1PJ2CT

Larrea Basterra, M. "La pobreza energética en la Unión Europea y el Reino Unido. El caso de Inglaterra". In *Revista ICADE*, No. 102, 2017. ISSN 1889-7045.

Lee, S. "Cybersecurity Strategy Advice for the Trump Administration: US-Mexico Relations". In *The Henry M. Jackson School of International Studies*. University of Washington. 2017. [Consulted at 20th December 2018]. Available at: https://jsis.washington.edu/news/cybersecurity-strategy-advice-trump-administration-us-mexico-relations/#_ftn21

Lété, B. "Addressing the Atlantic´s emerging security challenges". 2015. Available at:http://www.gmfus.org/sites/default/files/1115-WP9_GMF_Addressing%20the%20Atlantic%E2%80%99s%20Emerging%20Security%20Challenges.pdf

Morello, L. "US science agencies hit by government shutdown". In *Nature*. 2018. [Consulted at 15th January 2019]. Available at: https://www.nature.com/articles/d41586-018-07836-6

NACEI. "North American Cooperation on Energy Information". 2018. [Consulted at 30th November 2018]. Available at: http://nacei.org/#!/overview

NATO. "What happens when a power plant comes under cyber attack?" 2016. [Consulted at 20th December 2018]. Available at: https://www.youtube.com/watch?v=bV47gBsrDkc

NSS. "National Security Strategy of the United States of America". 2017. [Consulted at 18th December 2018]. Available at: https://www.whitehouse.gov/wp-content/uploads/2017/12/NSS-Final-12-18-2017-0905.pdf

NSSA. "National Security Strategy Archive". 2018. [Consulted at 19th December 2018]. Available at: http://nssarchive.us/

Presidency of US. "Reliable, Affordable, and Environmentally Sound Energy for America's Future". 2001. Available at: https://www.wtrg.com/EnergyReport/ National-Energy-Policy.pdf

Presidency of the US. "National Cyber Staretgy of the United States of America". 2018. Available at: https://www.whitehouse.gov/wp-content/uploads/2018/09/ National-Cyber-Strategy.pdf

Sodupe, K. "Gobernanza en situaciones de emergencia energética". In *Gobernanza para un sistema energético sostenible*. Universidad del País Vasco, 2018, 17.

Sodupe, K., & Molina, G. "Gobernanza, seguridad energética y sostenibilidad". In *Gobernanza para un sistema energético sostenible*. Universidad del País Vasco, 2018, 31.

Sovacool, B. K., & Mukherjee, I.. "Conceptualizing and measuring energy security: A synthesized approach". In *Energy. The International Journal*. Vol. 36, 2011, 5343-5355.

The White House. "The President's Energy Legislative Agenda". 2001. [Conulted at 5th December 2018.] Available at: https://georgewbush-whitehouse.archives.gov/news/releases/2001/06/energyinit.html

The World Bank. "Access to electricity (% of population)". 2018. [Consulted at 25th November 2018]. Available at: https://data.worldbank.org/indicator/ EG.ELC.ACCS.ZS

Times Premium. "Nigeria lost $2.8 billion to 'oil-related crimes' in 2018. UN". 2019. [Consulted at 30th January 2019]. Available at: https://www.premiumtimesng.com/news/headlines/304717-nigcria-lost-2-8-billion-to-oil-related-crimes-in-2018-un.html

UNOWA. "Maritime security in the Gulf of Guinea". 2019. [Consulted at 29th January 2019]. Available at: https://unowa.unmissions.org/maritime-security-gulf-guinea

US Mission To Mexico. "Secretary Perry Remarks at Press Event with SENER". 2017. [Consulted at 10th December 2018]. Available at: https://mx.usembassy.gov/secretary-perry-remarks-press-event-sener/

Wasson, E., Litvan, L. and Flavelle, C. "Here's What Would Happen If There's a Government Shutdown in December". In *Bloomberg*. 2018. [Consulted at 10th January 2019]. Available at: https://www.bloomberg.com/news/articles/2018-12-11/shutdown-impact-would-be-limited-as-only-some-agencies-unfunded

Wayne, E. A. "The Economic Relationship Between the United States, Canada, and Mexico': Earl Anthony Wayne Testifies before the US Senate Committee on Foreign Relations". Mexico Institute, Wilson Center. 2018. Available at: https://www.wilsoncenter.org/article/the-economic-relationship-between-the-united-states-canada-and-mexico-earl-anthony-wayne

Wayne, E. A. and Shedd, D. R. "Assuring Energy Security with a Modern NAFTA". In *Forbes*. 2018. [Consulted at 10th December 2018). Available at: https://www.forbes.com/sites/themexicoinstitute/2018/05/09/assuring-energy-security-with-a-modern-nafta/#35f3e5983019

Weir, B. "More coal-fired power plants have closed under Trump than in Obama's first term". In *CNN*. 2019. [Consulted at 25th January 2019]. Available at: https://edition.cnn.com/2019/01/07/politics/pennsylvania-coal-plants-weir-wxc/index.html

Woertz, E. "Has the Shale Revolution Really Led to US Disengagement from the Middle East?". In *CIDOB*. 2016. Available at: https://www.cidob.org/en/articulos/monografias/elecciones_presidenciales_en_estados_unidos/has_the_shale_revolution_really_led_to_us_disengagement_from_the_middle_east

Wood, D. "Integrating North America's Energy Markets: A Call for Action". In Wilson Center, Mexico Institute. 2014. Available at: https://www.wilsoncenter.org/sites/default/files/Integrating%20North%20America%27s%20Energy%20Markets.pdf

Part II

Facing New Challenges to Human Security

Chapter 4

Addressing New Threats in the Atlantic Basin Security Environment: The Role of Emerging Technologies in the Fight Against Illicit Arms Trade

Leonardo Paz Neves

The Atlantic Basin is widely considered a stable and pacific space when comes to inter-state conflicts. Since the end of World War II, the region witnessed only a handful of small scale wars, such as the Football War between El Salvador and Honduras in 1969 and the Falklands/Malvinas War between the UK and Argentina in 1982.

Unfortunately, despite the low frequency of wars, Atlantic countries are not unknown to violence. Two dynamics are responsible for the larger part of the societal violence that plagues the Atlantic continents. The first is the occurrence of civil wars. From 1945, nearly twenty open civil conflicts took place, both in the South and North part of the Atlantic Ocean: Costa Rican Civil War, 1948; La Violencia (Colombia), 1948–1958; Congo Crisis, 1960–1966; Guatemalan Civil War, 1960–1996; Nicaraguan Civil War, 1962–1990; Dominican Civil War, 1965; Nigerian Civil War, 1967–1970; The Troubles (Northern Ireland), 1969–1998; Angolan Civil War, 1975–2002; Salvadoran Civil War (El Salvador), 1979–1992; First Liberian Civil War, 1989–1996; Casamance Conflict (Senegal), 1990–2006; Sierra Leone Civil War, 1991–2002; Republic of the Congo Civil War, 1997–1999; Guinea-Bissau Civil War, 1998–1999; Second Congo War, 1998–2003; Second Liberian Civil War, 1999–2003; First Ivorian Civil War, 2002–2007; Second Ivorian Civil War, 2010–2011.

The second dynamic is the steadily increase in traffic flows. Trafficking of people, arms, drugs, wildlife, etc. are operated by complex and robust criminal networks that uses the Atlantic as its center stage.[1] The dynamic of those illicit flows has been integrating the region and developing interdependence between the criminal networks in all three continents, as the United Nations Office on Drugs and Crime annual report from 2010 stated:

---

1. May, Channing. "Transnational Crime and the Developing World". In *Global Financial Integrity Report*, 2017.

> West Africa is a paradise for organized crime, offering ideal condi-
> tions for trafficking contraband: a strategic location, porous borders,
> weak governance, wide- spread poverty and extensive corruption. As
> a result, criminals and insurgents are exploiting the region. West Af-
> rica serves as a transit point between Latin America and Europe for
> US\$ 1 billion-worth in cocaine, as a destination for counterfeit med-
> icines and toxic waste, and as a source of stolen natural resources,
> particularly oil. Human trafficking, whether for forced labor or sexual
> exploitation, also occurs in the region. [2]

The convergence of a high frequency of civil wars with the increasing
levels of illegal flows results in a worrisome combination which seems to
be the responsible for, not only the alarming rates of violence, but also the
levels of corruption and weak governance identified in most countries in
Western Africa and Latin America. Moreover, civil wars and illegal flows
tend to reinforce each other, operating in a vicious circle, since illicit activities are instrumental for the occurrence and the support of internal conflicts,
where the warring parties need to find alternative ways to finance their
efforts and guarantee their steady supply of weapons and other resources.

In this context, it seems essential to point out the role of Small Arms and
Light Weapons (SALW) in the Atlantic security environment. Unlike traditional wars, where heavy weaponry plays a leading role in the hostilities, in
light conflict situations and criminal activities, small arms are responsible
for the larger share of the damage. In fact, illicit flow of SALW has an
important peculiarity of having a cross-cutting impact in all other criminal
activities, which makes its steady flow fundamental for them. It also has
the most harmful and direct impact on societies security and development.

Despite the importance of illicit weapons trafficking for other criminal
activities, it ranks quite low in comparison with others illegal activities in
terms of the money it moves. According to the *Transnational Crime and
the Developing World* Report from Global Financial Integrity, the overall
estimate of the annual value of transnational crime is \$1.6-2.2 trillion. In
this research, SALW trafficking would rank in 9th place and would worth
\$1.7-3.5 billion.

According to a Report from the Small Arms Survey,[3] from 2010 to 2015
an average of 526,000 people died violently each year. The same Report

2. See http://www.nta.ng/news/20171208-the-needs-of-west-africa-to-combat-prolifera-
   tion-of-weapons-dogara/
3. Evoy, C. and Hideg, G. *Global Violently Deaths 2017: Time do Decide*. Geneva: Small
   Arms Survey Report, 2017.

Table 1. Annual Estimated Value of Illegal Trafficking by Activity

Transnational Crime	Estimated Annual Value (US$)
Counterfeiting	$923 billion to $1.13 trillion
Drug Trafficking	$426 billion to $652 billion
Illegal Logging	$52 billion to $157 billion
Human Trafficking	$150.2 billion
Illegal Mining	$12 billion to $48 billion
IUU Fishing	$15.5 billion to $36.4 billion
Illegal Wildlife Trade	$5 billion to $23 billion
Crude Oil Theft	$5.2 billion to $11.9 billion
Small Arms & Light Weapons Trafficking	$1.7 billion to $3.5 billion
Organ Trafficking	$840 million to $1.7 billion
Total	$1.6 trillion to $2.2 trillion

Source: May, Channing, "Transnational Crime and the Developing World". In *Global Financial Integrity Report, 2017.*

stated that in 2016 over 560,000 people were killed. From those, about 90,000 lives were claimed each year in conflict situations and 385,000 were causes by intentional homicides. Regarding to the role of SALW in this context, both Small Arms Survey reports and the Global Burden of Armed Violence[4] found that, in average, SALW were used in almost 50% of those homicides. In some conflict cases SALW may "produce" up to 93% of casualties, such as the situation in the Republic of Congo.[5]

Those numbers might be considered only a pale illustration of the link between violence and deaths to the use of SALW. The sharp increase armed violence in the last decades has brought this phenomenon to a greater scrutiny, both from academic and policy perspectives.

SALW is a complex matter. As mentioned before, it is not only related to armed violence, but it is intertwined with a wide range of illicit activities, including its own trafficking. In that sense, illicit arms trade has a cumulative effect on violence. It not only allows other criminal enterprises

---

4. See Geneva Declaration Secretariat. "Global Burden of Armed Violence 2015: everybody counts". 2015. [Consulted at: http://www.genevadeclaration.org/measurability/global-burden-of-armed-violence/global-burden-of-armed-violence-2015.html]
5. Cîrlig, Carmen-Cristina. *Illicit Small Arms and Light Weapons: International and EU Actions*. Brussels: European Parliament Research Service, 2015.

to thrive and civil wars to endure, but also have a significant impact on domestic violence—especially in gender violence, since armed violence (and conflicts) seems to have a disproportionate impact on girls and women.[6]

Besides the obvious human cost of the armed violence phenomenon, there are other human factors that also should be considered in the overall equation. The wide availability of SALW, especially from illicit background, is considered a major obstacle for human development.[7] It was directly associated with the obstacles of most countries in achieving the Millennial Development Goals.[8] Criminal activities and general violence quite often divert "unproductive" public administrations resources from others much needed public goods, such as health, education, sanitation, etc. A report from the Organization for Economic Co-Operation and Development (OECD) identified that between 10 to 15% of gross domestic product is directed to law enforcement activities in developing countries, opposed to 5% in developed countries.[9]

The overall cost of armed violence (and the role SALW plays in it) is currently a major issue on the international security agenda. Even in the Security Council, dealing with the SALW issue has become a common denominator of its debates and actions. It seems to be a reasonable consensus that the level of availability of SALW and ammunition and the frequency and scale of the weapons diversion are determinant factors in the dynamics of conflicts and the level of societal violence.[10] Moreover, in a given context, even if alternative solutions manage to reduce the level of violence and/or halt the conflict, if the arms availability issue is not addressed the risks that the conflict and violence re-emerge are more than significant.

The Atlantic Basin is home of the world most intense flux of weapons trade. It includes seven of the top 10 largest exporters of conventional arms. This information is not only relevant for the risk of piracy, but especially because the level of opacity of the weapons business. Despite the fact that

6. OECD. *Conflict and Fragility Armed Violence Reduction enabling development*. Paris: OECD Publishing, 2009.
7. A program of action to address the human cost of SALW. Inter-Agency Standing Committee, Unicef.
8. Cîrlig, Carmen-Cristina. *Illicit Small Arms and Light Weapons: International and EU Actions*. Brussels: European Parliament Research Service, 2015.
9. OECD. *Reducing the Involvement of Youth in Armed Violence: Programming Note, Conflict and Fragility Series*. Paris: OECD Publishing, 2011.
10. UNSC. *Small arms and light weapons Report of the Secretary-General*. S/2015/289. 2015. [Consulted at: http://www.securitycouncilreport.org/atf/cf/%7B65BFCF9B-6D27-4E9C-8CD3-CF6E4FF96FF9%7D/s_2015_289.pdf]

Table 2. The 10 largest exporters of conventional arms, 2013–17

	Exporter	Share of arms exports (%) 2013-2017	Share of arms exports (%) 2008-2012
1	United States	34	30
2	Russia	22	26
3	France	6.7	5.8
4	Germany	5.8	7.4
5	China	5.7	4.6
6	United Kingdom	4.8	3.8
7	Spain	2.9	2.9
8	Israel	2.9	2.1
9	Italy	2.5	2.4
10	Netherlands	2.1	2.1

Source: SIPRI Fact Sheet, 2018

there are already regimes (as we will see further) that determines obligations related to marking, tracking and reporting arms trade, the regime depends on voluntary participation. The pervasive lack of transparency from the arms trade business allows an easier transition from the white market to the 'grey market', and consequentially to the black market.[11]

The steady and poorly controlled flux of arms led to a massive influx of SALW in those region's societies. Latin America and West Africa have been particularly affected by this phenomenon. In West Africa, the SALW matter is intimately related to the continuation of civil wars, gross violation of human rights and even support of terrorist groups. In Latin America, gun violence is connected to the world's highest levels of societal violence. The Latin America homicide rate is on average 28 deaths per 100,000 people, contrasted with the world's average of almost 7 deaths per 100,000 people. Moreover, almost 75% of all homicides in this region are gun-related. This picture gets even grimmer once we acknowledge that half of the world's gun-related deaths comes from only four Latin American countries: Brazil, Colombia, Mexico and Venezuela.[12]

---

11. Jacobson, Mark R. and Daurora, Max. "Significant Trends in Illicit Trafficking: A Macro View of the Problem and Potential Means to Address It." In *Atlantic Future Scientific*. Paper 8, 2014.
12. See by Robert Muggah, Robert. "Latin America's Fatal Gun". In *Igarapé Institute Op-Ed*. 2016. [Consulted at: https://igarape.org.br/en/latin-americas-fatal-gun-addiction/]

This chapter focuses on this issue. The diversion of SALW and ammunition is a massive problem. It affects nearly all regions of the world and is present in nearly all armed violence. The apparent easy access to SALW by all sorts of criminals, gangs, pirates, terrorists, hate groups, extremists and rebels is a major cause on the escalation of violence, perceived both in open conflict situations and in many countries supposedly in peace, but plagued by societal violence.

Unfortunately, there are many ways in which the diversion of weapons might occur. Here we understand diversion as 'unlawful or intentionally unrecorded transfer of weapons and ammunition', e.g. theft, smuggling, barter, hand out to rebels or militias and even "military aid" for proxies in conflict. Diversion is generally a result of criminal activities, corruption and covert support of allies. Tackling the diversion issue could greatly reduce the access of weapons to those groups, hence reducing considerably the level of armed violence.

It is with that spirit that this chapter aims to explore more efficient alternatives to cope with the diversion problem. My intent is to present/explore some emerging technologies that might offer possible contributions to cope with the diversion issue. This effort is particularly important once considered that in the realm of technologies, weapons enhancement seems to be constantly beating the efforts to control it.[13] Technological progress is increasingly affecting SALW, including ways to avoid its marking, detection and traceability. Technologies such as 3D printing, techno-polymers and modular structures offer considerable challenges to control and track SALW flows.

Emerging technologies such as Blockchain, the Internet of Things (IoT), nanotechnology and Artificial Intelligence (AI) are already starting a revolution in many sectors of our society. Unfortunately, so far, it seems that the arms control area is lagging behind in using cutting-edge technology to develop innovative solutions to cope with one of its major problems, the diversion of weapons and ammunitions.

The Novelty of International Arms Control Regimes

The focus of the international community towards small arms and light weapons is rather recent. Only in the 1990s did SALW figure as a priori-

---

13. King, Benjamin and MCDonald, Glenn (ed). *Behind the Curve: New Technologies, New Control Challenges*. Geneva: Small Arms Survey, 2015.

ty in the international security agenda. Its insertion seems to be a consequence of the complex environment of the immediate post-Cold War period, in which international society witnessed a sharp increase in the number of intra-state conflicts. Many of those internal conflicts resulted in tragic events regarding the massive violation of human rights. Some of the most infamous examples of these events were the ethnic cleansing episodes in Bosnia (1991); first and second wars in Congo (1996-97 and 1998-2003) derived from ethnic strife; and the widespread crimes against humanity in the Somali civil war during the 1990s. The atrocities committed in those conflicts and the role that SALW had in them were instrumental in mobilizing the international community to address the issue.

In that sense, regulation of the arms trade, fighting the illicit proliferation of SALW and denying their access to criminals were some of the major goals of the first debates. It was within that context that some important initiatives started to take place, such as:

- Ninth UN Congress on the Prevention of Crime and the Treatment of Offenders.[14] Its report launched in 1995 was one of the first calls for the adoption of international regulations of firearms and combat its illicit trade.

- United Nations Economic and Social Council (ECOSOC) Report to the Secretary-General on Legal Institutions Measures to Regulate Firearm.[15] Presented in 1997, the ECOSOC report aimed to propose initiatives to develop measures aiming to regulate the international fluxes of firearms, in order to prevent the trafficking of SALW and its uses by criminal activities.

- UN Panel of Governmental Experts on Small Arms.[16] Firstly, tasked to identify the defining problems linked with the SALW, the panel focuses its efforts in establishing a definition to small arms and light weapons; identify the consequences of the proliferation of SALW; and propose means to prevent the excessive accumulation of SALW. The panel released its report in 1997.

---

14. UNGA. *Report of the Ninth United Nations Congress on the Prevention of Crime and the Treatment of Offenders.* A/CONF.169/16. Rev.1 of 8 May 1995.
15. ECOSOC. *Criminal Justice Reform and Strengthening of Legal Institutions Measures to Regulate Firearms: Report to the Secretary-General.* E/CN.15/1997/4 of 7 March 1997
16. UNGA. *Report of the Panel of Governmental Experts on Small Arms.* A/52/298 of 27 August 1997.

- UN Convention against Transnational Organized Crime.[17] It is considered the first international instrument aiming to prevent and combat transnational organized crime, in its various forms. It was complemented by several protocols, most notably the Firearms Protocol.

Those initiatives laid the foundation for the design and implementation of several international instruments that would build the current international architecture to support the control of arms and the prevention of illicit trafficking. Aside from regional initiatives, currently the international architecture for arms control is composed by four instruments, all established quite recently, in the 21st century.

- **UN Program of Action to Prevent, Combat and Eradicate the Illicit Trade in Small Arms and Light Weapons in All Its Aspects (Program of Action).**[18] Adopted in 2001, it establishes a politically binding normative framework for the control of small arms and light weapons. It determines a set of international commitments that covers a large array of issues concerning SALW, for instance: manufacturing, stockpiling, identification, surplus disposal and disarmament. Additionally, the Program of Actions calls on states to (voluntarily) submit national inventory reports every two years, coinciding with the biennial meetings which aimed to debate the regional and global implementation efforts of the Program of Action.

- **UN Protocol against the Illicit Manufacturing of and Trafficking in Firearms, Their Parts and Components and Ammunition (Firearms Protocol).**[19] Adopted in 2001, it was largely inspired in the Inter-American Convention against the Illicit Manufacturing of and Trafficking in Firearms, Ammunition, Explosives, and Other Related Materials (CIFTA) established by the Organization of the American Countries in 1997. The Firearms Protocol main objective is to foster cooperation among the states parties in preventing and

---

17. UNTOC. *United Nations Convention against Transnational Organized Crime*. Resolution 55/25 of 15 November 2000.
18. UNGA. *Programme of Action to Prevent, Combat and Eradicate the Illicit Trade in Small Arms and Light Weapons in All Its Aspects ('UN Programme of Action')*. A/CONF.192/15 of 20 July 2001. [Consulted at: http://www.poa-iss.org/poa/poahtml.aspx]
19. UNGA. *Protocol against the Illicit Manufacturing of and Trafficking in Firearms, Their Parts and Components and Ammunition, Supplementing the United Nations Convention against Transnational Organized Crime ('Firearms Protocol')*. A/RES/55/255 of 8 June 2001. [Consulted at http://www.unodc.org/pdf/crime/a_res_55/255e.pdf]

combating illicit manufacturing and trafficking of firearms, their parts and ammunition.

• **International Instrument to Enable States to Identify and Trace, in a Timely and Reliable Manner, Illicit Small Arms and Light Weapons (International Tracing Instrument - ITI).**[20] Adopted in 2005, the ITI is an instrument that derives from then Program of Action thread. It is also a politically binding instrument that recognized the importance of marking and record-keeping for the purpose of tracing arms, thus combating illicit flows of arms. The ITI states that the parties should ensure that all weapons manufactured in their territory have to be marked with serial number and country of origin—markings of the weapon model, year and caliber were also encouraged. Yet, it determines that countries should keep their records of their manufactured weapons for at least 30 years and 20 years for those imported or exported. Finally, the ITI elaborates on how countries should cooperate with regards of weapon tracing and exchange of information.

• **Arms Trade Treaty (ATT).**[21] Broader in its scope, the ATT, adopted in 2013, determines legally binding commitments that governs the international trade of conventional weapons, their parts and ammunition. It seeks to determine standards on exports, imports, transit and negotiations of such weapons. Among its main goals, the ATT seeks to foster greater confidence among countries and transparency on international conventional weapons trade.

The collection of international instruments aiming arms control illustrates the importance of the transparency in arms flows and its traceability. Arms and ammunition are, after all, evidence.[22] Their markings are unique and could be instrumental in identifying their points of diversion, which by its turn could provide to be valuable to efforts in combating illicit arms trade and their use for criminal activities.

---

20. UNGA. *Report of the Open-ended Working Group to Negotiate an International Instrument to Enable States to Identify and Trace, in a Timely and Reliable Manner, Illicit Small Arms and Light Weapons.* A/60/88 of 27 June 2005. [Consulted at: http://www.un.org/events/smallarms2006/pdf/A.60.88%20(E).pdf]
21. UNGA. *The Arms Trade Treaty.* Adopted 2 April. A/RES/67/234 B of 11 June 2013. [Consulted at: http://www.un.org/en/ga/search/view_doc.asp?symbol=A/RES/67/234%20B]
22. Small Arms Survey. *Documenting Small Arms and Light Weapons: A Basic Guide.* Issue Brief Number 14, 2015.

Marking weapons and proper record-keeping are essential for import and export purposes, so is for countries stockpiles management. Weapons stocks management and control are a considerable challenge.[23] They are fairly vulnerable (especially in a war-torn states) in corrupt environments and are a common target for non-state combatants and criminals—and could be a main source of ammunition for illicit activities.

Although often playing a secondary role, ammunitions control matters greatly. The handling of ammunitions generally has a fundamental part in SALW negotiations, since their real value derives from the availability of their respective ammunitions. Consequently, their inclusion on the above cited international instruments were paramount for the national and international efforts combat of illicit fluxes.

Although ammunitions are present in such instruments, its inclusion was not obvious. The International Tracing Instrument is an interesting example of how the ammunitions issue could be a source of divide. The inclusion or not of ammunitions on the ITI generated a sharp debate. Aside political interests, ammunitions, in essence, provide different and greater technical challenges if compared to SALW, especially regarding to marking efforts.[24]

Despite the technical differences and individual challenges, arms control international instruments and local policies alike should take in account the ammunitions issue. Effective measures to curb the illicit use of small arms and light weapons necessarily must include, and even focus on, efforts to avert the supply of ammunition. A tight control on the supply of ammunition might have an immediate and decisive impact on the intensity and course of a given conflict.

The recent development of the international framework for arms control is a fundamental effort to coerce illicit flows of arms and ammunition. Its establishment was essential for the creation of international standards in arms trade and management, but still is falling short of offering the much need transparency and still struggles to keep a reliable traceability from both arms and ammunition.

---

23. UNSC. *Small arms and light weapons Report of the Secretary-General*. S/2015/289. 2015. [Consulted at: http://www.securitycouncilreport.org/atf/cf/%7B65BFCF9B-6D27-4E9C-8CD3-CF6E4FF96FF9%7D/s_2015_289.pdf]

24. McDonald, Glenn. *Connecting the Dots: the international tracing instruments*. Geneva: Small Arms Survey Report, 2006.

Emerging Technologies and their Breakthrough Prospects

Emerging technologies are technical innovations generally character-ized by its fast growth and with high expectation in addressing society's current problems and generating a radical impact in the socio-economic space—changing the *status quo*. The current generation of emerging tech-nologies has been related to the 4th Industrial Revolution, which stands out for is interconnection or even fusion of the physical/biological and virtual worlds.

The disparate development of those disruptive technologies, both col-lectively and individually, heralds radical changes in the nature, properties and applications of future security sector. Some of these technologies, such as artificial intelligence and big data analytics, additive manufacturing and advanced and smart materials, Blockchain, virtual and augmented reality, the Internet of Things, nanotechnology and remote sensing, etc. will be critical to most modern militaries and security forces.

To address the arms control issue, we believe that some of those emerg-ing technologies from the 4th Industrial Revolution could provide a para-mount aid in powering innovative solutions that until now were not possi-ble or feasible. Among the possible major 'contributors', this chapter will highlight four cutting-edge technologies:

Blockchain

The Distributed Ledger Technology (also known as Blockchain) has been hailed as a revolutionary decentralized trust system, although until recently it was unknown for most people. It also has been identified as the precursor of a possible revolution of the way the Internet functions and opens infinite possibilities. The Blockchain technology essentially works upon a series of networks of databases that allows a virtual distributed ledger to store data while recording information from every transaction/in-sertion done in the ledger, which is continuously reconciling itself with the network. The recording structure of the Blockchain technology is built in a way that periodically a given amount of information is "compressed" into a block through a complex cryptography process called proof of work.[25] Once finished, those blocks are sent to the network where it could be vali-dated by its participants. If the information in the block is sound, it gets val-idated and then the block is inserted chronologically into the Blockchain.

---

25. Currently there are other processes other than proof of work, such as the proof of stake.

Blockchain has been particularly praised for the transparency and thus the accountability that this technology confers to transactions.

In relation to the security sector, Blockchain technology is expected to play a large role in areas such as cyber defense, secure messaging, logistical and supply chain support, data base networking, authentication among others.

Nanotechnology and Nano Sensors

The next step after the miniaturization revolution, nanotechnology has allowed scientists to reduce items, such as sensors, from millimeters or microns, to the nanometer scale. The new generation of nano sensors has even enabled us to create sensors small enough to be inserted within human bodies or to be mixed directly into construction materials. Nano sensors connected to the network are able to sense and signal information. Due to their diminutive size they may collect information from many different points, putting them in a unique position to create an incredibly detailed map or capture even the slightest changes in the environment. Nano sensors are revolutionizing tracking devices as they can not only determine a given item its location and course, but also it may determine changes in its circumstances, as a weapon's discharge.

Internet of Things

The Internet of Things (IoT) is the extension of the traditional Internet that goes beyond computers and communications systems to connect everyday objects. It is a communication network that connects devices (especially those which have a primary function that does not need to rely on internet, such as phones, cars, etc.) and enables them to share data and 'orders'. Intimately related with the phenomenon of the smart devices, the IoT is rapidly expanding the online universe due to its broad application that is capturing not only communication devices but a host of other more ordinary equipment as door locks and refrigerators. It allows smart devices to inter-operate within the existing internet infrastructure, where objects may be sensed or controlled remotely - greatly enhancing efficiency, accuracy and saving time and resources. IoT is already a reality all over the world since currently there are billions of objects/devices that are connected with the internet, sharing data and executing commands.

The IoT will most probably affect greatly in the next generation of military and security intelligence. Combined with advanced sensors technology, it will enable a full situational awareness and control over diverse settings, from urban scenarios to large remote areas.

Artificial Intelligence

Artificial Intelligence (AI) is intimately related to the machine learning revolution, which enables programs and/or objects to 'acquire' knowledge on their own, therefore acting even when they are not directly programed to do so. This process exists through the development of algorithms that can learn from the massive accumulation of data and identify patterns and even make predictions. By almost instantly assimilating enormous volumes of information and learning from it, AI allows programs and devices to engage in certain tasks faster and without human bias (whether emotional or intentional). The establishment of an open AI ecosystem would allow the connection of not only of our smartphones and computers through themselves, but also to other objects such as smart watches, cars, etc.

The AI potential for the defense domain is gigantic, although hard to measure properly. AI solutions are projected to impact in critical fields such as cyber defense, risk management, decision-support systems, pattern recognition, projection, and data correlation, among many others. The fact that AI-powered computers are able to outperform humans in many fields, from data analysis to playing chess, and are also able to develop new systems unknown to us (Facebook chatbots case) makes it impossible for us to determine and predict the level of disruption that this technology will cause.

Emerging Technologies and their Possible Contributions to the Arms Control Efforts

Arms trade is by nature an opaque business. It is generally protected with many layers of confidentiality and national interests or hidden under the shadows of illicit activities. Transparency and accountability are not often present in arms transactions, which favor diversion and the appropriation of weapons by criminal actors or non-state combatants.

Governments have always struggled to deny access of weapons to criminals and trace them back to those actors. Those efforts have been further challenged by recent developments in technology such as 3D printing, techno-polymers and modular structures, since they create new obstacles for arms control efforts regarding ways to avoid its marking, detection and traceability. Marking, record-keeping, managing of national stockpiles and attend to international standards for import and export is, therefore, a persistent challenge.

Fortunately, there are already innovative ways for governments to address the arms control question. Among others, the technologies presented here are transforming other sectors and are even already present in our daily lives. In that sense, their features could provide an invaluable aid to governments and the international community to increase the level of transparency and accountability for arms control efforts. The combination of those technologies could provide a real boost in current control mechanisms and even create a platform for innovative solutions.

Record-keeping is by far the stage that could benefit most. Blockchain technology, for instance, could create a unique and secure history of each weapon—since its production, passing from sales and for each of its owners/end users. In that way, each firearm would have all its information registered in real time and it could even be so accordingly the standards determined by international instruments.

Managing national stockpiles and import/export transactions share most of the challenges that record-keeping is confronted with. Here, nanotechnology could be instrumental in creating better marking solutions for tracking and storing data purposes. Connecting it with Blockchain, this data would be registered in a secure and untampered manner, which is fundamental for controlling activities as packing, shipping and transfers. It would create an important "paper trail" by storing all necessary documents and information on weapons shipments. An illustrative use case could be the reorganization of arms inventories before lifting international embargo and sanctions of a given country. It would be invaluable to international inspections aiming to verify the compliance of a given agreement.

The use of those emerging technologies for control solutions applied to record-keeping, managing stockpiles and transfers activities could became instrumental for identifying points of diversion, trafficking routes, embargo violations, among others illegal activities. In that sense, it could serve as a practical tool to the International Tracing Instrument and other regimes efforts. The same logic could be applied to a conflict context, for instance, arms used for human rights violations could be traced back to its last lawful custodian, which could be paramount for investigations.

Aside from recording arms and ammunitions flows, the technology could also increase accountability from defense and security forces and private security companies regarding their uses of weapons. Events such as custody of a given weapon and even weapons discharges could be identified with nano sensors and IoT-based solutions and recorded on the Blockchain for transparency purposes. In fact, the military, private security forces and law enforcement could provide an ideal place for launching pilot initiatives, before developing a broader solution.

There are already some initiatives in place, more focus on tracking that could benefit greatly in adopting some of those technologies-based solutions. ITrace,[26] iArms[27] and MAD[28] are some of those initiatives. ITrace is a project funded by the European Union and developed by the Conflict Armament Research (CAR). With iTrace the CAR seeks "quantified data on transfers of diverted conventional weapons, ammunition, and related materiel"[29] from conflict situations. IArms is an Interpol initiative that consists of a database where illicit arms are registered. It aims to facilitate the information exchange with national law enforcement agencies. MAD (Mapping Arms Data) is a visualization App developed by the Brazilian Think Tank Igarapé that records information on exports and imports of small arms and ammunition worldwide, covering 262 countries and territories.

Limits and Challenges for Emerging Technologies Applications to SALW Control Efforts

Despite the fact that these emerging technologies may present some useful contributions to arms control efforts, they do not come without limitations and points of concern. All of them are relatively new technologies. Most of their current applications, regardless of the sector, are still in proof of concept or testing stages.

Therefore, is possible to identify some limitations also with regard to arms control initiatives. The first limitation is probably the most obvious one: the requirement of a proper *network infrastructure*. Most of those technologies relies on internet connection, without it, it would be impossible to record any data in the ledger or to allow devices to connect with other devices or the network. That limitation is somehow 'limited', since it

---

26. See http://www.conflictarm.com/itrace/
27. See https://www.interpol.int/Crime-areas/Firearms-trafficking/INTERPOL-Illicit-Arms-Records-and-tracing-Management-System-iARMS/About-iARMS
28. See https://igarape.org.br/en/video-mapping-arms-data/
29. See http://www.conflictarm.com/itrace/

would probably affect only a few possible contributions. The managing of national stockpiles, for instance, probably would not be affected.

A second limitation would be regarding to the *markings on the weapons*. Frequently, when non-state actors and criminals gain possession of weapons, they remove or "erase" the guns markings (especially the serial number) in order to conceal its origins and the circumstances they were acquired. An apprehended weapon with no markings would be almost useless for the purposes of tracing investigations. Although here the nanotechnology could prove to be particularly useful, it would also have to face challenges from modular weapons technologies and locally manufactured weapons (being this last one a growing concern in West Africa).

An important point of concern is the issue of the *durability of the SALW*. Quite often SALW have a use life of several decades. That contrasts with the possible applications of some of those technologies mentioned here, which would require to be introduced during the manufacture of a given weapon, for instance the introduction of nano sensors or the development of a smart gun. On the other hand, there are alternatives using the Blockchain technology, for example, that could enhance the control of older weapons by registering their original markings.

Another pint of concern is the data *privacy dilemma*. An underlining feature from almost all of those technologies is the sharing of data, therefore they would enable unwelcome surveillance. The dilemma resides especially in the need to maintain the privacy of the user versus the possible law requirements that would give the authorities the power to access a given piece of information.[30] This is generally a point of concern between the clashes of individual fundamental right to privacy and the ability of governments to combat illicit activities.

Final Considerations

Due to the sensitive nature and relatively young age of those technologies, more pragmatic approaches could be addressed first. Approaches with less resistance and limitations could work as trailblazers allowing the first signs of success (or failures) to be instrumental to determine the next steps. Managing national stockpiles could be considered the 'lowest hanging

---

30. ASTRI. "Whitepaper on Distributed Ledger Technology". 2016. [Consulted at: http://www.hkma.gov.hk/media/eng/doc/key-functions/finanical-infrastructure/Whitepaper_On_Distributed_Ledger_Technology.pdf]

fruit' due to the near lack of limitations and points of concern. Registering private firearms requires a much larger effort and poses several dilemmas. In that sense, starting to register military, private security companies and law enforcement weapons would be a reasonable place to start. Registering import and export activities is another fertile field, although it would require some preparation and cooperation to be fully and successfully implemented, since it would require some level of international agreement within the international architecture of arms control.

Those ideas are aligned with the international instruments presented here. In fact, a more careful comparative analysis from those instruments shows that although they have broadly similar and complementary goals, and even some overlapping issues, they also present some important gaps. More specifically, each of those instruments tries to deal with a different part or stage of the regulations related to the registry, trade, import/export, storage, marking, tracking, and other management categories. So, in that sense they all manage to reinforce each other by covering their "gaps".

Nonetheless, given their different natures, each exhibits some particularities that hinders a full comparative exercise, for instance, some of them are legally binding (ATT, UNTOC and Firearms Protocol), while others do not impose any legal obligations (ITI and PoA). They also have different scopes of application, for instance: the UNTOC does not determine their scope of application, the Firearms Protocol focuses on SALW, their components and ammunition, the PoA and ITI concentrate only on the SALW (leaving aside their components and ammunition) and the ATT covers a wide array of weapons, from battle tanks, passing from warships, to SALW.

That difference in the scope of application from each instrument leads to two different issues that deserve attention. The first is the problem with definitions. The lack of proper definition poses some obstacles for the regulation process (to be incorporated by countries), such as registering, marking, trading, etc. The second element is the lack of verification mechanisms from those instruments. Most of them fall short of elaborating effective systems to monitor and ensure compliance. And it is here that emerging technologies could impact positively on arms management and combat illicit weapons trafficking.

It is important not to regard emerging technologies as a panacea. Even more aggressive application and solutions based in those and/or others emerging technologies will not solve completely the illicit trafficking of weapons. For that, a greater level of political work and will from countries and international institutions is required. While some international initiatives are blocked by political hurdles, technical solutions could find an easier path for implementation. Storing transactions or recording transfer of weapons in a given virtual ledger powered by Blockchain technology, tracking guns through nano sensors, identifying real-time discharge events using IoT, comprehending trends and identifying diversion points through Artificial Intelligence are solutions that are already available, or at the very least ready for testing. Most importantly, those technologies could be instrumental for the recent international institutional architecture of arms control. In the end, emerging technologies will not provide "teeth" for international regimes, but they could dramatically improve its "scent".

References

Ahlstrom, Christer. *Casualties of Conflict: Report for the World Campaign for the Protection of Victims of War*. Uppsala: Department of Peace and Conflict Studies, 1991.

ASTRI. "Whitepaper on Distributed Ledger Technology". 2016. [Consulted at: http://www.hkma.gov.hk/media/eng/doc/key-functions/finanical-infrastructure/Whitepaper_On_Distributed_Ledger_Technology.pdf]

Atlantic Basin Initiative. Eminent Persons Group. *A New Atlantic Community: Generating Growth, Human Development and Security in the Atlantic Hemisphere*. Washington, DC: Center for Transatlantic Relations, 2014.

Atlantic Future. Maritime Security in the Atlantic. European Policy Brief, 2014.

Bauer, Sibylle; Beijer, Paul and Bromley, Mark. "The Arms Trade Treaty: Challenges for the First Conference of States". In SIPRI, *SIPRI Insights on Peace and Security*. No. 2014/2, 2014.

Cîrlig, Carmen-Cristina. *Illicit Small Arms and Light Weapons: International and EU Actions*. Brussels: European Parliament Research Service, 2015.

Collier, Paul; Elliott, V. L.; Hegre, Håvard; Hoeffler, Anke; Reynal-Querol, Marta; Sambanis, Nicholas. Breaking the Conflict Trap: Civil War and Development Policy. A World Bank policy research report. Washington, DC: World Bank and Oxford University Press, 2003.

ECOSOC. Criminal Justice Reform and Strengthening of Legal Institutions Measures to Regulate Firearms: Report to the Secretary-General. E/CN.15/1997/4 of 7 March 1997

Evoy, C. and Hideg, G.. *Global Violent Deaths 2017: Time to Decide*. Geneva: Small Arms Survey Report, 2017.

Faria, Fernanda. "Fragile States: Challenges and Opportunities for Atlantic Relations." In *Atlantic Future Scientific*. Paper 9, 2014.

Geneva Declaration Secretariat. "Global Burden of Armed Violence 2015: everybody counts". 2015. [Consulted at: http://www.genevadeclaration.org/measurability/global-burden-of-armed-violence/global-burden-of-armed-violence-2015.html]

Hamilton, Daniel S.. Promoting Human Security and Effective Security Governance in the Atlantic Hemisphere, in *Dark Networks in the Atlantic Basin*. Washington, DC: Center for Transatlantic Relations, 2015.

Jacobson, Mark R. and Daurora, Max. "Significant Trends in Illicit Trafficking: A Macro View of the Problem and Potential Means to Address It." In *Atlantic Future Scientific*. Paper 8, 2014. [Consulted at: http://www.atlanticfuture.eu/files/326-ATLANTIC%20FUTURE_08_Transnational%20threats.pdf]

Kaldor, M. *New and Old Wars: Organized Violence in the Global Era*. 1st edition. California: Stanford University Press, 1999.

King, Benjamin and McDonald, Glenn (ed). *Behind the Curve: New Technologies, New Control Challenges*. Geneva: Small Arms Survey, 2015.

Lété, Bruno. "Addressing the Atlantic's Emerging Security Challenges." In *Atlantic Future*. No 34, 2015.

May, Channing. "Transnational Crime and the Developing World". In *Global Financial Integrity Report, 2017*.

McDonald, Glenn. *Connecting the Dots: the international tracing instruments*. Geneva: Small Arms Survey Report, 2006.

OECD. *Conflict and Fragility Armed Violence Reduction enabling development*. Paris: OECD Publishing, 2009.

OECD. *Reducing the Involvement of Youth in Armed Violence: Programming Note*, Conflict and Fragility Series. Paris: OECD Publishing, 2011.

Oliver, Cann. "Top 10 Emerging Technologies of 2016 Report". In *World Economic Forum*. 2016. [Consulted at: https://www.weforum.org/agenda/2016/06/top-10-emerging-technologies-2016/]

Parker, Sarah and Wilson, Marcus. *A Guide to the UN Small Arms Process*. 3rd edition. Genova: Small Arms Survey, 2016.

Roberts, Adam. "Lives and Statistics: Are 90% of War Victims Civilian?". In *Survival*. Vol 52, No. 3, 2010, 115-136.

Sivard, Ruth L. *World Military and Social Expenditures 1991.*, Washington DC: World Priorities, 1991.

Small Arms Survey. *Documenting Small Arms and Light Weapons: A Basic Guide*. Issue Brief Number 14, 2015.

SIPRI Fact Sheet, 2018. [Consulted at: https://www.sipri.org/sites/default/files/2019-04/fs_1904_milex_2018.pdf]

UNDP. *Human Development Report 1998: Consumption for Human Development Technical Report*. New York: UNDP, 1998.

UNGA. Programme of Action to Prevent, Combat and Eradicate the Illicit Trade in Small Arms and Light Weapons in All Its Aspects ('UN Programme of Action'). A/CONF.192/15 of 20 July 2001. [Consulted at: http://www.poa-iss.org/poa/poahtml.aspx]

UNGA. Protocol against the Illicit Manufacturing of and Trafficking in Firearms, Their Parts and Components and Ammunition, Supplementing the United Nations Convention against Transnational Organized Crime ('Firearms Protocol'). A/RES/55/255 of 8 June 2001. [Consulted at: http://www.unodc.org/pdf/crime/a_res_55/255e.pdf]

UNGA. Report of the Ninth United Nations Congress on the Prevention of Crime and the Treatment of Offenders. A/CONF.169/16.Rev.1 of 8 May 1995.

UNGA. Report of the Open-ended Working Group to Negotiate an International Instrument to Enable States to Identify and Trace, in a Timely and Reliable Manner, Illicit Small Arms and Light Weapons. A/60/88 of 27 June 2005. [Consulted at: http://www.un.org/events/smallarms2006/pdf/A.60.88%20(E).pdf]

UNGA. Report of the Panel of Governmental Experts on Small Arms. A/52/298 of 27 August 1997.

UNGA. Report of the United Nations Secretary-General on Small arms and light weapons. 2015. [Consulted at: http://www.un.org/ga/search/view_doc.asp?symbol=S/2015/289&referer=/english/&Lang=E]

UNGA. The Arms Trade Treaty. Adopted 2 April. A/RES/67/234 B of 11 June 2013. [Consulted at: http://www.un.org/en/ga/search/view_doc.asp?symbol=A/RES/67/234%20B]

UNODC. Comparative Analysis of Global Instruments on Firearms and other Conventional Arms: Synergies for Implementation. Vienna: UNODC, 2016.

UNSC. *Small arms and light weapons Report of the Secretary-General*. S/2015/289. 2015. [Consulted at: http://www.securitycouncilreport.org/atf/cf/%7B65BF-CF9B-6D27-4E9C-8CD3-CF6E4FF96FF9%7D/s_2015_289.pdf]

UNTOC. United Nations Convention against Transnational Organized Crime. Resolution 55/25 of 15 November 2000.

Chapter 5

Human (In)security and Irregular Migration: The Atlantic Basin

João Estevens

Both voluntary and forced migration remain among the most divisive issues among states today. Though not a new phenomenon, migration flows have been increasing over the last three decades. Since 9/11 and the subsequent 'Global War on Terrorism', migration has become an intense object for security analysis as it is undeniable how terrorism shapes public opinion on migration and affects political movements inside civil society and party systems. But does all migration matter for security? The answer is a clear no, since most of the flows are regular and will create neither a risk nor a threat for the state and its population. We live in a time of global human mobility and the twenty-first century is indeed the century of the migrant, but migration is a complex and highly stratified phenomenon. It affects political boundaries left from the days of imperialism and colonialism, producing multicultural societies with shifting ethnic or religious compositions.[1] Global human mobility is a key feature of our world, albeit it includes many different dynamics, from the global tourist to the undocumented employee, and from human trafficking to refugees forced to leave their country of origin because of climate changes, poverty or wars.[2] Hence, migration is contributing to many changes inside structures and institutions acting on global political, economic and social relationships.[3]

In this chapter we focus on the migration-security nexus and so we are mostly referring to irregular migration flows that happen due to mass displacements (forced migration), cross-border asylum seekers and refugees, cross-border contract workers, migrants seeking better social and economic opportunities, and migrants with an irregular administrative status in the receiving countries.

---

1. Goldstone, Jack A. "A Theory of Political Demography. Human and Institutional Reproduction". In *Political demography: How population changes are reshaping international security and National Politics*. New York: Oxford University Press, 2012, 12.
2. Castles, Stephen & Miller, Mark J. *The age of migration: International population movements in the modern world* (4ᵗʰ ed.). New York: Palgrave Macmillan, 2009.
3. Castles, Stephen. "Understanding global migration: A social transformation perspective". In *Journal of Ethnic and Migration Studies*. Vol. 36, No. 10, 2010, 1566.

Scholars need to be careful when associating migration and security because of the negative effects that may arise on migrants. But a lot of research has been developed in the last decades, especially in the security studies field, leading the migration-security nexus to be perceived mostly through a national security lens. The interest in how population dynamics and security studies are connected is increasing very fast, enhanced by the expansion of political demography as field of study within international relations and political science. We have now a vast literature on this subject allowing us to explore how these two areas may be connected.[4] The concept of securitization comes from the Copenhagen School and concerns focus on a specific subject beyond ordinary policies.[5] When applying it to migration, it may be translated into securitarian frameworks to address migration-related issues.[6] Migration can matter for national security in situations when migrants or refugees are opposed to their home country's regime, when they are perceived as a security risk or a cultural threat in the home country, when immigrants cause social and economic pressure in host societies, or when the host society use immigrants as an instrument against the country of origin.[7] Ceyhan and Tsoukala[8] approach the securitization of migration along four different axis: (i) socioeconomic,

---

4. Huysmans, Jef. "The European Union and the Securitization of Migration". In *Journal of Common Market Studies*. Vol. 38, No. 5, 2000, 751-777; Huysmans, Jef. *The Politics of Insecurity: Fear, migration and asylum in the EU*. Abingdon: Routledge, 2006; Weiner, Myron & Russell, Sharon Stanton (Eds.). *Demography and National Securit*. New York: Berghahn Books, 2001; Bigo, Didier. "Security and immigration: Toward a critique of the Governmentality of unease". In *Alternatives*, Vol. 27, 2002, 63-92; Goldstone, Jack A. "Population and security: How demographic change can lead to violent conflict". In *Journal of International Affairs*. Vol. 56, No. 1, 2002, 3-22; Goldstone, Jack A. "A Theory of Political Demography. Human and Institutional Reproduction". In *Political demography: How population changes are reshaping international security and National Politics*. New York: Oxford University Press, 2012, 10-28; Guild, Elspeth & Van Selm, Joanne (Eds.). *International migration and security. Opportunities and challenges*. Abingdon: Routledge, 2005; Adamson, Fiona B. "Crossing borders: International migration and national security". In *International Security*. Vol. 31, No. 1, 2006, 165-199; Guild, Elspeth. *Security and Migration in the 21ˢᵗ Century*. Cambridge and Malden: Polity Press, 2009; Bourbeau, Philippe. *The Securitization of Migration: A study of movement and order*. Abingdon: Routledge, 2011; Rodrigues, Teresa Ferreira. "Population dynamics: Demography matters". In *Globalization and international security. An overview*. New York: Nova Science Publishers, 2015, 33-49.
5. Buzan, Barry, Waever, Ole, & De Wilde, Jaa *Security: A New Framework for Analysis*. Boulder, CO: Lynne Rienner, 1998.
6. Ferreira, Susana. *Humans Security and Migration in Europe's Southern Borders*. Cham: Palgrave Macmillan, 2019, 37.
7. Weiner, Myron. "Security, stability, and international migration". In *International Security*. Vol. 17, No. 3, 1992, 105-106.
8. Ceyhan, Anastassia & Tsoukala, Ayse. "The securitization of migration in western societies: Ambivalent discourses and policies". In *Alternatives*. Vol. 27, 2002, 24.

due to unemployment, the rise of informal economy and underground economic activities, welfare state crisis, and urban environment deterioration; (ii) securitarian, considering the loss of a control narrative that associates sovereignty, borders, and both internal and external security; (iii) identitarian, where migrants are considered as being a threat to the host societies' national identity and demographic equilibrium; and (iv) political, as a result of anti-immigrant, racist, and xenophobic discourses. Therefore, since migration can impact in different areas as state sovereignty, the balance of power among states and the nature of conflicts in the international system, national security may also be affected.[9] Lastly, increasing human mobility has been associated with: urban clusters for migrants,[10] difficulties in the capacity of states to control who can enter their territories,[11] and asymmetries in the ethnic-religious population composition.[12] And if immigrants are not integrated into host communities, particularly if they come from a completely different cultural environment, the potential risk of religious and ethnic conflicts tends to be higher, demanding new governmental integration efforts of ethnic minorities into national communities.[13] So, according to this body of work, there are possible risks for a hosting society.

Security is built on a set of discourses or narratives and historical practices based on institutionally-shared understandings, therefore becoming a political and social construct.[14] During this process, elites in power, as well as analysts and experts, define the existing risks and threats in a certain moment and for different levels (national, regional, global). They then justify their validity alongside the community, subsequently activating, when possible, the means to neutralize them. Thus, the inclusion of a specific approach to security, in state practices or in international organisations, tends to be derived from an existing structure of power. And with increasing globalization, the state has changed some of its functions and developed new ones, since the traditional function to guarantee the defense of its territory

9. Adamson, Fiona B. "Crossing borders: International migration and national security". In *International Security*. Vol. 31, No. 1, 2006, 165-199.
10. Rodrigues, Teresa Ferreira. "Population dynamics: Demography matters". In *Globalization and international security. An overview*. New York: Nova Science Publishers, 2015, 45-46.
11. Mabee, Bryan. *The globalization of security: State power, security provision and legitimacy*. New York: Palgrave Macmillan, 2009, 123-124.
12. Tragaki, Alexandra. "Demography and migration as human security factors: The case of South Eastern Europe". In *Migration Letters*. Vol. 4, No. 2, 2007, 10.
13. Savage, Timothy M. "Europe and Islam: Crescent waxing, cultures clashing. In *The Washington Quarterly*. Vol. 27, No. 3, 2004, 25-50.
14. Waever, Ole. "Securitization and Desecuritization". In *On security*. New York: Columbia University Press, 1995, 46-86.

and political independence is now attached to the obligation of assuring economic independence, cultural identity and social stability. Transnational interdependences have been transforming existing risks and threats, which are impossible to neutralize by only focusing on the state and with a national security strategy limited to national boundaries.[15] Therefore, new approaches may be considered, and human security has been one of the strongest alternative paradigms emerging in international relations. Human security combines security, development and human rights, changing the referent for security from the state to the human. This people-oriented philosophy offers an alternative approach to tackle mass irregular migration, demanding a multilevel intervention and cooperation among states, international institutions and NGOs.[16] However, due to the absence of a concrete framework, human security remains a somehow fuzzy concept that requires a greater understanding of what it is today in a very different global environment than the one existing by the end of twentieth century when the concept has burst to the surface with astonishing force within the international relations. Also, human security still needs further developments in terms of operational tools and concrete action plans to assure its implementation.

So, since human security emerged in a multilateral context, are states really committing to it? Is human security really challenging the dominant paradigm of national security existing since the Peace of Westphalia? What does it bring to the migration-security nexus? Is it more effective to assess irregular migration? These are the questions addressed in this chapter. We try to look on how the human security paradigm penetrated the traditional paradigm of national security in the geographical context of the Atlantic Basin. To do so, we considered the national security and defence strategies from countries belonging to different regions, some regional powers, some with a strong historical Atlantic path. Further, we examined in which terms migration, especially irregular migration, was considered within the national security strategies of Argentina, Brazil, Canada, France, Mexico, Nigeria, Norway, Portugal, South Africa, Spain, the United Kingdom and the United States of America. We argue that human security, as national security, has a global, preventive and cooperative nature and it is comple-

---

15. Sorensen, Georg. "State transformation and new security dilemmas," In *Globalization, security, and the nation-state. Paradigms in transition.* New York: State University of New York Press, 2005, 81-98; Mabee, Bryan. *The globalization of security: State power, security provision and legitimacy.* New York: Palgrave Macmillan, 2009.
16. Ferreira, Susana. *Humans Security and Migration in Europe's Southern Borders.* Cham: Palgrave Macmillan, 2019.

mentary to national security. So far, the later tends to prevail when states deal with the migration-security nexus, especially during a crisis scenario, though we can observe some principles and values of human security in countries' security strategic documents. This merging is vital in a time of rising nationalism and increasing separation between us (nationals) and them (non-nationals). Irregular mass migration is a consequence of a globalized interdependent world, being also a paradox of globalization since it is reinforcing the Nation-state and fuelling national sovereignty debates. The more effective way to securitize irregular migration is through a comprehensive approach of the migration-security nexus combining both national security and human security. States keep focusing more on securitizing their territory and citizenry. Hence, human security is fundamental to protect migrants, asylum seekers and refugees facing vulnerability and insecurity. And the combination of both provides the securitization of different territories and of all individuals (nationals and non-nationals).

Human security, migration and migrants: a missing framework for analysis

During the 1990s, after the peaceful ending of the Cold War, the growth in intra-state conflicts, Western societies' fear of immigration, the decaying environment and the acceleration of the HIV/AIDS epidemic, it was inevitable to include new strategic factors associated with human security in the security agenda. The acknowledgement of a new world led to new developments in security, from its traditional political-military conception centred in the state and its sovereignty to a more inclusive and holistic view of peace and international stability based on the protection of individuals.[17] The state stopped being the only referent for security, since human security is a people-centered concept. Nonetheless, human security did not replace national security, integrating new dimensions as the protection of human rights, economic development and individual security. Though the term emerged in the 1980s, it was not until 1994 that it had an institutional conceptualization in the UN 1994 Human Development Report. There was not a concrete framework, but the core ideas were established. It was characterized by a universal, broad and flexible approach and by the interdependencies among the seven components: economic security, food secu-

---

17. Buzan, Barry & Hansen, Lene. *The evolution of international security studies*. Cambridge: Cambridge University Press, 2009, 187.

rity, health security, environmental security, personal security, community security and political security.[18]

The broadening of the security concept was pushed by the Copenhagen School, a school of academic thought on critical security studies that emphasized the social dimensions of security and rejected the sovereign state as the primary referent for and agent of security,[19] also defending increasing difficulties to sustain an enduring and reliable national security strategy without a strong response to human insecurity.[20] That was a key point: assuming national security paradigm was being inefficient to deal with environmental disasters, famine, disease epidemics, refugee flows, and other dynamics that were putting people's security at stake.[21] So, human security has brought the assumption of contemporary risks that demand new processes of securitization, spurring preventive diplomacy, good governance and economic and social development to save a society from reaching a crisis point. Hence, cooperation and prevention are fundamental principles of human security. They are also fundamental to national security.

Human insecurity is a major driver of migration, and the promotion of human security seems to be one fundamental path to manage and control mass irregular migration.[22] It should be obvious to most political actors that people caught up facing a civil war, or violent conflict in general, or targeted with political/ethnic/religious persecution, or facing economic deprivation, or dealing with famine, or migrating in very poor health conditions are dealing with human insecurity. Human survival, human dignity and human development are many times at stake for those migrating or being irregular inside a receiving or transit country. Two research contributions that clearly dealt with global mobility and human security were Bach[23] and Clark.[24] They concluded that to assess the problem in the most vulnerable

18. Und *Human Development Report 1994*. New York: UNDP, 1994.
19. Buzan, Barry, Waever, Ole, & De Wilde, Jaa *Security: A New Framework for Analysis*. Boulder, CO: Lynne Rienner, 1998.
20. Vietti, Francesca & Scribner, Todd. "Human insecurity: Understanding international migration from a human security perspective". In *Journal on Migration and Human Security*. Vol. 1, No. 1, 2013, 27.
21. Owen, Taylor. "Human Security - Conflict, Critique and Consensus: Colloquium Remarks and a Proposal for a Threshold-Based Definition". In *Security Dialogue*. Vol. 35, No. 3, 2004, 374.
22. Ferreira, Susana. *Humans Security and Migration in Europe's Southern Borders*. Cham: Palgrave Macmillan, 2019, 195.
23. Bach, Robert. "Global Mobility, Inequality and Security". In *Journal of Human Development*. Vol. 4, No. 2, 2003, 227-245.
24. Clark, Michele Anne. "Trafficking in Persons: an issue of human security". In *Journal of Human Development*. Vol. 4, No. 2, 2003, 247-263.

populations it is necessary to work with countries of origin, transit, and destination. Due to its preventive nature, much of the focus on human security is to address the conditions of human insecurity before people are forced to migrate. Ferreira[25] followed that and conceptualized a model of Minimum Standards based on human security and dignity principles that could be applied by the EU. But who can enforce human security? As Vietti and Scribner concluded,[26] human security goes beyond the limits imposed by the problems of state sovereignty and border control, leading to a deeper connection between irregular migration and human security that demands multilevel governance, strong cooperation and accountability.

Many of the images in our minds today about mass irregular migration evidence human insecurity both as a cause and an outcome of mass irregular migration. If irregular migration is fuelled by human insecurity in different areas, it is necessary to weigh up the security of migrants themselves that face numerous non-human conditions in many deterrence centres, refugee camps, or when they are subject to criminal networks involved in migrants smuggling and human trafficking.[27] A human security approach based on principles of social justice of various kinds will consider national security and human security as mutually supportive.[28] When migrants get to a country irregularly, some reports indicate cases of illegal work, labor exploitation, involvement in prostitution and human organ trafficking networks,[29] which generate a space for the legal marginalisation of migrants based on nationalistic values that may ignite xenophobic practices inside hosting societies.[30] Indeed, the development of underground economic activities has been reported in some studies, allowing both the lack of labour and socioeconomic security for the immigrants, plus labor abuse and tax evasion for those (individuals or companies) hiring them. So,

25. Ferreira, Susana. *Humans Security and Migration in Europe's Southern Borders*. Cham: Palgrave Macmillan, 2019.
26. Vietti, Francesca & Scribner, Todd. "Human insecurity: Understanding international migration from a human security perspective". In *Journal on Migration and Human Security*. Vol. 1, No. 1, 2013.
27. Ferreira, Susana. *Humans Security and Migration in Europe's Southern Borders*. Cham: Palgrave Macmillan, 2019, 5.
28. Truong, Thanh-Dam. "The Governmentality of Transnational Migration and Security: The Making of a New Subaltern". In *Transnational Migration and Human Security. The Migration-Development-Security Nexus*. Berlin: Springer, 2011, 36.
29. Burgess, J. Peter. "Introduction: Security, migration and integration". In *A threat against Europe? Security, migration and integration*. Brussels: Institute for European Studies, 2011, 15.
30. Geddes, Andrew. *The politics of migration and immigration in Europe*. London: SAGE Publications, 2003, 22.

human insecurity does not just come from origin countries, nor from the journey of moving in an irregular path, but also from the conditions many immigrants face within hosting societies. Irregular migrants or semiskilled temporary workers often work under profoundly precarious and dangerous conditions, and at the same time are excluded from such social welfare protection structures existing in the receiving countries as health, education and housing. So, even if they find a job that temporary fulfils national labor market needs, therefore adding value to the national economy, their economic security is also temporary and not structural.[31] For the benefit of immigrants and hosting communities, prevention of marginalization, discrimination, urban segregation and social disruption are essential to ensure social stability. If the economic and social security of these individuals is granted, not only is the area of socio-economic exclusion limited, they are less vulnerable to transnational organized crime. However, so far the path followed by many states does not seem very inclusive, as some countries in the global North lately rely on growing punitive governance, which illustrates the cycle of labor marginalization, radicalization and criminalization. The politics of immigration control and the criminalization of irregular and illegal immigrants derive mostly from a social-legal system that allows their marginalization and their labour exploitation.[32]

Migration policies go beyond economic and security issues as they enlighten the ethics of a given polity. From a human security approach, states are not only responsible to ensure the security of its borders and its citizens, but also of their residents. The resident population is made of nationals and non-nationals and both should be able to rely on the state to guarantee/ safeguard their human rights and to help them when dealing with vulnerable conditions. But even beyond this domestic compromise, states should also act on human security internationally at different levels: within international institutions, bilaterally or supporting NGOs. If we analyze the migration-security nexus through human security, the conclusion is clear: migrants tend to be the weakest link. A new migrant-centred approach to the migration-security nexus through human security is therefore very much needed since migrants' security is not a reference point for national security. Since there is widespread research on the topic and no common shared framework among countries and institutions, what does human security add to the migration-security analysis? Even before migrants move, there

---

31. Levoy, Michele, Verbruggen, Nele, & Wets, Johan (Eds.). *Undocumented Migrant Workers in Europe*. Brussels: PICUM, 2004.
32. Melossi, Dario. *Crime, punishment and migration*. London: SAGE Publications, 2015, 60.

is a commitment to ensure better standard of lives in developing countries by assuring human rights, development and humanitarian assistance. When they are moving, support and cooperation among countries of origin, transit and destination is provided to create safe legal routes, to fight migrants smuggling and human trafficking networks, and to assure basic human conditions in deterrence centres or refugee camps. And when migrants are in a receiving country, they can count on integration policies that encourage fair labor conditions and social welfare protection.

Thus, we now proceed to show how migration is considered in the national security strategic documents of selected countries.

Institutional approach: migration and national security strategies

Though security has a deeply political nature, the ways states approach it vary in time and space, and so we may assume it as a continuum involving various degrees of intensity.[33] National security strategies are not the only resource to assess the human security of migration, albeit they are key instruments to understand the principles, the values and the institutional prerogatives structuring the securitization of migration developed by each state. Also, national security has been changing over the time, including some elements of individual security. These strategic documents are essential to understand states' strategic cultures and institutional view over global human mobility by analysing the security environment, prioritizing necessary actions, and defining domestic and international cooperation. All documents reflect each state decision-makers and experts' preferences in security and defence policy at a specific moment in time about different issues, being migration one of those. These documents (White Papers, Defense Agreements, Defense Concepts or similar strategic reports) were planned and implemented at different times but try to give a persistent security strategy projection as they are expected to last around five to ten years. So, here is how selected states approach migration in their security and defense strategies:

Argentina (2015)

The White Book for defense of Argentina ignores the migration-security nexus when approaching the existing risks for the country, as well the prin-

---

33. Bourbeau, Philippe. *The Securitization of Migration: A study of movement and order*. Abingdon: Routledge, 2011, 18.

ciples of human security, though a lot of ideas are explored under humanitarian aid and assistance and international cooperation.[34]

Brazil (2016)

Brazilian PND and END do not mention migration as an issue for security, neither the official version of 2012, nor the unofficial public draft under analysis of 2016. In these documents, both human security and irregular migration were absent, though some assumptions of human rights and global security cooperation in terms of peacekeeping were mentioned.[35]

Canada (2017)

The quite recent strategy for defense of Canada does not consider any references to human security nor to the migration-security nexus, though there is a major premise regarding the necessity of international cooperation with regard to humanitarian assistance and disaster relief, as well as peacekeeping missions.[36]

France (2017)

The migration crisis in Europe is understood as one of the tough subjects nowadays that has created a lot of tensions inside the EU, while challenging the sovereignty over the national territory of France, demanding stronger border control from the French Armed Forces. Demographic factors, especially migration flows, are understood as factors that exacerbate crisis situations. So, migration and refugee flows are posing challenges not only to France but to fragile developing countries with low absorptive capacity. Thus, the action needs to happen in neighboring countries as well in terms of migration without ignoring its humanitarian dimension. In the document, it also mentions increasing organized crime involving migrants smuggling and human trafficking.[37]

---

34. República Argentina, Ministerio de Defensa. "Libro Blanco de la Defensa 2015" [Consulted at: December 5, 2018]. Available at: http://ceed.unasursg.org/Espanol/09-Downloads/Info-Pais/Arg/LB/Libro_blanco_2015.pdf.
35. Ministério da Defesa. "Política Nacional de Defesa e Estratégia Nacional de Defesa" (Versão Preliminar) [Consulted at: December 5, 2018]. Available at: https://www.defesa.gov.br/noticias/29093-minutas-do-livro-branco-da-pnd-e-da-end-estao-disponiveis-para-leitura.
36. Minister of National Defence. "Strong, Secure, Engaged. Canada's Defence Policy" [Consulted at: December 5, 2018]. Available at: http://dgpaapp.forces.gc.ca/en/canada-defence-policy/docs/canada-defence-policy-report.pdf.
37. République Française. "Revue stratégique de defense et de sécurité nationale 2017" [Consulted at: January 3, 2019]. Available at: https://www.defense.gouv.fr/espanol/

Mexico (2014)

The regional context of North America presents several economic inequalities as well as existing intense regular and irregular flows. The Mexican strategy develops a full autonomous section dedicated to migration. Due to its huge flows under severe conditions, Mexican authorities must fight migrant smugglers and human trafficking networks, as well as provide humanitarian aid to those moving and support to those settling in to prevent labor and sexual exploitation, as well as participation in organized transnational crime networks. Controlling the borders and increasing surveillance, especially along Mexico's southern border, is necessary, but the focus should rely on the migrants facing the most vulnerable conditions in order to achieve an efficient human mobility system. As a transnational phenomenon, cooperation between origin, transit and hosting countries is essential and they should work together to create conditions that enhance legal migration. Repatriation programs of Mexican citizens could be enforced if required by external countries and accepted by national authorities.[38]

Nigeria (2014)

Irregular migration is perceived as a threat to national security in Nigerian strategy. Nigeria's inadequately policed land and maritime borders have resulted in numerous illegal border crossings and irregular migration associated with transnational crimes, also favouring the illegal movement of arms, terrorists and other criminals. The approach to migration is perceived as being mainly "*a matter of law enforcement*"[39] that is necessary to tackle since criminal organizations and terrorist groups use migration channels to establish and reinforce their positions within the region. It should be handled within a framework of bilateral, multilateral and international cooperation, that can lead to the suppression of transnational organized crime and the prevention of acts of terrorism. Internally, the practices of the Islamist terrorist group Boko Haram have had consequences on migration too, as mass displacements occurred, as well as the creation of refugee populations under non-human conditions, and the expansion of famine and poverty.[40]

---

dgris/politique-de-defense/revue-strategique/revue-strategique.

38. Presidencia de la República. "Programa para la Seguridad Nacional 2014. 2018. Una política multidimensional para México en el siglo XXI" [Consulted at: December 5, 2018]. Available at: http://cdn.presidencia.gob.mx/programa-para-la-seguridad-nacional.pdf.

39. Federal Republic of Nigeria. "National Security Strategy 2014 [Consulted at: December 5, 2018]. Available at: http://ctc.gov.ng/nigerian-national-security-strategy-2014/. 21.

40. *Ibid.*

Norway (2017)

The Norwegian foreign and security policy document states that the security environment is changing and one of the reasons is the strong indication that migratory pressure on Europe will increase as the political context in the MENA region is not yet stabilized. During the last years, new challenges relating to migration and integration emerged due to increasing terrorism and organized crime. Therefore, the control of Schengen's external borders and cooperation in the area of asylum are necessary, as countries need to improve their joint system for processing asylum applications and to deport migrants who have had their asylum applications rejected. Also, the Government is following the Nordic cooperation project on the integration of refugees and immigrants inside Norway to prevent social marginalisation and fertile ground for radicalization. The issue of migrants and refugees demands a strong international response based on cooperation to deal with a humanitarian crisis and the need of further development programmes in weak and fragile states. "Better coordination of development aid and humanitarian assistance for refugees and migrants could help to ensure a more sustainable approach to dealing with flows of refugees and migrants in the neighbouring areas."[41]

Portugal (2013)

The Portuguese strategic concept claims its commitment to human security as it is a principle followed by the UN (United Nations), NATO (North Atlantic Treaty Organization) and the EU (European Union) security strategies. As an active member of the global security system, cooperation in international missions and humanitarian aid programmes has been pursued by the Portuguese Armed Forces. The impact of failed states and civil wars on migrant and refugee flows is perceived as a global security risk. The consequences of climate change and transnational organized crime on human migration are also considered. Therefore, Portugal needs to commit to maritime security to fight transnational organized crimes, also concerning irregular migration and human trafficking. Population aging is understood as a major national challenge and the suggested way to cope with it is to promote new immigration policies, reinforcing integration policies to

---

41. Norwegian Ministry of Foreign Affairs. "Setting the course for Norwegian foreign and security policy" [Consulted at: December 5, 2018]. Available at: https://www.regjeringen.no/en/aktuelt/future_course/id2550127/. 38.

avoid the rise of extremism, xenophobia and nationalism movements that can compromise social cohesion.[42]

South Africa (2014)

The South African Defence Review considers human security, identifying the need for a shift from solely national security to the provision of security for its people by addressing critical political, socio-economic and environmental problems as many African countries suffer with human insecurity. Human security is approached as "a component of a wider national security."[43] In terms of regular migration, one of the main worries is the internal flows from rural to urban spaces that are challenging the existing urban infrastructures. As for irregular migration, it is addressed in relation to the expansion of the informal labour market, illicit economic activities, disease control, migrants smuggling and human trafficking. To manage irregular migration flows, border control and safeguard must be achieved, in many cases with the cooperation of neighbouring countries. Social instability, the growth of terrorist cells, the financing of terrorism activities and other criminal activities, as well as the development of no-go areas are other problems emerging from irregular migration in South Africa. South Africa remains a destination country for many neighbouring migrants. Intolerance and violence against non-nationals is another strong issue in social relations, entrenched in "negative perceptions and stereotypes about foreigners, business rivalry, criminality, population density and pressure on scarce resources, particularly where perceptions of relative deprivation are sharpened by high unemployment and strong migratory pressure."[44]

Spain (2017)

Irregular migration flows demand a comprehensive approach that advocates safeguarding the human dimension and strong international cooperation. Through better understanding about the causes of migration, "improving channels of legal migration, protecting migrants, combating exploitation and people smuggling, and cooperating in terms of return and

---

42. Governo de Portugal. "Conceito Estratégico de Defesa Nacional [Strategic Concept of National Defense]". [Consulted at: December 5, 2018]. Available at: http://www.portugal.gov.pt/pt/ministerios/mdn/quero-saber-mais/sobre-oministerio/20120223-conceito-estrategico/20130416-conceito-estrategico.aspx.
43. South African Government. "South African Defence Review 2014" [Consulted at: December 5, 2018]. Available at: https://www.gov.za/sites/default/files/dfencereview_2014.pdf. 3-1.
44. *Ibid*, 2-17.

readmission"[45] might be possible. The North Africa region and the Sahel present unstable political contexts that enable mass migration flows, many of them being irregular. Spain's direct interest in order to address irregular immigration demands cooperation with those countries and with the EU to advance towards greater regional stability. In recent years, "criminal networks have taken advantage of the migrant and refugee crisis, and their extreme vulnerability, to open human trafficking routes to Europe."[46] These irregular migration networks use maritime routes that create a vulnerability in the Spanish maritime space, demanding stronger border control.

Irregular migration flows come from conflicts and regional instability, poverty and environmental degradation. Without lasting solutions, forced displacements may affect the political stability and social cohesion of the receiving countries. But the migration crisis management cannot ignore the protection of human rights of those who are in the most vulnerable situations. Also, the integration of immigrants in Spain is important to promote the country's prosperity and diversity, respecting different values, lifestyles and freedom. The goal is to prevent, control and organize irregular migration flows at borders, and ensure appropriate integration of immigrants, asylum seekers and refugees. For that to happen further cooperation is needed, among states, the EU, with transit and origin countries, and by encouraging the private sector to participate. Complying with all national and European legal provisions, developing safe routes for legal migration, combating human trafficking networks, and monitoring Spanish external borders are also part of the Spanish lines of action.[47]

United Kingdom (2015)

Migration is understood as a major global and national security challenge, whether directly or because of political-social instability in conflicts such as the ones in Syria and Iraq, which led to increasing mass migration and human trafficking. Instability, extremism and conflict in the Middle East and Africa have displaced millions of people in recent years. Transnational organized crime and climate change can also be a driver of migration that needs to be securitized. There is a strong humanitarian challenge in Europe, pressing the EU and demanding coordinated work with multilater-

---

45. Gobierno de España. "National Security Strategy 2017" [Consulted at: December 5, 2018]. Available at: http://www.dsn.gob.es/sites/dsn/files/2017_Spanish_National_Security_Strategy_0.pdf. 24.
46. *Ibid*, 60.
47. *Ibid*.

al agencies and countries that are hosting large numbers of refugees. There is the goal to help improving livelihoods and give displaced people the best possible prospects, but as close to home as possible. It is also vital to further strengthen the ability to control migration, to offer asylum, and to ensure that the border, immigration and citizenship systems can manage migration overseas, at the UK border and within the UK.

The UK is not part of Schengen's open borders agreement and has an independent way of dealing with the migration crisis in Europe, but remains working with NATO and the EU, as well as bilaterally (though no countries are mentioned within the document for bilateral cooperation). All in all, there is a comprehensive approach to migration that ensures investment in countries of origin to help reducing forced displacement and migration over the long term, to provide humanitarian aid to those who are forcibly displaced, as well as education and livelihood opportunities. Tackling the capacity of origin and transit countries to manage their borders more effectively and organised immigration crime are priorities. And to do so, humanitarian aid, disaster response, and especially development assistance is needed. Therefore, the UK is committed to those principles in fragile states with vulnerable populations since "it makes a significant contribution to long-term national security and prosperity. Tackling poverty and instability overseas means tackling the root causes of many of the global challenges that we face including disease, migration and terrorism"[48].

United States of America (2017)

The document tries to put the idea of 'America First' in terms of security and the first pages clearly state that the fundamental responsibility is to protect the American people, the homeland, and the American way of life, adding the need to strengthen border control and reform the immigration system. A full section is dedicated to that issue since it is perceived as central to national security, economic prosperity, and the rule of law. Though the document has an autonomous section analyzing migration, the border issue is considered when approaching terrorism, drug trafficking, and criminal cartels. Therefore, affirming the need to enforce national sovereignty and the right to determine who should enter the US and under what circumstances is a key priority.

---

48. HM Government. "National Security Strategy and Strategic Defence and Security Review 2015. A Secure and Prosperous United Kingdom" [Consulted at: December 5, 2018]. Available at: https://www.gov.uk/government/publications/national-security-strategy-and-strategic-defence-and-security-review-2015. 48.

Another issue is irregular migration and the way it "burdens the economy, hurts American workers, presents public safety risks, and enriches smugglers and other criminals."[49]. So, it is fundamental that the state can decide about who to admit legally for residency and citizenship based on the migrants' merits and abilities and not allowing an extended-family chain of migration. Though regular migration may be stimulated according to the national interest, there is a need to enhance border control (construction of a border wall), the screening and vetting of travellers, close dangerous loopholes, and revise outdated migration laws and policies.

In another section, when exploring the priority actions, the document states that the US is committed to reduce human suffering. Even if expecting stronger shared responsibilities with other states and institutions, the US will continue its humanitarian assistance, trying to ignite international responses to natural disasters and to provide food security and health programs that save lives. The support to displaced people will be close to their homes until they can safely and voluntarily return home.[50]

We believe this analysis shows how human security managed to (or failed to) penetrate the dominant national security paradigm. In the next section, we explore how migration can be framed within national security and human security and highlight which countries are considering and which are ignoring human insecurity.

National Security and/or Human Security: A Comparative Approach

Through a comprehensive approach to the literature review, Table 1 considers fourteen dimensions, half of them linked to national security and the other half to human security. In terms of national security, we considered irregular migration as: (A) threatening social cohesion due to shifting ethnic and religious population composition; (B) requiring a focus on deterrence centres and repatriation programmes; (C) demanding stronger border control; (D) facilitating terrorism; (E) increasing transnational organized crime; (F) increasing small criminality and internal insecurity; and (G) pressuring the social welfare protection instruments. As for human security, we focused on (A') assuring human rights, dignity and humanitarian assistance to migrants moving or trying to enter a country; (B') commit-

49. The White House. "National Security Strategy of the United States of America 2017" [Consulted at: December 5, 2018]. Available at: https://www.whitehouse.gov/articles/new-national-security-strategy-new-era/. 9.
50. *Ibidem*.

Table 1. Migration-security nexus: a framework for analysis

Country	National security							Human security						
	A	B	C	D	E	F	G	A'	B'	C'	D'	E'	F'	G'
Argentina														
Brazil														
Canada														
France				+	+				+					
Mexico			+		+				+	+				
Nigeria			+		+				+					
Norway			+		+			+	+			+		
Portugal			+		+				+	+		+		
South Africa	+		+	+	+	+			+			+		
Spain	+		+		+			+	+	+	+	+		
U.K.			+		+			+	+	+				
U.S.A.		+	+	+	+	+	+		+	+				

ting to development support and cooperation with countries of origin and transit; (C') combating migrants smuggling and human trafficking; (D') developing new safe legal routes; (E') fostering integration policies that protect immigrants from social marginalization and urban segregation; (F') assuring fair labor conditions and protection to migrants; and (G') persuading socioeconomic integration through social welfare protection. We use (+) to identify when countries consider one these fourteen dimensions in their strategic documents.

One of the first ideas derived from Table 1 is that although most states are not following a concrete framework to promote human security, they consider certain elements of it when approaching the migration-security nexus. We can perceive a light penetration of human security within national security strategies. This is relevant since human security may re-orient the values and principles guiding national security strategic cultures and hence be enforced by states in their security practices, avoiding being just a dream of the international community. The presence of human security in these documents is fundamental to commit states to it and to make them accountable for it in the national political arena and in the international system.

Only three countries totally ignore the migration-security nexus according to their documents, namely Argentina, Brazil and Canada. When considering human security, what prevails is ensuring development, support and cooperation with countries of origin and transit to stabilize them or the regions under deep political turmoil. We can also observe that countries are more focused on the dynamics with origin and transit countries than to deal with the human insecurity of migrants, asylum seekers and refugees when they are inside their countries, especially if they are a destination country. Nevertheless, Norway, Portugal, South Africa and Spain stress the importance and the necessity of strong integration policies. Nonetheless, it is harder to find references about enabling the access to housing, employment and other social programs, as well as opening and regulating safe routes for migrants. Only Spain establishes the development of legal safe routes as a priority action.

Hence, we conclude that the focus on the migration-human security nexus tends to work on a previous stage, before irregular migrants arrive in the country. Countries rely on international cooperation and global migration governance, especially through the promotion of stronger aid and human rights' programs in countries of origin to promote human security. All in all, these documents end up reassuring the restrictive character of migration control policies, as many countries are committing to intense border control, stronger asylum and citizenship vetting; while others, like the US, are now focusing on deterrence centers and repatriation programs to manage irregular migration. Another important conclusion is that although there is no direct evidence connecting recent mass migration flows and terrorism, many countries keep associating irregular migration with a growing terrorist threat, except for Mexico, Portugal and Spain. One common ground seems to exist around the fight against migrants smuggling and human trafficking since there is intense criminal transnational activity going on today and, at the same time, it imposes great vulnerability on the migrants themselves. The humanitarian consequences of avoiding human security are not fully detailed in these documents. So, we must trust that more and better international cooperation will be the key to manage irregular migration flows and to overcome the obstacles existing to access asylum. Considering dangerous border crossings and the risk of exploitation as inherent to irregular migration, if the first can be dealt with international cooperation and better border control, the last seems to remain under-securitized.

Conclusion

We live in a time of rising nationalism in the world while we have contributed to a crisis of multilateralism. If we agree that stronger global cooperation is the key to manage irregular migration on a global level, the truth is that the actual context is presenting more difficulties to impose human security both internationally and domestically since states have different priorities and views with regard to the migration-security nexus and are committing more to the traditional national security paradigm. The causes of migration are now well established and are mostly the same. Ongoing research on push-pull factors has now produced a solid body of work that allows us to conclude that the main drivers of migration rely on societal inequalities that have been expanding with asymmetric developments of capitalism. Also, irregular mass migration tends to come from crisis scenarios such as civil wars, political persecution and environmental degradation. Cross-border human mobility implies the merging of different cultural environments since migration flows are global and not only regional or limited to people sharing the same broad cultural values. So, multicultural societies are the way to go. Of course, this challenges established ideas of national identity, but one may say that this is a tough concept to measure in the information age and within transnational societies. One thing is for sure, national identity is more than citizenship and a passport. Or maybe, nowadays, that is all it is and nothing more.

If we accept globalization and the free circulation of goods, services and capital, we cannot allow double standards regulating the circulation of people. On the one hand, a shared system for migrants that are already part of the global productive apparatus and on the other hand a very divisive system full of cultural boundaries, contradictions and discriminations towards non-productive individuals. The choice that we must make collectively cannot be confined to economic benefits and we cannot route for an ugly globalization that leaves powerless individuals out of it. Globalization is also for asylum seekers and refugees. Either we embrace it fully or we are using our privileges to choose the "good part" and leave the "bad part" out for others to deal with. The ethics must always prevail in national and international policy making and if that happens, if societies stick to globalization, they will demand an alternative path to migration governance. To achieve better integration and to promote a globalization of humanitarianism, human security may just be the key to manage global migration and the migration-security nexus. Nevertheless, without a clear and strong commitment of states to human security (making them accountable for it), recent history proves that will be an enormous and arduous task.

References

Adamson, Fiona B. "Crossing borders: International migration and national security". In *International Security*. Vol. 31, No. 1, 2006, 165-199.

Adelman, Howard. "From refugees to forced migration: The UNHCR and human security". In *The International Migration Review*. Vol. 35, No. 1, 2001, 7-32.

Bach, Robert. "Global Mobility, Inequality and Security". In *Journal of Human Development*. Vol. 4, No. 2, 2003, 227-245.

Bigo, Didier. "Security and immigration: Toward a critique of the Governmentality of unease". In *Alternatives*, Vol. 27, 2002, 63-92.

Bourbeau, Philippe. *The Securitization of Migration: A study of movement and order*. Abingdon: Routledge, 2011.

Burgess, J. Peter. "Introduction: Security, migration and integration". In *A threat against Europe? Security, migration and integration*. Brussels: Institute for European Studies, 2011, 13-15.

Buzan, Barry & Hansen, Lene. *The evolution of international security studies*. Cambridge: Cambridge University Press, 2009.

Buzan, Barry, Waever, Ole, & De Wilde, Jaa *Security: A New Framework for Analysis*. Boulder, CO: Lynne Rienner, 1998.

Castles, Stephen. "Understanding global migration: A social transformation perspective". In *Journal of Ethnic and Migration Studies*. Vol. 36, No. 10, 2010, 1565-1586.

Castles, Stephen & Miller, Mark J. *The age of migration: International population movements in the modern world* (4th ed.). New York: Palgrave Macmillan, 2009.

Ceyhan, Anastassia & Tsoukala, Ayse. "The securitization of migration in western societies: Ambivalent discourses and policies". In *Alternatives*. Vol. 27, 2002, 21-39.

Clark, Michele Anne. "Trafficking in Persons: an issue of human security". In *Journal of Human Development*. Vol. 4, No. 2, 2003, 247-263.

Federal Republic of Nigeria. "National Security Strategy 2014 [Consulted at: December 5, 2018]. Available at: http://ctc.gov.ng/nigerian-national-security-strategy-2014/.

Ferreira, Susana. *Humans Security and Migration in Europe's Southern Borders*. Cham: Palgrave Macmillan, 2019.

Geddes, Andrew. *The politics of migration and immigration in Europe*. London: SAGE Publications, 2003.

Goldstone, Jack A. "Population and security: How demographic change can lead to violent conflict". In *Journal of International Affairs*. Vol. 56, No. 1, 2002, 3-22.

Goldstone, Jack A. "A Theory of Political Demography. Human and Institutional Reproduction". In *Political demography: How population changes are re-shaping international security and National Politics*. New York: Oxford University Press, 2012, 10-28.

Gobierno de España. "National Security Strategy 2017" [Consulted at: December 5, 2018]. Available at: http://www.dsn.gob.es/sites/dsn/files/2017_Spanish_National_Security_Strategy_0.pdf.

Governo de Portugal. "Conceito Estratégico de Defesa Nacional [Strategic Concept of National Defense]". [Consulted at: December 5, 2018]. Available at: http://www.portugal.gov.pt/pt/ministerios/mdn/quero-saber-mais/sobre-oministerio/20120223-conceito-estrategico/20130416-conceito-estrategico.aspx.

Guild, Elspeth. *Security and Migration in the 21st Century*. Cambridge and Malden: Polity Press, 2009.

Guild, Elspeth & Van Selm, Joanne (Eds.). *International migration and security. Opportunities and challenges*. Abingdon: Routledge, 2005.

HM Government. "National Security Strategy and Strategic Defence and Security Review 2015. A Secure and Prosperous United Kingdom" [Consulted at: December 5, 2018]. Available at: https://www.gov.uk/government/publications/national-security-strategy-and-strategic-defence-and-security-review-2015.

Huysmans, Jef. "The European Union and the Securitization of Migration". In *Journal of Common Market Studies*. Vol. 38, No. 5, 2000, 751-777.

Huysmans, Jef. *The Politics of Insecurity: Fear, migration and asylum in the EU*. Abingdon: Routledge, 2006.

Levoy, Michele, Verbruggen, Nele, & Wets, Johan (Eds.). *Undocumented Migrant Workers in Europe*. Brussels: PICUM, 2004.

Mabee, Bryan. *The globalization of security: State power, security provision and legitimacy*. New York: Palgrave Macmillan, 2009.

Melossi, Dario. *Crime, punishment and migration*. London: SAGE Publications, 2015.

Minister of National Defence. "Strong, Secure, Engaged. Canada's Defence Policy" [Consulted at: December 5, 2018]. Available at: http://dgpaapp.forces.gc.ca/en/canada-defence-policy/docs/canada-defence-policy-report.pdf.

Ministério da Defesa. "Política Nacional de Defesa e Estratégia Nacional de Defesa" (Versão Preliminar) [Consulted at: December 5, 2018]. Available at:

https://www.defesa.gov.br/noticias/29093-minutas-do-livro-branco-da-pnd-e-da-end-estao-disponiveis-para-leitura.

Norwegian Ministry of Foreign Affairs. "Setting the course for Norwegian foreign and security policy" [Consulted at: December 5, 2018]. Available at: https://www.regjeringen.no/en/aktuelt/future_course/id2550127/.

Owen, Taylor. "Human Security - Conflict, Critique and Consensus: Colloquium Remarks and a Proposal for a Threshold-Based Definition". In *Security Dialogue*. Vol. 35, No. 3, 2004, 373-387.

Presidencia de la República. "Programa para la Seguridad Nacional 2014. 2018. Una política multidimensional para México en el siglo XXI" [Consulted at: December 5, 2018]. Available at: http://cdn.presidencia.gob.mx/programa-para-la-seguridad-nacional.pdf.

República Argentina, Ministerio de Defensa. "Libro Blanco de la Defensa 2015" [Consulted at: December 5, 2018]. Available at: http://ceed.unasursg.org/Espanol/09-Downloads/Info-Pais/Arg/LB/Libro_blanco_2015.pdf.

République Française. "Revue stratégique de defense et de sécurité nationale 2017" [Consulted at: January 3, 2019]. Available at: https://www.defense.gouv.fr/espanol/dgris/politique-de-defense/revue-strategique/revue-strategique.

Rodrigues, Teresa Ferreira. "Population dynamics: Demography matters". In *Globalization and international security. An overview*. New York: Nova Science Publishers, 2015, 33-49.

Savage, Timothy M. "Europe and Islam: Crescent waxing, cultures clashing. In *The Washington Quarterly*. Vol. 27, No. 3, 2004, 25-50.

Sorensen, Georg. "State transformation and new security dilemmas". In *Globalization, security, and the nation-state. Paradigms in transition*. New York: State University of New York Press, 2005, 81-98.

South African Government. "South African Defence Review 2014" [Consulted at: December 5, 2018]. Available at: https://www.gov.za/sites/default/files/dfencereview_2014.pdf.

The White House. "National Security Strategy of the United States of America 2017" [Consulted at: December 5, 2018]. Available at: https://www.whitehouse.gov/articles/new-national-security-strategy-new-era/.

Tragaki, Alexandra. "Demography and migration as human security factors: The case of South Eastern Europe". In *Migration Letters*. Vol. 4, No. 2, 2007, 103-118.

Truong, Thanh-Dam. "The Governmentality of Transnational Migration and Security: The Making of a New Subaltern". In *Transnational Migration and Human Security. The Migration-Development-Security Nexus*. Berlin: Springer, 2011, 23-37.

UND *Human Development Report 1994*. New York: UNDP, 1994.

Vietti, Francesca & Scribner, Todd. "Human insecurity: Understanding international migration from a human security perspective". In *Journal on Migration and Human Security*. Vol. 1, No. 1, 2013, 17-31.

Waever, Ole. "Securitization and Desecuritization". In *On security*. New York: Columbia University Press, 1995, 46-86.

Weiner, Myron. "Security, stability, and international migration". In *International Security*. Vol. 17, No. 3, 1992, 91-126.

Weiner, Myron & Russell, Sharon Stanton (Eds.). *Demography and National Security*. New York: Berghahn Books, 2001.

Chapter 6

Connecting Shores:
Migration and Human Security in the Atlantic Basin

Susana Ferreira

Human mobility has become a defining feature of this new millennium. It has become increasingly more complex, with varying geographies and motivations. More people than ever are on the move, in a scenario of large displacements stemming from wars and transnational conflicts, social and political instability and environmental and climatic changes, often within a context of deprivation of human security.

Most international migration takes place within legal channels. Irregular migration, however, is often associated with insecurities and public concerns about this phenomenon. During this last decade we have seen a substantial increase in forced displacement, within and across national borders, in different regions of the globe. Against this backdrop a whole set of challenges emerge, particularly regarding the safeguarding of the individual's human rights and dignity.

Geography is a fundamental axiom of migration as it shapes the different patterns of human mobility and involves the movement between numerous origins and destinations. Migration channels create a set of interconnections and spatial linkages that are designed by people on the move. Within this set we will adopt a geographic perspective to approach the phenomenon of migration in the Atlantic Basin, which includes a complex web of migration patterns and trends across and between three different continents—Europe, Africa and America (here divided as Latin America and Caribbean—LAC—and North America).

The Atlantic Ocean has a central role in the geography of international migration. It is an area of exchanges, linking distant regions and connecting its shores through trade and cultural relations, going all the way back to the Portuguese and Spanish discoveries and the Atlantic slave trade.

The period between the mid-19th century and the early 20th was one of intense emigration across the Atlantic by Europeans, known as the 'Age of

Mass Migration'.[1] Ever since, the geography of migration in this basin has changed dramatically and nowadays the majority of flows take place at the South-South and South-North level, but to a lesser extent at a West-East or East-West level.[2]

For many of the individuals on the move nowadays, migration is their own approach to safeguard their human security, it is a survival strategy. Nevertheless, it might come along with other threats to their personal security. What are the main threats to human security connected to migration in the Atlantic basin? Through the analysis of migration across the Atlantic region, specifically of three critical hotspots identified, this chapter will assess the different regional realities and the main challenges to human security emerging, offering an innovative comparative analysis of migratory flows in this large region, through the lenses of human security.

The hotspot analysis facilitates the identification and prioritization of critical points with significant sustainability challenges, which enables the focus on priority issues such as a humanitarian crisis or conflicts.[3] Therefore, three critical unrest points in terms of human mobility have been identified in the Atlantic Basin and a comparative analysis has been adopted, through the evaluation of different phenomena by similar features, to assess the main human security challenges arising in such contexts. Furthermore, this approach also aims to facilitate the sharing of the learning between different experiences as a means of prioritizing a humanitarian dimension in migration policies and strategies.

The research is based on the analysis of primary sources—databases and reports by the International Organization for Migration (IOM), the United Nations Population Department, Amnesty International, International Federation of Red Cross and Red Crescent Societies and Reliefweb—as well as on a review of the state of the art of academic works. However, while carrying out the research some methodological obstacles showed up, particularly regarding the compilation of data about the Venezuela crisis, given the difficulties for international agencies to gather data on the ground and also given the fact that this is a too recent event.

---

1. Keeling, D. "Transatlantic shipping cartels and migration between Europe and America, 1880-1914". In *Essays in Economic & Business History*, 17, 195.
2. United Nations, *International Migration Report 2017*. New York, 2017, 5. Retrieved from https://www.un.org/en/development/desa/population/migration/publications/migrationreport/docs/MigrationReport2017.pdf.
3. United Nations Environment Program, *Hotspot Analysis. An overarching methodological framework and guidance for product and sector level application*. United Nations Environment Program, 2017.

The chapter is structured in three sections. The first one will look at the nexus between migration and human security, which provides a framework for the research; the second will focus on three critical migratory hotspots—Central America, Venezuela and the Mediterranean—through an analysis of the main trends in these migratory corridors; and the third one will make an assessment of the main challenges to human security in a context of irregular migration based on the study made in the previous section.

The Nexus Between Migration and Human Security

The individual gained momentum in the late 20th century, becoming a subject of security, as human life turned into a referent object.[4] In a time of international migration crisis, with critical hotspots for migration and forced displacement throughout the world, the preservation of individuals' life and dignity and the safeguarding of their human rights is often at risk.

Since international migration questions state capacities to manage migratory flows, the strategies adopted by states are increasingly more focused on contention and deterrence. In a VUCA[5] (volatility, uncertainty, complexity and ambiguity) world, with increasingly complex transnational threats that present unique challenges to the international system, the feeling of insecurity arises, bringing population movements into the spotlight. Such threats are more severe to specific vulnerable populations such as forced migrants, irregular migrants, women and children.[6]

Human security can be roughly understood as individuals' 'freedom from want' and 'freedom from fear', which include the preservation of people's livelihoods (including dimensions such as economic, food, environmental or personal).[7] The human security framework emphasizes the protection of individuals from violence and respect for fundamental rights.

---

4. Buzan, Barry; Waever, Ole & De Wilde, Jaap, *Security: a new framework for analysis*. Boulder: Lynne Rienner Publishers, 1998.
5. The acronym VUCA originated in the US military (Bennett & Lemoine, 2014, 1).
6. Vietti, Francesca & Scribner, Todd, "Human Insecurity: Understanding International Migration from a Human Security Perspective". In *Journal on Migration and Human Security*, 1, 1, 2013, 26.
7. Gómez, Oscar A. & Des Gasper, "Human Security. A Thematic Guidance Note for Regional and National Human Development Report Teams". United Nations Development Programme (UNDP), Human Development Report Office, 2013, 1-2 [Consulted at: 25 March 2019]. Available at: http://hdr.undp.org/sites/default/files/human_security_guidance_note_r-nhdrs.pdf.

Thus, human security focuses on the survival, livelihood and dignity of individuals, acknowledging the interconnections between peace, development and human rights.[8]

The human security paradigm goes beyond a traditionally state-centric approach to security and encompasses the security of individuals and communities. Nonetheless, a comprehensive approach to the contemporary transnational threats entails the interconnection between both frameworks—state and human security. Thus, states should ensure the safeguard of the rights of all individuals in their territory, regardless of their status, protecting them from violations to their personal dignity and safety.[9]

Within a broad conceptualization, threats to human security range from deprivation of human rights, terrorism, drugs, pollution, among others.[10] Its consequences have repercussions not only on the individual but beyond borders, within a logic of 'freedom from want'. Yet, a narrow approach focuses on violent threats to the individual, within the paradigm of 'freedom from fear'.[11] As stressed by Bilgic, "(...) life under fear is not a life. It is reductive and restrictive, and makes an individual susceptible to hate, distrust, paranoia, and suspicion", which requires a comprehensive approach to human security.[12]

Des Gasper and Sinatti[13] offer a comprehensive conceptualization of the intersection between migration studies and the human security approach, which includes the linkages between deprivation and vulnerability; the interaction between several separate domains; a psychological analysis of individuals' social security considerations and the role of human actors and evolution of migrant communities. In the end, it highlights the added value a human security framework brings to the exploration of the different dimensions of migration.

Irregular migration is frequently regarded as an element of insecurity, as migrants' irregular arrival to a certain territory might pose a direct or urgent

8. UNIDO, *UNIDO's Contribution to Human Security*. Vienna: United Nations Industrial Development Organization, 2015, 5.
9. Ferreira, Susana, *Human Security and Migration in Europe's Southern Borders*. Cham: Palgrave Macmillan, 2019, 33. DOI: 10.1007/978-3-319-77947-8
10. Ibid, 34.
11. Xavier, Ana Isabel, *A União Europeia, Actor de Segurança Humana. O Futuro Da Segurança*. Lisboa: Universidade Lusófona de Humanidades e Tecnologia, 2013, 59.
12. Bilgic, Ali, *A Human Security Perspective on Migration: A Compass in the Perfect Storm*. International Institute of Social Studies, 2018, 1.
13. Des Gasper & Sinatti, Giulia, "Investigating Migration within a Human Security Framework". In *Revista de Migración y Desarrollo*, 2016.

challenge to state's internal security. A securitarian approach to migration can be framed within four different axes: socio-economic, relating migration with unemployment, increase in informal economies and the crisis of the welfare state; securitarian, relating with the loss of the control narrative that links questions of sovereignty, borders and internal and external security; identitarian, where migrants are considered a threat to host societies for their national identity; and, political, resorting to anti-immigration and racist discourses to acquire political benefits.[14] Paradoxically, irregular migration comprises a myriad of threats to migrants' human security given their vulnerable situation, as will be assessed throughout this chapter.[15]

Irregular flows are often correlated with trafficking and smuggling of people. Migrants often engage in 'survival crimes', jeopardizing their own human security, by resorting to smuggling in an attempt to reach a safe harbor and survive. Human smuggling networks are service providers, who facilitate migrants' crossing throughout a route. Nevertheless, abuses might take place sometimes, such as deprivation from water or food, bad transportation or accommodation conditions, harassment or rape, or in extreme cases leading to coercion and enslaving migrants.[16] In this sense, human smuggling and human trafficking are often interconnected, within a continuum that goes from deception to complete coercion.[17] Trafficking in human beings involves coercion and different forms of exploitation, violating human dignity and fundamental rights.[18]

Both traffickers and smugglers are known to use (excessive violence) against their victims to exert power and control. All this raises human rights concerns. Therefore, human rights should be at the core of the human security concept, as this body of rights aims "(...) to make human beings secure in freedom, in dignity, with equality, through the protection of their basic human rights".[19] Nevertheless, those are two distinct concepts. On the one

14. Ceyhan, A & Tsoukala, A., "The securitization of migration in western societies: Ambivalent discourses and policies". In *Alternatives*, 27, 2002, p.24. DOI: 10.1177/03043754020270S103.
15. Ferreira, Susana, *Human Security and Migration in Europe's Southern Borders*. Cham: Palgrave Macmillan, 2019, 33. DOI: 10.1007/978-3-319-77947-8.
16. Ibid, 45.
17. Aronowitz, Alexis A., "Smuggling and trafficking in human beings: The phenomenon, the markets that drive it and the organizations that promote it". In *European Journal on Criminal Policy and Research*, 9, pp. 163–195, 2001, 166.
18. Vietti, Francesca & Scribner, Todd, "Human Insecurity: Understanding International Migration from a Human Security Perspective". In *Journal on Migration and Human Security*, 1, 1, 2013, 27.
19. Ramcharan, Bertrand, *Human rights and human security*, M. Nijhoff Publishers, 2002, 40.

hand, human rights consists in a defined legal framework comprised by declarations and international treaties; on the other hand, human security has a broader scope, including a wide set of threats.[20]

All in all, the paradigm of human security offers an invitation to rethink the security of individuals, addressing cross-cutting challenges to survival from a bottom-up approach. The adoption of this concept advances the multidimensional causes and consequences of such complex flows, calling for integrated multilevel actions (local, national and regional).

Migration hotspots across the Atlantic Basin

Migration is a global phenomenon that affects every single region on the globe. It has undergone significant changes in recent years. Population movements in the Atlantic Basin are motivated by different forces, from economic reasons and prosperity to conflicts, inequalities and insecurity that have highly contributed to the important shifts in migration patterns over the last three decades.

On both sides of the Atlantic the size and scope of forced migration and irregular flows are extraordinary, and migration has emerged as a central but contentious issue for regional stability. By the end of this second decade of the 21st century, three migration crisis hotspots can be identified in both sides of the Atlantic: the Central American caravans; the Venezuela humanitarian crisis; and the so-called European migration crisis.

Central American migration has received increased public attention with Trump's administration enforcing a 'zero-tolerance' policy at its southern border, raising walls, separating families and deterring irregular migration. Further south, Venezuela's political and social instability is turning into a humanitarian crisis with growing displacements to neighboring countries, which might affect regional (in)stability. Across the Atlantic, the number of irregular migrants crossing the Mediterranean has decreased drastically since reaching its peak in 2015, with new significant changes in the routes moving westward to Morocco.

These are mostly mixed migration flows, encompassing forced and voluntary movements of migrants, refugees and asylum seekers, as well as

---

20. Figueira, Rickson Rios, "Tensões e distensões entre a segurança do estado-nação e os direitos humanos: segurança humana e migrações internacionais sob o olhar da teoria dos direitos fundamentais de Robert Alexy". In *Revista de Direitos Humanos Em Perspectiva*, 1, 2, 2015, 100. DOI: 10.21902.

victims of human trafficking and internally displaced persons. While the management of these flows is one of the greatest challenges states currently face, it also places serious concerns regarding the protection of migrants' human rights and the safeguarding of their human security. As these migration crisis mount, questions regarding migrants' human security arise.

Central America, Mexico and the Caribbean

The predominant trend in Central America is northward migration. Mexico is no longer only the main country of origin but plays a prominent role as transit country for migrants travelling to the US (United States).[21] New and diversified flows throughout the region have emerged in the last decades, particularly composed by irregular migrants. Albeit not being a recent phenomenon, migration flows from the 'Northern Triangle'—the region of Guatemala, Honduras and El Salvador—to the US have acquired a new humanitarian dimension, with thousands of people fleeing violence. The pervasive violence in those countries has led to a dramatic humanitarian crisis.[22]

Given the complexity and magnitude of human mobility in this region and its dynamic and transnational character, the capacity of protection by transit and destination countries is still very limited. Migrants from the Northern Triangle countries display special 'risk profiles', such as individuals persecuted by gangs (*maras*) or victims and witnesses of gang crimes. However, only a small portion of those individuals in need of protection are recognized as refugees or are subject to some sort of additional protection.[23]

These flows gained greater visibility with the 'Migrant Caravan' in 2018. In October 2018, a group of migrants left Honduras and others have joined them throughout the route, estimated in 7,000 when they reached Mexico, including minors. These caravans have been organized during the last decade although no other has had this dimension and visibility, motivated by migrants own conviction and despair.[24]

---

21. IOM, *World Migration Report 2018*. Geneva: International Organization for Migration, 2017, 76.
22. Amnistía Internacional, ¿Hogar dulce hogar? El papel de Honduras, Guatemala y El Salvador en la creciente crisis de refugiados. London: Amnistía Internacional, 2016, 6.
23. Ibid, 5.
24. Ramírez Gallegos, Jacques, "De la era de la migración al siglo de la seguridad: el surgimiento de 'políticas de control con rostro (in)humano". In *Revista Latinoamericana de Estudios de Seguridad*, 23, 2018, 10–28. DOI: 10.17141/urvio.23.2018.3745.

The caravans of migrants are organized group mobilizations that aim to ensure protection throughout the journey to make it safer. These mobilizations involve the participation of migrants themselves and in some cases their relatives and aim to provide protection to make the trip a little more safely. This way, when walking in a moderately organized group, migrants do not need to resort to the services of human smugglers (known as *coyotes* in Mexico) and are not subject to the violence of smuggling industry. It is important to stress that people resort to this migration strategy because of insecurity in transit countries, particularly in Mexico.[25]

In El Salvador and Honduras, violence is the key factor behind these flows. According to Amnesty International, the expanding violence in territories controlled by gangs affects the right of people to life, their physical integrity, access to education and even their freedom to movement.[26] In Guatemala, the increasing inequalities are the main driver of human mobility.

Women and children are the most vulnerable groups to the different forms of violence and political instability in the Northern Triangle. Gender-based crimes often go unpunished and the region registers one of the highest femicide rates in the world, which creates a constant feeling of insecurity among women.[27]

One of the critical dimensions of this phenomenon are the unaccompanied minors (boys and girls) travelling and crossing the border alone. Children escaping poverty and violence at home, separated from their families, who risk their lives in this dangerous route to get to the US. In 2014, the US Border Patrol detained nearly 70,000 unaccompanied children and in 2016 almost 60,000, the majority of them coming from the Northern Triangle (80%) and the others from Mexico (20%).[28]

A study from the Congressional Research Service (Kandel et al., 2014) has pointed out that 75 -80% of unaccompanied minors are victims of human trafficking, as they resort to smugglers throughout the journey who

25. Martínez Hernandéz-Mejía, Iliana, "Reflexiones sobre la caravana migrante". In *Análisis Plural*, 1st semester, 2018, 232–248.
26. Amnistía Internacional, ¿Hogar dulce hogar? El papel de Honduras, Guatemala y El Salvador en la creciente crisis de refugiados. London: Amnistía Internacional, 2016, 5.
27. Ibid.
28. Ataiants, Janna, Cohen, Chari, Riley, Amy Henderson, Lieberman, Jamile Tellez, Reidy, Mary Clare, & Chilton, Mariana, "Unaccompanied Children at the United States Border, a Human Rights Crisis that can be Addressed with Policy Change". In *Journal Immigrant Minor Health*, 20, 4, 2018. DOI: 10.1007/s10903-017-0577-5, 1000–1010.

later coerce them into forced labor or prostitution. This reveals the vulnerability of these children and their exposure to numerous forms of trauma.

The progressively restrictive immigration policies implemented by the Trump administration have placed the world's attention on the migration system comprised by Central America-Mexico-United States and Canada. Nevertheless, Trump's threats to finish the wall along the border between Mexico and the US and denying refugee status to those in need of protection seem to have had the contrary effect in international public opinion, strengthening solidarity among civil society.[29]

The deterrent policies adopted by the White House have three main axes: 1) massive illegal expulsions of asylum seekers at the US-Mexico border; 2) thousands of illegal separation of families; and, 3) increasingly arbitrary and indefinite detention of asylum-seekers. These practices have been condemned by Amnesty International for the extreme suffering they inflict on families and the inhuman and degrading treatment asylum seekers receive.[30]

Mexico plays a more and more crucial role in the management of these migratory flows, both as country of transit and because migrants are often stranded in Mexico with no possibilities to go back to their countries of origin or continue forward. The crossing through Mexico is increasingly more dangerous, in a context of instability and violence leaving migrants in a situation of greater vulnerability. In this sense, Martínez Hernandéz-Mejía highlights that "[t]he Mexican government has not clearly implemented a policy that has a vision of human security (…). On the contrary, it privileges its national security (…) since it does not seek to protect the human rights of people in transit but, instead, arrests and expels them from Mexican territory".[31]

Given all the difficulties in the routes along this migratory corridor, the smuggling business model has become a highly profitable industry, which has learned how to play with the growing instability of the region. The 'coyotes' have acquired relevance with the strengthening of surveillance in the US southern border, adapting their strategies to the different cir-

29. Martínez Hernandéz-Mejía, Iliana, "Reflexiones sobre la caravana migrante". In *Análisis Plural*, 1st semester, 2018, 235.
30. Amnistía Internacional, *Estados Unidos: "Tú no tienes ningún derecho aquí"*. London: Amnistía Internacional, 2018a.
31. Martínez Hernandéz-Mejía, Iliana, "Reflexiones sobre la caravana migrante". In *Análisis Plural*, 1st semester, 2018, 237.

cumstances, which might involve "(...) predatory practices ranging from demands for bribes to mass kidnapping and extortion".[32]

Venezuela and South America

Political and social instability in Venezuela has led to a serious deterioration of the population's living conditions, which prompted a humanitarian emergency with over three million refugees by the end of 2018.[33] Representing already one of the largest forced displacements in the Southern Hemisphere, this crisis affects its neighboring countries as well as regional stability in South America.

The deep gap created by hyperinflation, shortage of food, water and medicine, along with growing violence among the population are driving millions of Venezuelans out of the country. During 2018, an estimated average of 5,000 people per day left the country in search of protection or a better life. The countries in the region have demonstrated an incredible solidarity granting protection to those migrants. Colombia alone hosts the largest number of refugees and migrants, with over 1.1 million. Overall, Latin America and the Caribbean countries host an estimated 2.7 million Venezuelans, while the rest are spread across other regions (mostly Europe).[34]

Violence has taken over the country, with rising criminality rates. Sharpening poverty has led to new forms of crime, with new actors: young men living in poverty, stealing basic goods, as food has become scarce. With over 81.4 violent deaths per hundred thousand inhabitants, Venezuela is currently the most violent country in Latin America.[35] These dramatic levels of violence question the security of the population in Venezuela, endangering their life and integrity. Under the presidency of Maduro, the state was not able to guarantee the right to life in a context of extreme violence.[36] Nowadays, in a scenario of uncertainty and discussed leadership,

32. IOM, *World Migration Report 2018*. Geneva: International Organization for Migration, 2017, 76.
33. UNHCR, "Number of refugees and migrants from Venezuela reaches 3 million". In UNHCR Press Releases, 8 November, 2018 [Consulted at: 20 February 2019]. Available at: https://www.unhcr.org/news/press/2018/11/5be4192b4/number-refugees-migrants-venezuela-reaches-3-million.html.
34. IOM and UNHCR, "Venezuelan Outflow Continues Unabated, Stands Now at 3.4 Million". *Reliefweb Updates*, Geneva, 22 February, 2019.
35. Observatorio Venezolano de Violencia, *Informe Anual de Violencia 2018*. Observatorio Venezolano de Violencia, 2018 [Consulted at: 25 February 2019]. Available at: https://observatoriodeviolencia.org.ve/ovv-lacso-informe-anual-de-violencia-2018/
36. Amnistía Internacional, *Esto no es vida. Seguridad ciudadana y derecho a la vida en Venezuela*. London: Amnistía Internacional, 2018b, 5.

with so many international pressures and interests, the situation remains volatile.

Given the recent events and the unpredictability of the evolution of the political situation, it is difficult to anticipate the development of these flows. Yet, it can be expected that this flow of people will persist, although migration routes might shift if restrictive migration policies are implemented in the region.[37]

European migration crisis

The Mediterranean is the world's deadliest migration corridor. Irregular migration is a present and future reality, but with shifting dynamics and geographies. Migratory pressure in this region has intensified during the last half of this decade, reaching its peak in 2015 with over 1.8 million illegal detections in the EU's southern and eastern borders.[38] Ever since, there have been geographic changes in the routes while the intensity of the flows decreased significantly.

Three main migratory routes cross the Mediterranean: the Western Mediterranean (crossing from Morocco to Spain), the Central Mediterranean (from Libya to Italy and Malta) and the Eastern Mediterranean (from Turkey to Greece). Variations across these routes depend on various external factors that range from conditions in the countries of origin and transit to the mechanisms and strategies implemented by the EU to manage these flows. Therefore, during the last four years, there have been shifts in the routes, although the Central Mediterranean has been the prevailing one. Nonetheless, in 2018 there was a dramatic drop in this route, while the western Mediterranean registered a significant increase and became the main route into Europe.[39]

As the number of departures from Morocco records an intense increase, Spain registers greater migratory pressure. The majority of the migrants travelling across this route come from sub-Saharan countries, although the number of Moroccan nationals is on the rise.[40]

The migratory pressure in Africa, with very young age structures and large income inequalities continues to boost economic migration and

---

37. IFRC, *Emergency Appeal Operarion Update. Americas: Population Movement*. International Federation of Red Cross and Red Crescent Societies, 2019.

38. FRONTEX, *Risk Analysis for 2019*. Warsaw: Frontex, 2019, 41. DOI: 10.2819/224322.

39. Ibid, 6.

40. Ibid.

South-North mobility, particularly from sub-Saharan countries. Furthermore, the existence of few legal immigration channels to the EU combined with these large income inequalities between origin and destination countries to diversify the causes of irregular flows beyond that of security.[41]

Conflict and violence within and in surrounding subregions have contributed to displacement in Central and North Africa. Furthermore, conflicts in the MENA (Middle East and North Africa) region, particularly in Syria where the civil war continues to destabilize the region and force outward migration, have a huge impact in human mobility across the African continent. Moreover, people smugglers have taken advantage of this situation of insecurity to facilitate migrant journeys, particularly in the crossing of the Mediterranean Sea.

As an important hub of transit movements, the African continent, in particular the North African subregion, encounters several protection challenges related with irregular migration to Europe.[42] The routes to Europe across Africa are long, harsh and dangerous. Migrants might come from countries such as Somalia or Nigeria and have to overcome several geographical obstacles, being the riskier parts of the journey the crossing of the Sahara desert and the crossing by boat of the Mediterranean Sea.[43] Therefore, migrants need to resort to 'intermediaries' who facilitate and arrange their journeys.

Along these routes, migrants are vulnerable to serious human rights violations, which might include "(…) deaths at sea, in the desert and in other transit locations; missing migrants, exploitation, physical and emotional abuse, trafficking, smuggling, sexual and gender-based violence, arbitrary detention, forced labor, ransom demands and extortion; and other human rights violations".[44]

Following repeated tragedies in the Mediterranean in the first semester of 2015, the European Commission adopted the European Agenda on Mi-

41. Ferreira, Susana, "Migratory Crisis in the Mediterranean: Managing Irregular Flows". In *Stability: International Journal of Security & Development*, 5, 1, 2016. DOI: 10.5334/sta.441, 2.
42. IOM, *World Migration Report 2018*. Geneva: International Organization for Migration, 2017, 72.
43. Lutterbeck, Drew, "A View from the Ground: Human Security Threats to Irregular Migrants across the Mediterranean". In O. Grech & M. Wohlfeld (Eds.), *Migration in the Mediterranean: human rights, security and development perspectives*. Msida: Mediterranean Academy of Diplomatic Studies, 2014, 125.
44. IOM, *World Migration Report 2018*. Geneva: International Organization for Migration, 2017, 72.

gration in May and adopted a set of urgent actions to face the crisis. One of the goals was also to give a comprehensive framework to those issues by presenting a new set of medium-term measures.[45] However, the EU's answer so far, has mostly been one of a deterrence-based approach, predominantly grounded on the dimensions of border management.[46]

Understanding threats to human security in the context of irregular migration

Each migrant lives a different story, one of adventures and risks, crossing deserts and seas or countries in conflict dominated by chaos, but not all of them survive to tell it. The reality of irregular migration is a harsh one, as migrants encounter extreme adversities due to the increasingly dangerous routes taken, risking their own lives.

Figure 1 highlights the three migratory hotspots in the Atlantic Basin previously analyzed and the main challenges to human security in the countries of origin and transit. The most problematic areas are the Gulf of Guinea and Central America with mounting instability and increasing levels of violence. The situation in Venezuela, albeit dramatic, is still too recent and not much reliable data is available.

Through the analysis of these three migratory crisis in the Atlantic Basin we have identified three main sources of threats to human security throughout migrants' journeys across Africa to Europe, and across the American continent: the extreme travel conditions, the insecurity in transit countries, and the mistreatment at the hands of smugglers.[47]

Regarding travel conditions, it is important to start by stressing that migratory routes are often long ones, therefore the journeys might take several months or even years, as the vicissitudes of the journey might make them even longer than originally planned. The most difficult part of the routes are the journeys across a desert or a sea. The trip across the Sahara desert

45. Ferreira, Susana, "Migratory Crisis in the Mediterranean: Managing Irregular Flows". In *Stability: International Journal of Security & Development*, 5, 1, 2016. DOI: 10.5334/sta.441, 4.

46. Ferreira, Susana, *Human Security and Migration in Europe's Southern Borders*. Cham: Palgrave Macmillan, 2019, 193. DOI: 10.1007/978-3-319-77947-8.

47. Lutterbeck, Drew, "A View from the Ground: Human Security Threats to Irregular Migrants across the Mediterranean". In O. Grech & M. Wohlfeld (Eds.), *Migration in the Mediterranean: human rights, security and development perspectives*. Msida: Mediterranean Academy of Diplomatic Studies, 2014, 124.

Figure 1. Human Security Threats in the Three Atlantic Hotspots

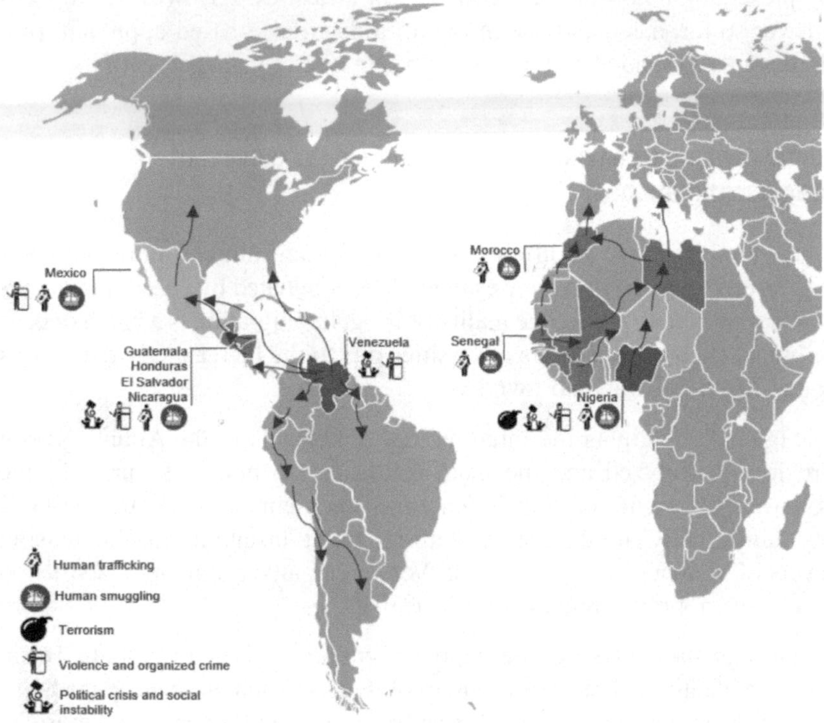

Source: Author's own ellaboration

or in Arizona (US) is a dangerous one due to the severe climatic conditions but also because of the lack of provisions such as water or food.[48] Here migrants are abandoned to their fate by smugglers and many perish along the way.

The crossing of a sea (the Mediterranean, the Caribbean or even the Atlantic Ocean) is a life-threatening journey. The risks of travelling across the sea include the danger of drowning and the exposure to severe weather conditions during sailing. Furthermore, the unseaworthy conditions of vessels, with migrants travelling in overcrowded boats, with limited supplies and insufficient lifejackets triggers situations of high distress. All in all, these crossings have a set of risks that directly affect migration as

---

48. Ibid, 127.

migrants are exposed to the dangers of the sea and deserts and completely unprotected.[49]

Despite these hazards, migrants continue to risk their lives in such dangerous journeys often pushed by structural factors in the countries of origin.[50] Those who perish in the desert are often left unaccounted and easily forgotten, while deaths in the Mediterranean Sea have gained growing visibility. Nevertheless, as smugglers adapt to strategies implemented by states, the crossings become increasingly more dangerous and the means of transportation increasingly more precarious, putting the right to life at risk.

As highlighted in the previous section, the majority of these routes cross along countries with 'structural violence'. Irregular migrants travelling along those routes are exposed to different hazards in a context of social vulnerability, given their migratory status. The violence perpetrated against migrants includes kidnapping or sexual violence, added to stigmatization and discrimination.[51] Organized criminal groups and drug cartels target migrants travelling across these countries, abducting them and imprisoning them. In November 2018, news on the migrant caravan reported that at least 100 members of the group had gone missing, "(…) suspected of having fallen prey to criminal gangs, who abduct migrants in order to extort their family members".[52] Furthermore, women and girls are particularly exposed to physical, sexual and psychological abuses.

The market for providers of irregular migration services has established itself in the different regions, adapting to the specificities of each route. Human smugglers exploit migrants' lack of legal opportunities and their willingness to take risks. These profit-seeking criminals treat migrants as mere commodities, transporting them in suffocating containers or vans, in unseaworthy vessels, leaving them to drown at sea or perish in the desert.[53] Furthermore, many people end up being stripped of their money and aban-

49. Jumbert, Maria Gabrielsen, "Control or rescue at sea? Aims and limits of border surveillance technologies in the Mediterranean Sea". In *Disasters*, 2018, 4. DOI: 10.1111/disa.12286.
50. Servan-Mori, E., Leyva-Flores, R., Infante Xibille, C., Torres-Pereda, P., & Garcia-Cerde, R. (2014). "Migrants suffering violence while in transit through Mexico: Factors associated with the decision to continue or turn back". In *Journal of Immigrant Minority Health*, (16), 53–59.
51. Ibid, 54.
52. Bonello, Deborah, "100 people "kidnapped" from migrant caravan by drug cartels in Mexico". In *The Telegraph*, Mexico City, 6 November, 2018.
53. UNODC, *Smuggling of migrants: the harsh search for a better life*. United Nations Office on Drugs and Crime, 2019. [Consulted at: 28 February 2019]. Available at: https://www.unodc.org/toc/en/crimes/migrant-smuggling.html

doned in the desert or along the way never reaching their final destination. Corruption has become a key element in the provision of facilitating services to irregular migration. Border officials, police, military and diplomatic agents may also be involved in providing documentation of facilitating the crossing.[54]

As destination countries adopt increasingly more restrictive immigration policies and enhance controls at the border, migrants and refugees seek riskier routes endangering their own lives. On the one hand, the shielding of the frontier, in an attempt to create 'hermetic borders', produces an inventive and adaptable underground business arranged by smugglers, often connected with criminal networks, which makes the journeys more dangerous for migrants.[55] On the other hand, the strengthening of border controls might also lead to the creation of borderlands as places of detention and immobility, with growing abuses by the authorities who control these border crossings.

Talking about irregular migration includes addressing the security and safety of migrants throughout the entire migratory process, as they are exposed to various threats to their human security. But, in the end, it is important to consider that human mobility is also a form of human security, it is a survival strategy for those who decide to move to another country.

Conclusion

Today's insecure world faces intense human mobility flows around the globe, which highlight the interconnection between migration (in particular, irregular migration) and human security. The three crises addressed in the Atlantic Basin are complex and varied, involving numerous forms of human insecurity and present great challenges to policy-making in migration management. In this sense, the human security approach to irregular migration provides a strong framework to support comprehensive responses and actions to the challenges arising from these flows. It offers a people-centered focus and a more holistic perspective, based on the importance of people's dignity.

---

54. OHCHR, *Situation of migrants in transit*. Geneva: Office of the High Commissioner for Human Rights, n.d., 9.
55. Danish Institute For International Studies, *Europe and the refugee situation. Human security implications*. Copenhagen: Danish Institute for International Studies, 2017, p. 6.

Despite the different geographies of the flows we have identified three main sources of threats to human security, which are common to all routes: the extreme travel conditions, the insecurity in transit countries, and the mistreatment at the hands of smugglers. This calls for integrated actions from the international community on these topics. Furthermore, each region has its own specificities and challenges and those should be addressed with all stakeholders involved in the migratory process.

Connecting shores involves the creation of synergies between countries of origin, transit and destination, to promote responses grounded on the particularities of each region. This requires the participation of all different actors, from governments, to the private sector and local communities, guaranteeing that no one is left behind.

References

Amnistía Internacional, ¿Hogar dulce hogar? El papel de Honduras, Guatemala y El Salvador en la creciente crisis de refugiados. London: Amnistía Internacional, 2016.

Amnistía Internacional, Estados Unidos: "Tú no tienes ningún derecho aquí". London: Amnistía Internacional, 2018a.

Amnistía Internacional, Esto no es vida. Seguridad ciudadana y derecho a la vida en Venezuela. London: Amnistía Internacional, 2018b.

Aronowitz, Alexis A., "Smuggling and trafficking in human beings: The phenomenon, the markets that drive it and the organizations that promote it". In *European Journal on Criminal Policy and Research*, 9, 163–195, 2001.

Ataiants, Janna, Cohen, Chari, Riley, Amy Henderson, Lieberman, Jamile Tellez, Reidy, Mary Clare, & Chilton, Mariana, "Unaccompanied Children at the United States Border, a Human Rights Crisis that can be Addressed with Policy Change". In *Journal Immigrant Minor Health*, 20, 4, 2018. DOI: 10.1007/s10903-017-0577-5, 1000–1010.

Bennett, Nathan, & Lemoine, G. James, "What a difference a word makes: Understanding threats to performance in a VUCA world". In *Organizational Performance*, 1–7, 2014. DOI: 10.1016/j.bushor.2014.01.001.

Bilgic, Ali, *A Human Security Perspective on Migration: A Compass in the Perfect Storm*. International Institute of Social Studies, 2018

Bonello, Deborah, "100 people "kidnapped" from migrant caravan by drug cartels in Mexico". In *The Telegraph*, Mexico City, 6 November, 2018.

Buzan, Barry; Waever, Ole & De Wilde, Jaap, *Security: a new framework for analysis*. Boulder: Lynne Rienner Publishers, 1998.

Ceyhan, A & Tsoukala, A., "The securitization of migration in western societies: Ambivalent discourses and policies". In *Alternatives*, 27, 21–39, 2002. DOI: 10.1177/03043754020270S103.

Danish Institute For International Studies, *Europe and the refugee situation. Human security implications*. Copenhagen: Danish Institute for International Studies, 2017.

Des Gasper & Sinatti, Giulia, "Investigating Migration within a Human Security Framework". In *Revista de Migración y Desarrollo*, 2016.

Ferreira, Susana, "Migratory Crisis in the Mediterranean: Managing Irregular Flows". In *Stability: International Journal of Security & Development*, 5, 1, 2016. DOI: 10.5334/sta.441, 1–6.

Ferreira, Susana, *Human Security and Migration in Europe's Southern Borders*. Cham: Palgrave Macmillan, 2019. DOI: 10.1007/978-3-319-77947-8.

Figueira, Rickson Rios, "Tensões e distensões entre a segurança do estado-nação e os direitos humanos: segurança humana e migrações internacionais sob o olhar da teoria dos direitos fundamentais de Robert Alexy". In *Revista de Direitos Humanos Em Perspectiva*, 1, 2, 90–109, 2015. DOI: 10.21902.

FRONTEX, *Risk Analysis for 2019*. Warsaw: Frontex, 2019. DOI: 10.2819/224322.

Gómez, Oscar A. & Des Gasper, "Human Security. A Thematic Guidance Note for Regional and National Human Development Report Teams". United Nations Development Programme (UNDP), Human Development Report Office, 2013 [Consulted at: 25 March 2019]. Available at: http://hdr.undp.org/sites/default/files/human_security_guidance_note_r-nhdrs.pdf

IFRC, Emergency Appeal Operarion Update. Americas: Population Movement. International Federation of Red Cross and Red Crescent Societies, 2019.

IOM, *World Migration Report 2018*. Geneva: International Organization for Migration, 2017.

IOM and UNHCR, "Venezuelan Outflow Continues Unabated, Stands Now at 3.4 Million". Reliefweb Updates, Geneva, 22 February, 2019.

Jumbert, Maria Gabrielsen, "Control or rescue at sea? Aims and limits of border surveillance technologies in the Mediterranean Sea". In *Disasters*, 2018. DOI: 10.1111/disa.12286.

Kandel, William A., Bruno, Andorra, Meyer, Peter J., Seelke, Clare Ribando, Taft-Morales, Maureen, & Wasem, Ruth Ellen, *Unaccompanied Alien Children: Potential Factors Contributing to Recent Immigration*. Washington D.C.: Congressional Research Service, 2014.

Keeling, D. (2012). "Transatlantic shipping cartels and migration between Europe and America, 1880-1914". In *Essays in Economic & Business History*, 17, 195–213.

Lutterbeck, Drew, "A View from the Ground: Human Security Threats to Irregular Migrants across the Mediterranean". In O. Grech & M. Wohlfeld (Eds.), *Migration in the Mediterranean: human rights, security and development perspectives*. Msida: Mediterranean Academy of Diplomatic Studies, 2014, 124–131.

Marc, Alexandre, Verjee, Neelam, & Mogaka, Stephen, *The Challenge of Stability and Security in West Africa*. Washington D.C.: World Bank, 2015.

Martínez Hernandéz-Mejía, Iliana, "Reflexiones sobre la caravana migrante". In *Análisis Plural*, 1st semester, 231–248, 2018.

Observatorio Venezolano de Violencia, Informe Anual de Violencia 2018. Observatorio Venezolano de Violencia, 2018 [Consulted at: 25 February 2019]. Available at: https://observatoriodeviolencia.org.ve/ovv-lacso-informe-anual-de-violencia-2018/

OHCHR, Situation of migrants in transit. Geneva: Office of the High Commissioner for Human Rights, n.d.

Ramcharan, Bertrand, *Human rights and human security*, M. Nijhoff Publishers, 2002.

Ramírez Gallegos, Jacques, "De la era de la migración al siglo de la seguridad: el surgimiento de 'políticas de control con rostro (in)humano". In *Revista Latinoamericana de Estudios de Seguridad*, 23, 10-28, 2018. DOI: 10.17141/urvio.23.2018.3745.

Servan-Mori, E., Leyva-Flores, R., Infante Xibille, C., Torres-Pereda, P., & Garcia-Cerde, R. (2014). "Migrants suffering violence while in transit through Mexico: Factors associated with the decision to continue or turn back". In *Journal of Immigrant Minority Health*, (16), 53–59. https://doi.org/10.1007/s10903-012-9759-3

UNHCR, "Number of refugees and migrants from Venezuela reaches 3 million". In UNHCR Press Releases, 8 November, 2018 [Consulted at: 20 February 2019]. Available at: https://www.unhcr.org/news/press/2018/11/5be4192b4/number-refugees-migrants-venezuela-reaches-3-million.html

UNIDO, UNIDO's Contribution to Human Security. Vienna: United Nations Industrial Development Organization, 2015.

United Nations, International Migration Report 2017. New York, 2017. Retrieved from https://www.un.org/en/development/desa/population/migration/publications/migrationreport/docs/MigrationReport2017.pdf

United Nations Environment Program, Hotspot Analysis. An overarching methodological framework and guidance for product and sector level application. United Nations Environment Program, 2017.

UNODC, Smuggling of migrants: the harsh search for a better life. United Nations Office on Drugs and Crime, 2019. [Consulted at: 28 February 2019]. Available at: https://www.unodc.org/toc/en/crimes/migrant-smuggling.html

Vietti, Francesca & Scribner, Todd, "Human Insecurity: Understanding International Migration from a Human Security Perspective". In *Journal on Migration and Human Security*, 1, 1, 17–31, 2013.

Xavier, Ana Isabel, *A União Europeia, Actor de Segurança Humana. O Futuro Da Segurança*. Lisboa: Universidade Lusófona de Humanidades e Tecnologia, 2013.

Chapter 7

Cities Under Pressure: Internal Migration in Latin American Metropolitan Areas

The case of Ciudad de México Metropolitan Area

Ramón Mahía and Rafael de Arce

Traditionally, studies on migration have focused more on international migration than on internal migration, and, in turn, the analysis of internal migration has given more importance to rural-urban migration as an essential pattern of human movement. In relative terms, attention to internal migration between urban centers has not gathered special attention. However, 80% of Latin American population resides in urban areas, 36% resides in large metropolises of more than one million inhabitants and almost 13% in just 5 megacities with 10 million inhabitants or more.[1] These data illustrate that, to a large extent, the most relevant migration patterns in the medium and long term will be those that connect some cities with others.

The causes of urbanization and its effects on economic and social development have been the subject of study for decades.[2] The conclusions observed in this regard depend, for obvious reasons, on the socio-cultural, political, regional and historical context. In general terms, an "optimal" population concentration can be assumed, from which appears the concept of "excess concentration" which, if exceeded, generates a potential loss of efficiency associated with diseconomies of scale linked to high infrastructural investment costs.[3]

The link between urbanization dynamics and migration in general (and inter-urban migration in particular) is today, by far, much more interest-

---

1. UN. *The World's Cities in 2016. Data Booklet.* 2016. (ST/ESA/ SER.A/392). United Nations, Department of Economic and Social Affairs, Population Division (2016).
2. See Spence et al. 2008 for a comprehensive thematic paper series on Urbanization and Growth edited by The Commission on Growth and Development from the International Bank for Reconstruction and Development (World Bank).
3. Atienza, M. & Aroca, P. "Concentración y crecimiento en Chile: una relación negativa ignorada". In *Revista Latinoamericana de Estudios Urbano Regionales EURE*. Vol. 38, No. 114, 2012, 257-277.

ing than the understanding of pure demographical changes.[4] Nevertheless, the complexity of contemporary migratory movements at different scales makes the study of effects of migration composition into hosting cities much more challenging that in the past under the simple framework of a rural-urban internal migration pattern. Inter-urban migration forces analysts to consider both incoming and outgoing flows, unlike rural-urban patterns in which the unidirectional flow implied a gradual pressure on the receiving cities. Large cities such as Ciudad de México, São Paulo or Rio de Janeiro attract and expel inhabitants at the same time and these inter-urban flows are combined with rural influences, even notable in some cases, interior residential mobility in large cities and flows of international migration, generating, all together, an increasingly complex urban demographic dynamic. The urbanization process, traditionally linked in the past to classical phenomena of rural-urban migration, looks nowadays to a much multifaceted episode that frequently coexists with sub-urbanization, counter-urbanization or re-urbanization that are the cause and consequence of complex migratory movements.[5]

In this text we will briefly review in a first section the trends in urbanization and internal migration in the case of Latin American continent. We will then concentrate the focus in the specific case of Mexican Metropolitan Areas ("Zonas Metropolitanas" or ZM in Spanish) with special attention to the misalignment between policies and real needs.

Trends in Urbanization and Internal Migration in Latin America

Heterogeneity is a remarkable feature of Latin America area but we observe that the region has reached high urbanization rates, with significant population concentration and territorial expansion of large cities. This urbanization can be explained by the particular pattern of industrialization adopted since the 1930s based on import substitution model[6] and by other important factors linked to demographic transition.[7]

4. Rodríguez Vignoli, J. *Migración interna y asentamientos humanos en América Latina y el Caribe (1990-2010)*. Santiago: CEPAL, 2017.
5. Galindo, A. M. C. [et al.]. "Migración interna y cambios metropolitanos:¿ qué está pasando en las grandes ciudades de América Latina?". In *Revista Latinoamericana de Población*. Vol. 10 No. 18, 2016, 7-41.
6. Cerrutti, M., & Bertoncello, R. "Urbanization and internal migration patterns in Latin America". In *Centro de Estudios de Población*. 2003, 1-24.
7. Rodriguez Vignoli, J. *Distribución Territorial de la Población de América Latina y el Caribe: Tendencias, Interpretaciones y Desafíos para las Políticas Públicas*. Santiago:

In the last six decades, urbanization in the Latin American and Caribbean area has slowed down slightly[8] (UN, 2015), although consensus forecasts agree that the urbanization process will continue in the future, especially in countries with lower development levels. The greatest relative growth will occur in medium-sized cities, although some Latin American cities such as Bogotá and Lima will become mega-cities (more than 10 million inhabitants) before 2030, joining others from the continent such as Buenos Aires, Ciudad de México, Rio de Janeiro and São Paulo.[9]

The deceleration in the urbanization process is linked to several factors. On the one hand, having reached very high aggregate urbanization levels limits new progress but, additionally, other factors are relevant. Among them, the change in some demographic patterns, and especially the one related to migration, is key for the correct understanding of the process. There is a certain consensus in considering a change in the internal migration dynamics that would imply that cities are becoming centers that expel population after a long period of immigration.[10]

A recent study[11] offers a quantification of internal migration between cities in Latin America by approximating origin-destination matrices based on the census data of ten Latin American countries, considering a list of 20,000 cities. The most remarkable finding is to confirm the change of migration patterns: a tendency towards urban deconcentration and very small and reverse migration balances. Indeed, most cities already have net emigration, especially those under 100,000 inhabitants. It is true that the largest cities, with more than one million inhabitants, still show net immigration but in very meager values and apparently at much lower scale than previously observed with the 2000 census data. Megalopolises (10,000,000 inhabitants or more) also show net emigration balances.

According to this study, the high net urban immigration registered in the past is not so evident today, and this could lead to a consequent relief of the potentially negative effects linked to the collapse of basic services, infrastructure and governance and security. The causes of this tendency

CEPAL/CELADE, 2002.
8. UN *World Urbanization Prospects: The 2014 Revision*. 2015. (ST/ESA/SER.A/366), New York, Department of Economic and Social Affairs, Population Division.
9. Ibid.
10. Galindo, A. M. C. [et al.]. "Migración interna y cambios metropolitanos:¿ qué está pasando en las grandes ciudades de América Latina?". In *Revista Latinoamericana de Población*. Vol. 10 No. 18, 2016, 7-41.
11. Rodriguez Vignoli, J. *Migración interna y asentamientos humanos en América Latina y el Caribe (1990-2010)*. Santiago: CEPAL, 2017.

towards net emigration could be endogenously related to the accumulation of the negative effects of excessive concentration and, therefore, linked to loss of efficiency and attractiveness of large cities. This would have involved phenomena of voluntary de-concentration with different patterns and intensities. Together with these endogenous causes, it is also possible to assume the success of some political plans and decisions that, explicitly, have achieved a greater regional migratory balance or a turn in the most harmful dynamics of urban concentration.

A second trend of interest is the consolidated predominance of urban-urban migration in the context of internal migration, although rural-urban migration also remains. Urban-urban migration, a pattern that started and accelerated with intensity between the 1970s and the 1990s, continues today, and can be thought as the main category of internal movement: with data related to censuses of 2010, 3 out of 4 migrants moved between cities.

The loss of relative importance of rural-urban migration has diverse causes depending on the different regional or historical contexts. The saturation of some predominant destination cities in the past, which favors urban migration to other nearby metropolitan areas, less congested and more accessible; the greater regional convergence, sometimes linked to labor market or to the evolution of prices of land and/or housing, the changes in the productive system, the decentralization of administrative policy or the implementation of active policies of spatial planning. The concept of counter-urbanization was in fact coined in 1976 [12] and frequently studied from late 1990's and empirically observed in various countries.

In any case, the phenomenon of net emigration from the cities must be redefined considering that the definition of city has been altered, making difficult a precise depiction of concepts such as concentration, migration or urban immigration. The traditional concept of "city" appears with other ideas of expanded concentration, diffuse city, metropolis-region,[13] multi-centered metropolis, archipelago of cities[14] or city-region, far away in any case from the classic idea of urbanization "center + suburb". The boundaries of large cities are now more blurred, including very large

12. Berry, B. "The Counter-urbanization Process: Urban America since 1970". In *Urban Affairs Annual Review*. Vol. 11, 1976, 17-30.
13. Sassen, S. "El reposicionamiento de las ciudades y regiones urbanas en una economía global: ampliando las opciones de políticas y gobernanza". In *Revista Latinoamericana de Estudios Urbano Regionales EURE*. Vol. 33, No.100, 2007, 9-34.
14. D Mattos, C.A., Fuentes, L. & LINK, F. "Tendencias recientes del crecimiento metropolitano en Santiago de Chile. ¿Hacia una nueva geografía urbana?". In *Revista INVI*. Vol. 29, No. 81, 2014.

peri-urban areas, entire population areas or even other cities that today appear to be integrated into a less compact definition of the city.

The apparent emigration observed from the cities would not imply, therefore, a clear de-concentration or de-urbanization but the result of the expansion of the limits of the previously compact city.[15] This conclusion is effectively illustrated by these authors for a study carried out in 18 cities in several Latin American countries, they find that "Without exception, the use of the bounded definition (of the city) offers an image of less attractive migratory or of more marked net emigration, which can certainly lead to mistaken or hasty conclusions about the loss of attractiveness of the big cities, since with the extended delimitation they still show their character of attraction."[16]

In this context, the phenomenon of inter-urban migration, which generally adopts the center-periphery pattern, had already been initiated and clearly detected in studies of the early 2000s. This phenomenon of "de-compaction" implies, therefore, that the pressure on the provision of services, governance and security would not have been reduced so clearly but would have mutated, claiming equally extensive resources and intense planning. Indeed, the "periphery" of important cities in Latin America, sometimes combined with intense immigration, has required attention and active policies for a long time depending on different patterns of consolidation. Sometimes the peripheries have been occupied by migrants (both internal and external) or by relatively more disadvantaged citizens who were "expelled" from the center, demanding active segregation related policies. Sometimes, segregation has followed other patterns and disadvantaged population has concentrated precisely in the center or in some older and worse endowed peripheral areas. In many cases, the peripheries have been gaining density over time becoming new satellite urban centers, densely populated, demanding substantive attention and coordinated decentralization in terms of planning and provision of resources of all kinds. In any case, this expansion model also requires active policies of balanced decentralization that provide the new infrastructural endowments required to communicate the areas that must be interconnected and provide them with basic services.

---

15. Galindo, A. M. C. [et al.]. "Migración interna y cambios metropolitanos:¿ qué está pasando en las grandes ciudades de América Latina?". In *Revista Latinoamericana de Población*. Vol. 10 No. 18, 2016, 7-41.
16. *Ibid.*

The Case of the Central Region and Ciudad de México Metropolitan Area

Migration is essentially a dynamic phenomenon that evolves by adjusting its volumes and shapes rapidly and adopting increasing complexity over time. The case of Mexico reproduces some of the patterns of change detected in general terms in Latin America and many other areas of the world. On the one hand, as is the case in other countries, international migration, mainly to the United States, captures most of the attention, debate and study. In addition, until relatively recently, rural-urban migration to Ciudad de México, and to a lesser extent to Guadalajara and Monterrey, had been predominant in terms of internal movements. More recently, however, we have also found contemporary phenomena common to other countries in the area. A greater role for internal migration as a factor of change, a progressive importance of urban-urban migration to the detriment of the classic rural-urban migration and a progressively more decentralized population with a greater role for medium-sized cities.[17]

In Mexico, four phases of development and specific migratory dynamics are usually identified. The period 1900-1940 would correspond to the early urbanization phase with very dynamic rural-urban flows that also continued to predominate between 1940-1980, a period of very intense industrialization. They are followed by a third period of 1980-2000 of economic openness and explosion of migration to the United States and the 2000-2016 period defined by political openness and moderate economic growth marked by the deceleration of interstate migration and the increase in close migration within the same entity.[18]

The amount of internal migration is, in any case, very significant. Between 2010 and 2015, around 3.2 million Mexicans changed their residence between states and a similar number changed municipality of residence within the same state; total internal migration between 2010 and 2015 therefore represents 6.4 million people.[19]

Together with these basic trends, and as we commented in previous paragraphs, the evolution of the concept of the classical city is confirmed, from mononuclear center-periphery design towards more contemporary

17. Pérez Campuzano, E., Castillo, G., & Galindo, M. C. "Internal Migration in Mexico: Consolidation of Urban–Urban Mobility, 2000–2015". In *Growth and Change*. Vol. 49, No. 1, 2018, 223-240.
18. De Anda, G. G., & Plassot, T. "Migraciones internas: un análisis espacio-temporal del periodo 1970-2015". In *Economía UNAM*. Vol. 14, No. 40, 2017, 67-100.
19. ENADID *Encuesta Nacional de la Dinámica Demográfica*. INEGI, 2014.

configurations and somewhat more diffuse city, emerging essential patterns to understand the processes of territorial concentration.

We are especially interested in the concept of city-region because of what it implies in terms of the emergence of patterns of population movements of diverse nature. These movements of people are in line with the interactions of economic nature between the entities of the city-region (trade and capital flows) and demand significant adjustments in the services and urban infrastructures of the urban nuclei that make up the city-region as well as in the communication routes that connect them. The appearance of new zones of economic growth stimulates internal migration and labor flows,[20] to which migratory flows must be added due to reasons of insecurity and violence or related to environmental deterioration or climatic catastrophes. Some of these movements correspond to the category of "circulation" and not so much to migration in the strict sense; they are pendular movements, essentially corresponding to the commuting of thousands of people that move from their areas of residence to those of work or commercial and leisure activities. Others take the form of a permanent rearrangement of the population that, abandoning the traditional center, moves to new urban centers on the periphery, leaves the state or changes municipalities in the same federal state. The reordering of the population in turn drives the economic dynamism of the new areas, generating a complex dynamic of cause and effect that requires constant attention in terms of urban and regional planning. For a correct planning and an adequate location of the resources it is necessary to know what role the big cities play as nodes of population concentration at the same time as attractors of migratory flows, and the type of migratory exchanges that they maintain with the rest of urban centers of their own region.[21]

Within the framework of this new concept of city, the concept of city-region is of special interest in the case of Mexico and even more interesting is the concept of Metropolitan Area (MA) ("metropolitan zone" or ZM in Spanish) common in this country. The definition of a MA in Mexico exceeds the scope of a single city and its close conurbation and does not necessarily adjust to that of state or region so that, de facto, an MA is configured based on economic and social relations between different municipalities in a given large area. There are 59 metropolitan areas in Mexico,

20. Aguilar, A. G., & Hernandez-Lozano, J. "La reorientación de flujos migratorios en la ciudad-región. El caso de la Ciudad de México en la Región Centro". In *Revista EU-RE-Revista de Estudios Urbano Regionales*. Vol. 44, No. 133, 2018, 135-159.
21. *Ibid.*

comprising 367 municipalities that together represent around 60% of the country's total population.[22]

We will focus this analysis in the Mexican city region called Central Region ("Región Centro" or RC in Spanish), an entity integrated by seven states: Ciudad de México, and the states of Mexico, Hidalgo, Morelos, Puebla, Querétaro and Tlaxcala. This enormous City-Region contains a third of the population of the whole nation although, nevertheless, it only represents a 5% of the extension of the country which gives an idea of its huge population concentration. The two major centers on which the development of this city-region has orbited are the urban agglomeration around Ciudad de México (MCMA or ZMCM in Spanish) and the metropolitan area Puebla-Tlaxcal (PTMA or ZMPT in Spanish).

The metropolitan area of Ciudad de México (MCMA), also known as "Zona Metropolitana del Valle de México", is made up of Ciudad de México and 76 agglomerated municipalities, all of them belonging to the State of Mexico (59) or Ciudad de Mexico (16) except for one of them in the state of Hidalgo. To the almost 9 million inhabitants of Ciudad de México would be added 14 million distributed in these 60 municipalities totaling a population of more than 22 million inhabitants (1 in 5 Mexicans). According to the United Nations,[23] this is one of the most populated urban agglomerations in the world and the second largest in Latin America, only below the Binational Metropolitan Area of San Diego-Tijuana. The metropolitan area Puebla-Tlaxcal (ZMPT) is a metropolitan area located in the center of the state of Puebla and the south of the state of Tlaxcala and agglutinates a total of 38 municipalities from Poblanos and Tlaxcaltecas located in the Valley of Puebla-Tlaxcala.

According to Aguilar and Hernandez-Lozano,[24] the process of urban de-concentration has been the predominant feature in the central region during the last thirty years with a gradual decrease in the participation of the MCMA in the urban growth of the region. The data of migratory net balances of the last twenty years between urban centers presented by these authors show that the MCMA has been expeller of migrating population

---

22. 2010 Census Data from National Institute of Statistics and Geography (INEGI).
23. UN *The World'sCities in 2016. Data Booklet*. 2016. (ST/ESA/ SER.A/392). United Nations, Department of Economic and Social Affairs, Population Di-vision (2016).
24. Aguilar, A. G., & Hernandez-Lozano, J. "La reorientación de flujos migratorios en la ciudad-región. El caso de la Ciudad de México en la Región Centro". In *Revista EU-RE-Revista de Estudios Urbano Regionales*. Vol. 44, No. 133, 2018, 135-159.

maintaining negative balances with the majority of metropolitan areas and smaller urban centers.

Ciudad de México, MA's main center of gravity, has evolved from a net receiver of population to an expeller of residents who move particularly towards neighboring agglomerations within the metropolitan area itself. Between 1970 and 1980 the number of arrivals began to decrease clearly and from 1980 the departures began to surpass the entrances. It would be in the 1985-1990 period that most departures from Ciudad de México to other states were recorded (more than 1 million departures in that period); migration to Ciudad de México went from representing 14% of total interstate flows between 1975 and 1980 to 10% between 2010 and 2015.[25] Despite its character as a net emitter of population, the rate of entries per thousand inhabitants is stable in comparison with the exit rate; that is, the negative net migratory balance of Ciudad de México is due to exits more than to entries.[26] This reveals difficulties in conserving its population as a consequence of a high cost of living (particularly in access to housing), competition for land use between commerce and housing, and the increase in tertiary activities.[27]

Despite this overall negative balance, Ciudad de México continues to receive migrants from other areas of the RC such as Puebla-Tlaxcala, the second most important metropolitan area in the region and with which it maintains a positive balance receiving a high number of migrants. In fact, although the resident population in Ciudad de México has decreased in absolute terms, its working population has increased, which means that a large part of the working population in Ciudad de México lives on the periphery.[28]

What is of interest in this phenomenon is not, however, the loss of relevance of Ciudad de México but the complex dynamics of change and interrelation between the different populations of the area. Aguilar and Hernandez-Lozano [29] have verified that together with the negative global balance

---

25. Ibid.
26. De Anda, G. G., & Plassot, T. "Migraciones internas: un análisis espacio-temporal del periodo 1970-2015". In *Economía UNAM*. Vol. 14, No. 40, 2017, 67-100.
27. Delgadillo, V. "Territorio, vivienda, infraestructura y transporte, el caso de la Ciudad de México y su área metropolitana". In *5 temas selectos del hábitat latinoamericano*. Río de Janeiro: ONU-Hábitat, 2010.
28. De Anda, G. G., & Plassot, T. "Migraciones internas: un análisis espacio-temporal del periodo 1970-2015". In *Economía UNAM*. Vol. 14, No. 40, 2017, 67-100.
29. Aguilar, A. G., & Hernandez-Lozano, J. "La reorientación de flujos migratorios en la ciudad-región. El caso de la Ciudad de México en la Región Centro". In *Revista EU-*

of Ciudad de México, processes of urban concentration in other metropolitan areas coexist with other metropolises of the same region, implying a movement of urban redistribution from the "center" to the "periphery" and towards the lowest levels of the urban hierarchy. The authors point out that metropolitan-metropolitan migration is the one that involves the greatest number of migrants (51.3% of the total). The conclusion is that the city-region of Mexico has become a territory of very high level of urbanization with the consolidation of several metropolitan areas and cities of various sizes, which already form a polycentric structure where the main centers act as nodes of strong urbanization and migratory attraction.

The logic of the city-region and the metropolitan area as an integrated entity essential to understand population dynamics necessarily implies an integrated planning. Decisions about where to locate scarce resources in terms of infrastructure and service improvements must be made at this same metropolitan area level. City-regions show at the same time, for interconnected areas, complementary processes of re-urbanization and de-urbanization that require an increasingly complex urban planning scheme, coordinated and integrated in a very large area. Municipal administration, essentially local, is fragmentary, ineffective, and clearly inefficient in terms of resource optimization, and the absence of an integrated administration at the metropolitan area level generates essential malfunctioning and inadequate, incomplete, and lacking continuity in infrastructure development.

One of the causes that explain the lack of a homogeneous management framework at metropolitan area level is the lack of legal recognition of the Metropolitan Area, which does not have a clear legal framework that allows its centralized management. In fact, institutional fragmentation is expressly derived from article 115 of the Mexican Constitution, which unambiguously prohibits, on the one hand, the establishment of government bodies between the municipality and the states of the Republic; and, on the other, only allows intergovernmental coordination and/or intermunicipal associationism.[30] This author points out that, while in Latin America a process of metropolization is been intensely lived, its political-administrative structures, on the one hand, and the understanding of the metropolitan phenomenon, on the other hand, are not convergent.

RE-Revista de Estudios Urbano Regionales. Vol. 44, No. 133, 2018, 135-159.

30. Arellano Ríos, A. "La coordinación metropolitana en el ámbito subnacional mexicano: un análisis institucional". In *Documentos y aportes en administración pública y gestión estatal*. Vol. 14, No. 23, 2014, 33-70.

Given the impossibility of setting up metropolitan or regional governments and the existence of a free municipality, Metropolitan governance in Mexico is only possible within minimal schemes and only under the mechanism of intergovernmental coordination or intermunicipal associationism.[31] In this sense, the lack of a solid framework of homogeneous management at the Metropolitan Zone level has led several states to promote their own initiatives to create different instances of metropolitan coordination: Metropolitan Councils, Metropolitan Commissions, Metropolitan Coordination Boards, Metropolitan Institutes, Metropolitan Citizen Councils, Metropolitan Development Councils, Metropolitan Planning Institute, Councils for Citizen Participation, etc.

Most of these bodies are only opinion and/or consultation bodies with little executive capacity to carry out projects and less still to intervene in the daily operation of the different issues with which they deal. The fragmentation and weakness of these intermunicipal coordination entities frequently leads to governance problems in metropolitan areas with imprecise urban planning, excessively sectoral management channeled through specific bodies and a lack of coordination and planning.[32]

The Mexican Institute for Competitiveness (IMCO) pointed out in a recent analysis that in the MCMA there is no agency that has the power to plan, execute joint projects or operate in key areas such as transportation, water services or security. The main implication is that instead of an integrated city there is an extensive universe of localities that provide public services and plan exclusively for the inhabitants of their demarcation. On the one hand, this limits the ability to execute more ambitious strategies to solve the problems of the City and, on the other hand, generates deficient services and bankrupt organisms, as in the case of the Ciudad de México water supply network (SACM) and some of the 56 water organisms that exist in the State of Mexico.[33]

The deficiencies in terms of metropolitan management are accentuated in the framework of internal migrations between different areas of the same metropolitan area. On the one hand, despite the net emigration of many cities such as Ciudad de México, they continue to receive a significant influx of new residents from other areas of the region, from other parts of the

31. Arellano Ríos, A. "La gobernabilidad metropolitana en México". In *Revista Analítica*. Vol. 1, No. 1, 2018.
32. Valenzuala Van Treek, E. V "Áreas metropolitanas, reflexión, evolución y casos de estudio (2ª Parte)". In *Urbano*. Vol. 10, No, 15, 2007, 7-19.
33. IMCO "Distrito Federal y Estado de México: la ciudad dividida". In *IMCO*. 2014.

country or from other countries. On the other hand, this process coexists with complex patterns of relocation of citizens between different areas of the metropolitan area itself, which requires an agile and flexible planning system that aligns with these patterns and, in a certain way, contributes to providing them with logic and viability. These dynamics generate, for example, important challenges in terms of transport infrastructure, especially in terms of public transport. The National Federation of Municipalities of Mexico itself recently pointed out a scarcity of resources for the construction and rehabilitation of infrastructures overexploited by the use of floating population as a consequence of a lack of coordination between the municipalities of the metropolitan areas themselves and with the state and federal governments, and the lack of a strategic metropolitan vision for the realization of long-term projects.

In line with IMCO's opinion, the public agenda must be adapted to the reality of the integrated city by developing metropolitan bodies capable of providing common services. This would imply that the authorities cede certain powers, such as the provision of water or public transport, to a metropolitan body in charge of providing them for all the inhabitants of the MCMA.

An essential starting point for proper planning is an accurate diagnosis of the situation based on real data and adapted to the geographical area of interest. In terms of mobility, this is precisely the objective of the last Origin-Destination Survey of the Metropolitan Area of the Valley of Mexico, referring to 2017 which, among its explicit objectives, serves as the basis for defining integral planning policies in the areas of transport and traffic, sustainable mobility and territorial ordering. The data from this survey confirms that, although there are approximately 4.4 million trips per day that cross the border between Mexico City and another political jurisdictions, the polycentric nature of the MCMA is clear: only one out of every eight trips that start in conurbated municipalities end in Mexico City and only one out of every seven trips that start in Mexico City ends in a conurbated municipality. Faced with this reality, IMCO experts [34] show the deficient design of the public transport system of the MCMA. While about 9 million people live in Mexico City, 14 million live in the metropolitan area, so the need for a peripheral-central connection is very evident. Approximately 20% of daily commuting involves municipalities other than Mexico City. However, the bulk of the stations are concentrated in Mexico City, leaving

---

34. Ibid.

millions of inhabitants of the MA without the options of mass transportation to connect them with the rest of the City. The subway network is considerable but not extensive enough and does not reach the state of Mexico and where the subway ends, major bus congestion begins.

In many of the world's major cities there are metropolitan planning and project execution agencies,[35] while in the MCMA there is no metropolitan transportation agency that plans and executes projects integrally. The Metro Collective Transport System is operated by Ciudad de México so that most of the investments and expansions are centered within this demarcation. There is therefore a misalignment between the reality of the MA and the administrative organization.

Perhaps because of this, data from the Origin-Destination Survey of the Metropolitan Area of the Valley of Mexico shows that despite investments in transport infrastructure in recent years, the travel times of citizens have worsened. In the previous ten years, the suburban train, Line 12, more than 100 kilometers of Metrobus and Mexibus, dozens of kilometers of urban highways, and the Ecobici bicycle lane were built. Despite all this, the 2017 survey documented a 3-minute increase in travel times, compared to the average recorded in 2007. Today people take an average of 57 minutes to get to work (60 minutes if you don't live in Ciudad de México). One in three trips to work in the MCMA require more than one hour, and 7.2% of trips to work that begin in conurbated municipalities last more than two hours.

In this sense, the bet on road infrastructure, which has been preferred in recent years, does not seem the best option. In recent years the budget for mobility allocated more than 65% to road infrastructure and less than 35% to collective and cycling and pedestrian infrastructures. The commitment to road infrastructure for the private vehicle contributes to the disproportionate increase in the number of cars: each year 250,000 additional cars are added to the circulation in the MCMA, a growth of 15% per year, which is much higher in comparison with the increase in population and well above the growth of any existing means of collective transport[36].

---

35. For instance Metropolitan Planning Organizations (MPO's) for metropolitan areas in United States, Metropolitan Area of Lisbon in Portugal, Greater London Authority for UK, Communauté urbaine de Lyon in France or Metropolitan Area of Barcelona in Spain.
36. See https://www.eleconomista.com.mx/politica/La-Ciudad-de-Mexico-duplico-el-parque-vehicular-en-10-anos-20170801-0114.html

This inadequate planning and betting on the private vehicle generates not only inefficient transport but serious damage of various kinds. From an environmental point of view, Ciudad de México has been facing a serious pollution problem for some time. In 1992, Mexico City received the "prize" of the most polluted city in the world by the United Nations and although a period of awareness and implementation of corrective measures began, its effectiveness was gradually decreasing and today the city faces episodes of environmental crisis increasingly frequent and serious.

Additionally, there is a problem regarding the quantity and quality of water available in Ciudad de México alone. There are more than 1,300,000 people who do not have drinking water in their homes and 1,500,000 do not receive water on a regular basis. The overexploitation of aquifers, the need to import it from remote basins, the recycling of gigantic volumes of wastewater and the absence of rainwater harvesting systems are some of the most pressing problems.

Security problems are also notable. INEGI, which regularly prepares the National Public Safety Survey, estimated at the end of 2018 that in the country's urban areas 74% of the adult population perceives that their city is unsafe to live in. In the case of Mexico City, the percentage even rises to 88% in the north or 86% in the west and west city areas.

Conclusions

The concept of city-region or Metropolitan Area is fully consolidated in Mexico and the data support that these demarcations have their own migratory dynamics that tend to very complex polycentric realities in which superimposed patterns of mobility coexist.

The case of the Central Region and the Metropolitan Area of Ciudad de México illustrates the complexity of the migratory dynamics that occur over time. While Ciudad de México has lost its relative weight as a migratory attractor for the benefit of other populations in the same metropolitan area, the city continues to be a focus of essential activity, registering a constant flow of immigrants and a high volume of circulation of people from conurbated areas and other more distant areas.

However, the brief analysis carried out for the case of the MCMA reveals a misalignment between this pattern of complex mobility of the city-region and its management architecture. The lack of regional coordination mechanisms at the MA level with a greater scope than the current ones reduces the effectiveness of infrastructure and service provision policies and seems to contribute to inefficient spatial planning.

On the one hand, the lack of coordination between the metropolitan area's own municipalities and with the state and federal governments impedes a strategic metropolitan vision that focuses on long-term projects that respond to the needs of the resident population, the new citizens arriving to each municipality and the immense floating population of the entire area. It therefore seems essential that the public agenda be adapted to the reality of this polycentric and integrated city, creating global metropolitan bodies capable of providing common services.

On the other hand, it seems evident that the paradigm of current urban planning is unsustainable in the medium and long term. Cities that have opted to increase road infrastructure have failed to achieve mobility objectives and have deteriorated environmental quality; it seems a fait accompli that the central axis of sustainable mobility is a commitment to collective transport.

Decisions on medium- and long-term environmental sustainability cannot wait and require coordinated action between the entities that make up the metropolitan area and in coordination with the state administration. The problems of circulatory collapse, pollution, lack of access to water and, in general, saturation of Ciudad de México threaten to collapse one of the greatest cities of the planet.

References

Aguilar, A. G., & Hernandez-Lozano, J. "La reorientación de flujos migratorios en la ciudad-región. El caso de la Ciudad de México en la Región Centro". In *Revista EURE-Revista de Estudios Urbano Regionales*. Vol. 44, No. 133, 2018, 135-159.

Arellano Ríoz, A. "La coordinación metropolitana en el ámbito subnacional mexicano: un análisis institucional." In *Documentos y aportes en administración pública y gestión estatal*. Vol. 14, No. 23, 2014, 33-70.

Arellano Ríoz, A. "La gobernabilidad metropolitana en México." In *Revista Analitica*. Vol. 1, No. 1, 2018.

Atienza, M. & Aroca, P. "Concentración y crecimiento en Chile: una relación negativa ignorada". In *Revista Latinoamericana de Estudios Urbano Regionales EURE*. Vol. 38, No. 114, 2012, 257-277.

Berry, B. "The Counter-urbanization Process: Urban America since 1970". In *Urban Affairs Annual Review*. Vol. 11, 1976, 17-30.

Cerrutti, M., & Bertoncello, R. "Urbanization and internal migration patterns in Latin America". In *Centro de Estudios de Población*. 2003, 1-24.

De Anda, G. G., & Plassot, T. "Migraciones internas: un análisis espacio-temporal del periodo 1970-2015". In *Economía UNAM*. Vol. 14, No. 40, 2017, 67-100.

De Mattos, C.A., Fuentes, L. & Link, F. "Tendencias recientes del crecimiento metropolitano en Santiago de Chile. ¿Hacia una nueva geografía urbana?". In *Revista INVI*. Vol. 29, No. 81, 2014.

Delgadillo, V. "Territorio, vivienda, infraestructura y transporte, el caso de la Ciudad de México y su área metropolitana". In *5 temas selectos del hábitat latinoamericano*. Río de Janeiro: ONU-Hábitat, 2010.

Delgado, J. *Ciudad-región y transporte en el México Central: un largo camino de rupturas y continuidades*. Madrid: Plaza y Valdés, 1998.

ENADID *Encuesta Nacional de la Dinámica Demográfica*. INEGI, 2014.

Galindo, A. M. C. [et al.]. "Migración interna y cambios metropolitanos:¿ qué está pasando en las grandes ciudades de América Latina?". In *Revista Latinoamericana de Población*. Vol. 10 No. 18, 2016, 7-41.

IMCO "Distrito Federal y Estado de México: la ciudad dividida". In *IMCO*. 2014.

Pérez-Campuzano, E., Castillo, G., & Galindo, M. C. "Internal Migration in Mexico: Consolidation of Urban–Urban Mobility, 2000–2015". In *Growth and Change*. Vol. 49, No. 1, 2018, 223-240.

Rodríguez Vignoli, J. *Distribución Territorial de la Población de América Latina y el Caribe: Tendencias, Interpretaciones y Desafíos para las Políticas Públicas*. Santiago: CEPAL/CELADE, 2002.

Rodríguez Vignoli, J. *Migración interna y asentamientos humanos en América Latina y el Caribe (1990-2010)*. Santiago: CEPAL, 2017.

Sassen, S. "El reposicionamiento de las ciudades y regiones urbanas en una economía global: ampliando las opciones de políticas y gobernanza". In *Revista Latinoamericana de Estudios Urbano Regionales EURE*. Vol. 33, No.100, 2007, 9-34.

Spence, M., Annez, P. C., & Buckley, R. M. (Eds.) *Urbanization and growth*. World Bank Publications, 2008

UN *The World's Cities in 2016. Data Booklet*. 2016. (ST/ESA/ SER.A/392). United Nations, Department of Economic and Social Affairs, Population Di-vision (2016).

UN *World Urbanization Prospects: The 2014 Revision*. 2015. (ST/ESA/SER.A/366), New York, Department of Economic and Social Affairs, Population Division.

Valenzuela Van Treek, E. "Áreas metropolitanas, reflexión, evolución y casos de estudio (2ª Parte)". In *Urbano*. Vol. 10, No, 15, 2007, 7-19.

Part III

Forging Human Security Networks

Chapter 8

Regions as Security Spaces: Taking External Actors and Incomplete Region-Building into Account

Frank Mattheis

Across the southern sections of the Atlantic space, the perception of a se-curity threat is often related to the demarcation of a region in which state control is lacking. These regional spaces enable actors other than central governments to establish competing forms of governance across national borders. This chapter explores how such regional spaces come into being and why they do not necessarily turn into autonomous territorial units. Particular attention is given to the involvement of external actors from across the Atlantic space in the creation of regional security spaces.

The question of how a regional space emerges has been vividly dis-cussed in seminal works in both international studies[1] and geography.[2] Yet studying regionalism within international studies has predominantly meant to study formal intergovernmental regional organizations. This has led to a substantial knowledge production on these organizations and their institutions but has marginalized other forms of regionalism that do not correspond to a state-centric expectation.[3] The dominant practices and theories of International Relations (IR) have throughout the 20th century marginalized the idea of space as an analytical category and the study of regions conducted as a subfield of IR has reproduced much of this bias.[4] The applied notion of regionalism has followed the dualistic epistemology of the nation state, as it has been prevalent in IR theories. The region is not understood as a space but as yet another pre-given container, whose inside can be clearly separated from the outside.

Beyond the spatial and state-centric bias that is deeply rooted in interna-tional relations and regionalism studies, there are avenues forward to chal-

1. Hettne, B., & Söderbaum, F. "Theorizing the rise of regionness". In *New political economy*. Vol. 5, No. 3, 2000, 457-472.
2. Paasi, A. "The resurgence of the 'region' and 'regional identity': Theoretical perspectives and empirical observations on regional dynamics in Europe". In *Review of international studies*. Vol. 35, No. S1, 2009, 121-146
3. Matheis, F., Raineri, L., & Russo, A. *Fringe Regionalism*. Palgrave Pivot: Cham, 2019.
4. Matheis, F. *New regionalism in the South–Mercosur and SADC in a comparative and interregional perspective*. Leipzig: Leipziger Universitätsverlag, 2014.

lenge such notions. Regions can be considered actors in their own right in negotiating spatial configurations and globalization processes.[5] As a consequence, regions are not understood as being in a zero-sum game vis-à-vis nation states but offer a new scale for actors to explore. These scales accumulate in a complex overlapping setting. [6] Regionalism is thus not limited to a negotiation between states or an imposition of one particular state. Territories might be shifting between different dimensions, including the regional one, but this does not undermine their relevance for the spatial configuration.[7] Under these conditions, those imagining and defining a region inevitably territorialize.[8] A regional space does not necessarily entail a delineated territory or pooling of sovereignty. The production of a region becomes tangible through cultural and social practices or can remain limited to a discursive expression. Regionalism is thus one of "different knowledge orders in the production of space."[9]

Unlike the field of international relations, political geography has focused on regionalism as a primarily sub-national phenomenon, paying less attention to the transnational dynamics at stake. This chapter acknowledges that the notion of regional space has been marginalized in the evolution of international studies as a field seeks to illustrate specific dynamics and limits of the production of regions, in particular the mutual relationship between external and internal imaginations in terms of demarcation, identity and function.[10] This is done by following MacLeod and Jones[11] and Beel et al.[12] in applying Paasi's four-stage framework[13] and broadening its

5. Engel, U., Zinecker, H., Matheis, F., Dietze, A., & Plötze, T. (Eds.). *The New Politics of Regionalism: Perspectives from Africa, Latin America and Asia-Pacific*. London: Routledge, 2016.; MIDDELL, M. (Ed.). *The Routledge Handbook of Transregional Studies*. Abingdon: Routledge, 2019.
6. Revel, J. *Jeux d'échelles: la micro-analyze à l'expérience*. Paris: Le Seuil, 1996.
7. Agnew, J. "Sovereignty regimes: territoriality and state authority in contemporary world politics". In *Annals of the association of American geographers*. Vol. 95, No. 2, 2005, 437-461.
8. Paasi, A. "Geography, space and the re-emergence of topological thinking". In *Dialogues in Human Geography*. Vol. 1, No. 3, 2011, 299-303.
9. Engel, U., & Nugent, P. (Eds.) *Respacing Africa*. Leiden: Brill, 2010.
10. Brenner, N., Jessop, B., Jones, M., & MacLeod, G. (Eds.) *State/space: a reader*. Malden: Blackwell, 2003.
11. MacLeod, G., & Jones, M. "Renewing the geography of regions". In *Environment and planning D: society and space*. Vol. 19, No. 6, 2001, 669-695.
12. Beel, D., Jones, M., & Jones, I.R. "City-Region Building and Geohistorical Matters". In *Reanimating Regions: Culture, Politics, and Performance*. Abingdon: Routledge, 2017. 194-2004.
13. Paasi, A. "The institutionalization of regions: a theoretical framework for understanding the emergence of regions and the constitution of regional identity". In *Fennia-International Journal of Geography*. Vol. *164*, No. 1, 1986, 105-146.

scope by exploring its relevance for international studies and vice-versa. However, rather than illustrating each stage with a different empirical case that best fit the description, one single case is analyzed through the lens of all four stages.

The intention of this chapter is thus to provide a bridge between the two disciplines. In geographical thought in general and regarding the declination of the four-stage model in particular, regions have usually been associated with sub-national entities, be they provinces [14], regions [15] or city-regions.[16] By contrast, the case analyzed through the four-stage framework in this chapter is a transnational regionalism, albeit one that is not led by formal regional organizations: the Triple Border region around the Iguazu river at the intersection of Argentina, Brazil and Paraguay. This regionalism emerges at a crossroads between deliberate practices of cross-border actors, overarching intergovernmental structures, external perceptions and representations as well as counter-imaginations against imposed conceived spaces.

The four-stage model has been used to analyze the entangled and complementary processes that enable a region to emerge and institutionalize into an established part of a spatial structure. The stages build on each other but they are not entirely sequential. Rather, they are staggered in a partly overlap manner, both interlacing and reinforcing each other at points of juncture. Regionalization is a complex process and to trace its emergence and evolution Paasi[17] proposes four analytical stages to grasp a process that spans over a long duration with overlapping features. Regions reflect a spatial structure that primarily manifests itself in institutions that create a collective that socializes its inhabitants and exercises control.

In the remainder of this chapter, the four-stage model outlined in Paasi[18] will be discussed from a regionalism point of view and applied to the Triple Border (*triple frontera* in Spanish or *triplice fronteira* in Portuguese), also called the Iguazu region, which refers to a transnational space that is

---

14. Ibid.
15. MacLeod, G., & Jones, M. "Renewing the geography of regions". In *Environment and planning D: society and space*. Vol. *19*, No. 6, 2001, 669-695.
16. Beel, D., Jones, M., & Jones, I.R. "City-Region Building and Geohistorical Matters". In *Reanimating Regions: Culture, Politics, and Performance*. Abingdon: Routledge, 2017. 194-2004.
17. Paasi, A. "The institutionalization of regions: a theoretical framework for understanding the emergence of regions and the constitution of regional identity". In *Fennia-International Journal of Geography*. Vol. *164*, No. 1, 1986, 105-146.
18. Ibid.

located around the border of the three South American countries Argentina, Brazil and Paraguay, but has strong ties across the entire Atlantic Basin.

First stage: consciousness the region as an idea

The first stage deals with the foundation of a region-building process: regional consciousness. This process is primarily understood as the emergence of the awareness among a collective to inhabit a region. A crucial element for the consciousness of a region is a prevalent idea of the shape of a region and common expectations concerning its defining characteristics. The shape of a region can already be territorial but vague and less exclusive connotations are likely to be prevailing. Regions are considered through a certain historical narrative, a landscape or cultural traits. Though theses defining characteristics suggest where a region begins or ends but its boundaries are usually not statically defined but are rather porous and shifting. The processes of cognitive mapping thus primarily entail an imagined region that established itself by increasing its relevance as a space and identity reference point for its inhabitants.

The lens of the first stage can be meaningfully applied to the Iguazu case. First, the Iguazu region surrounds the border between Argentina, Brazil and Paraguay. The idea of the region is thus connected to the status of a borderland in a remote situation vis-à-vis the national capitals.

Second, the Iguazu region is topographically characterized by the Parana and Iguazu rivers that also constitute the national boundaries. The rivers lead to the world's largest waterfalls, the Iguazu waterfalls, which are located at the heart of the region and constitute the main landmark. The idea of the region is thus also structured around elements of nature and landscape.

Third, the Iguazu region as an economic space is primarily characterized by activities of transnational nature, chiefly energy production and commerce. The Iguazu waterfalls fuel massive hydropower plants that constitute a major source of electricity for all three countries. In terms of commerce, Ciudad del Este not only is the main urban center of the region but also an important market where large amounts of illicit and licit goods attract traders from beyond the region. To that end, the idea of the region is characterized by the permeability of borders, which underpins the economic practice and the social fabric.[19]

Fourth, the Iguazu region as an infrastructure is forms a triangle between three cities connected by the transnational bridges that span the two rivers. In decreasing order of size, the cities are Ciudad del Este in Paraguay, Foz do Iguazu in Brazil and Puerto Iguazu in Argentina. The idea of the region is thus a transnational and transurban one.

Fifth, the Iguazu region as a socio-cultural space is characterized by a multitude of migrations throughout the 20th century leading to cultural, ethnic and linguistic diversity. The idea of the region is thus not defined by a homogenous society, although certain patterns, such as the dominance of Portuguese and Spanish, embody the region as a whole.

Second stage: objectification the region as a shape

The second stage refers to a process of objectification or fetishization of the region. The core mechanisms are conceptualization and symbolism. The second stage builds on the first stage, as it tries to embody the elements on which regional consciousness relies on creating names and labels that embody the idea of the region. At the same time, the second stage also curbs the first stage. Providing a symbolic shape to the region entails putting on hold the dynamic and porous processes, as the conceptualization of the region proposes to freeze the region in its current shape. Symbols aim to reproduce and legitimize the practices of the region-building process. The conceptualization of the inhabitants of the region as a social group guides political and economic action. Through symbolism such as flags or maps the inside of the region becomes more tangible and thus also more distinguishable from the non-region. Social and physical demarcations delimiting the region become more visible. At the same time, the label of a region is applied retroactively to forge the concept of a common history, even if the region might not have been a relevant entity in the past.

The second stage thus requires considerably more deliberativeness than the first stage. In addition, it entails a formalization of the regional space both in terms of cartography and social structure. Out of the many available characteristics of regional consciousness existing in the first stage, only a selection is carried over. Power relations become visible as the selection

---

19. Ribereio Nogueira, B.F., & Clemente, C. C. "Etnografia da Tríplice Fronteira: Primeiras aproximações". In *Horizonte Científico*. Vol. 5, No. 2, 2011.

is negotiated between an existing elite that includes elements that confirm and expand their control in the current spatial format and an aspiring elite that seeks to disrupt existing administrative delineations.

Applying the second stage to the Triple Border yields a number of insights.

First, the Iguazu region surrounds the border between Argentina, Brazil and Paraguay. The idea of the region is thus connected to the status and self-identification of a borderland in a remote situation vis-à-vis the national capitals. The shape of the region is thus defined by its transnational and distant position. The national borders are not considered dividing and sealed demarcations. Rather, it is their porosity that underpin the socioeconomic shape of the region.

Second, the region did not have a strong label until demand for a term to refer to this space emerged in the mid-1990s when the region was designated as the Triple Border. A term was required not so much to give shape to a regional consciousness but to delineate a problem to be solved: the external perception of a transnational lawless territory outside the control of national capitals. The primary purpose of creating the term Triple Border was thus not for purposes of internally driven region-building or cohesion but to be able to grasp a space that could be set apart from surrounding areas by the flourishing of specific illicit activities.[20] As such, the name Triple Border did not emerge as an aspiration towards regional identity but rather as an external denomination used to delineate a negative space.[21]

Third, the spatial narrative of the Triple Border was autonomously promoted by actors - primarily national governments and foreign powers - that had become aware of their limited influence in the area and aimed to pave the way to re-establish territorial control. The bias in framing a region around the illicit character of economic practices entailed that other region-building aspects, including crucial existing cross-border activities such as tourism and energy, were largely negated. Furthermore, the definition about what qualifies as illicit was driven externally [22]. This all corresponds to the selective process in stage 2, albeit driven by actors outside

---

20. Rabossi, F. "En las calles de Ciudad del Este: una etnografía del comercio en la frontera". In *Suplemento antropológico*. No. 43, 2008, 1-282.
21. Montenegro, S., & Béliveau, V. G. La Triple Frontera: *Globalización y construcción social del espacio*. Buenos Aires: Miño y Dávila editors, 2006.
22. Jusionyte, I. "On and off the record: The production of legitimacy in an Argentine border town". In *PoLAR: Political and Legal Anthropology Review*. Vol. 36, No. 2, 2013, 231-248.

the region. Equalizing the region from the outside with a perceived lack of control led to policy solutions being brought from outside.

Fourth, the region was not designed as a long-lasting political, social or cultural space. Instead, it was conceived as an ephemeral entity and the main purpose of this framing was to address illicit activities. Once the illicit aspects were solved and external control was reinstated, the need for referring to the Triple Border as a region would vanish. By consequence the region itself would disappear, as soon it did not represent a problem anymore. This observation adds to Paasi's model, as not all region-building is designed to advance through all stages.

Fifth, this external and state-led narrative of the Triple Border had the unintended consequence of creating a backlash of region-building, thus leading to the negotiation process highlighted in stage 2. The denomination of the Triple Border as a lawless heartland of underground activities also generated a somewhat romantic imaginary of a space in which the otherwise prohibited is conceivable, enabling inhabitants and transients to change their identity in other words a "South American version of Casablanca in the 1940s".[23] However, this romanticized reinterpretation only had a limited impact on the external perception and did not lead to notably increase the attraction of the region.

Sixth, instead of establishing a monopoly on defining the region from the outside as a problem, the external frame gave rise to a local counter-narrative as an exercise of regional appropriation. Being externally perceived as a problem triggered two intertwined reactions. The first one was to reject the reductionist vision and the second one was to tap into existing cross-border dynamics in order to create an alternative regional frame. This frame would be congruent with the scope of the Triple Border and based on the same categories yet coined in positive terms as commonalities. The idea of a regional consciousness and a regional economy were an attempt to directly speak to the external perception of ethnic links to terrorism and illicit trade and turn them around. Rather than defending that the idea of the Triple Border was only an external frame, the existence of the region was accepted but filled with a different meaning. This appropriation would thus challenge the external definition and produce its own from the inside. Rather than giving in to be a playing field for external actors, the region tried to promote its own agency and coherence. The negotiation does thus not only happen among internal actors, as stage 2 formulates, but also between

---

23. Lyman, M., & Potter, G. *Organized Crime*. Boston: Pearson, 2015.

external and internal actors. A central instrument in this endeavor was to relabel the region. Instead of appropriating the term Triple Border and reversing its negative connotation the strategy consisted of replacing it altogether. Appropriation would have entailed to continue framing the region around the border as the central feature. The proposed alternative was to replace the term Triple Border with Iguazu region (or Iguaçu in Portuguese). Iguazu is the name of the river that crosses the region and partly serves as borderline. The claim of the new name thus refers to a physical topography rather than an administrative demarcation. It suggests the existence of a seemingly more natural, long-standing and less controversial region. Naming nations and other administrative entities after rivers is common in the Southern Cone of South America (e.g. the country names of Paraguay and Uruguay). In addition, the term evokes an association with the nearby Iguazu Falls, which are one of the major tourist attractions in South America and thus positively connotated internationally. This reframing from a borderland to a topographic identity also resonated with local administrations that rejected the idea that the space they governed was lawless. The idea of an Iguazu region could rely on already established multiple formal frameworks for mutual cooperation.[24]

Third stage: institutionalization—the production of a region

The third stage refers to the institutionalization that further engrains the region. This third stage also builds on the ideas and symbols of a region from the first and second stage, but it also partly occurs in parallel to the second stage by accompanying and reinforcing it. Symbols and labels of a region are institutionalized by using them in all spheres of societal life from media to education to legislation. The region also becomes a tool that is exploited to advance other spatial processes such as marketisation or territorialization. Stage 3 is a steady process during which the region can acquire a legal status that allows it to be represented vis-à-vis other institutionalized spaces. A region-based social system is established, often to the detriment of (or at least at odds with) other overlapping spatial categories such as local communities or nation states. Expectations towards the inhabitants of the region are formulated and codified. The selective process of stage 2 is more rigidly adhered to, as the selection gains a dom-

24. Rhi Sausi, J.L., & and Oddone N. "MERCOSUR: El Caso de la Triple Frontera Argentina-Brasil-Paraguay". In *Gobernanza y Prevención Transversal en la Frontera Norte de México*. Mexico: Centro de Alta Dirección Pública, 2013, 157–204.

inant status. The historicizing, visualization and stereotyping of the region emerging from the second stage enshrined in institutions and reproduced through school curricula or official maps. The third stage not only enables the production of a region but also its social reproduction by formally establishing the region as a political and social entity through institutions and by granting the region as such an economic, social and political purpose. Region-based institutions turn into the most powerful entities in the region. They for instance establish who is part of the region and how one can become a part of it. In this respect, Paasi also highlights the third stage as a transformation from nature as part of the idea of a region in stage one towards the abstraction of landscape. The concept of landscape embodies the expectations towards the internal and external representation of a region and the iconography forging a set of values that eventually can be used for a regional ideology - a regionalism in a meaning akin to nationalism. The antagonism between those advocating the region and those that defend other spatial formats gradually comes to the fore, sometimes overshadowing but not replacing the competition inside the region concerning the shape and purpose of the region.

The Iguazu case appears to have only partly gone through the third stage. Nevertheless, certain elements emerged.

First, the internal regional counter-narrative of a cross-border alternative to the Triple Border was driven in particular by the Brazilian and Paraguayan population of Arab descendant, who mainly settled in the area from the 1950s onwards and worked as small-scale merchants. The idea of a positive notion of the Triple Border materialized in the movement "Peace without Frontiers", which held mass gatherings and cultural festivals, thus indicating a first step of institutionalizing activity. In line with stage 3, the rationale was to tap into an existing sense of community along the border and to mobilize citizens on a common basis that would supersede ethnicity, nationality or religion and other identities fragmenting the population [25]. In the end, however, the internal glue holding together a regional community remained feeble and volatile. The attempt to create a more formal Iguazu region was not able to supersede existing antagonisms. Notably, the latter do not primarily mirror the existing borders, as they do not follow lines of nationality. Also, religion appears to only play a secondary role. By contrast, social and economic divisions are deeply rooted and cut across

---

25. Karam, J. T. "Crossing the Americas: The US War on Terror and Arab Cross-Border Mobilizations in a South American Frontier Region". In *Comparative Studies of South Asia, Africa and the Middle East*. Vol. *31*, No. 2, 2011, 251-266.

the other categories. For instance, large-scale soy farmers and indigenous peasants form transnational groups that are difficult to curb within one regional frame [26]. The strongest asset of a formal Iguazu proposal was thus to embody a reaction to external narratives that used the region as a danger zone, although internal divisions prevented further institutionalization.

Second, although criminal actors in the Triple Border do not relate to a specific institutional region-building process per se, there is a convergence around a specific characteristic, namely, to establish a region devoid of a state presence capable or willing to interfere with illicit cross-border activities. The activities chiefly consist in trafficking drugs, weapons and people, but also include counterfeiting and money laundering. These illegal aspects of transnational economic activities have become institutionalized in the region, where they are not necessarily concerned illicit, benefiting over time from the limited interventions by governments to an extent to be able to resist the actions of international organizations and even specialized task forces.[27] There is no coherent or unitary actor representing this specific institutionalization of the region. Rather, numerous organized groups that at times compete, at times collaborate and at times directly conflict, share a specific interest in maintaining the porous character of the Triple Border or Iguazu.[28] A large part of the actors is located outside the region, including criminal networks originated from China, Korea, Russia, Italy or Nigeria [29]. They typically do not conceive the Triple Border as a region to be considered in its own right but rather as a region that is integrated in a larger notion of transcontinental space that is not geographically continuous. The geographic aspect of this global integration is fluid and amendable but serves the purpose of stage 3 to institutionalize a spatial economy. Many forms of mapping overlap depending on the activity or goods at stake. One of the main purposes of the Triple Border is to connect the Andean hinterland to the economic capitals of the continent Sao Paulo and Buenos Aires and from there further overseas. The connection also proceeds vice-versa. The region in its economic institutionalization performs two key functions for illicit activities and goods. The first constitutes a market, which in-

26. Fogel, R. "La región de la triple frontera: territorios de integración y desintegración". In *Sociologias*. Vol. 10, No. 20, 2008.

27. Jusionyte, I. "On and off the record: The production of legitimacy in an Argentine border town". In *PoLAR: Political and Legal Anthropology Review*. Vol. 36, No. 2, 2013, 231-248.

28. Costa, T.G., & Schulmeister, G.H. "The puzzle of the Iguazu tri-border area: many questions and few answers regarding organized crime and terrorism links". In *Global Crime*. Vol. 8, No. 1, 2007, 26-39.

29. Lyman, M., & Potter, G. *Organized Crime*. Boston: Pearson, 2015.

cludes a strong element of barter, for instance directly swapping weapons against drugs. The second one constitutes a transformative space. Channeling people, money or stolen goods through the Triple Border does not only occur in view of a changing ownership but also to blur and replace previous identities. Local organized crime has also taken advantage of the situation and constitutes a relevant element in many economic activities. However, the importance of external actors in this realm underlines the previously unveiled notion of a region that is primarily built from outside rather than from within.

Third, the main official project to formalize a cross-border region was the establishment of Ciudad del Este as a free trade zone, an arrangement that facilitated both informal and formal, licit and illicit economic activities. The free trade zone has however not coincided with a political project seeking representation or administration and did not rely on a historic narrative to claim its existence as a political space. This practice is not unique to the region but often occurs in the context of special economic zones [30] or development corridors.[31]

Fourth, institutionalization in terms of exercising regional control was further advanced, as the Triple Border attracted international attention, in particular in the US. The narrative that successfully achieved this was to depict a "black hole", a secluded den that harbored terrorists with impunity, where attacks were conceived and where financial and logistical support was organized (Zinno 2008). This narrative benefited from referring to the existence of a large Arab minority in the Triple Border as well as from allegations that some organized crime groups operating in the region were linked to the economic and financial activities of the Islamic group Hizbollah (Hudson 2010). The Triple Border as an external frame is thus based on a perception of a security threat linked with a focus on specific elements of identity and economy.

Fourth stage: the region as a system

The fourth stage is interlocked with the third stage and starts while the latter is still in process but has already reached an advanced stage of in-

---

30. Maruschenk, M. "Special economic zones and transregional state spatiality". In *The Routledge Handbook of Transregional Studies*. Abingdon: Routledge, 2019. 221-227
31. Söderbaum, F., & Taylor, I. "Transmission belt for transnational capital or facilitator for development? Problematising the role of the state in the Maputo Development Corridor". In *The Journal of Modern African Studies*. Vol. 39, No. 4, 2001, 675-695.

stitutionalization. Although the region does not gain a monopoly in terms of spatialization, it becomes an essential unit in the spatial structure and unavoidable by any participant in that structure.

Regionalization as a process can be considered as having been achieved, in the sense of successfully installing a regional structure and dominant imagination of the region as a reference framework for the main social institutions that thus inevitably reinforce the social reproduction of stage 3. Even movements opposing the regional system contribute to its reproduction by acknowledging and engaging with its dominant position. The scattered regional consciousness of stage 1 has given way to a consciousness of one particular region the institutionalized, formalized and thus controlling region. The region becomes a given and can from now on be mobilized as an ideology to attain resources and power. The region acquires an identity on its own, which is fundamentally different from the regional consciousness and imagination of stage 1, in which it is the inhabitants' identification with the region that plays a key role. The identity of a region in stage 4 is primarily a matter of communication and perception, both externally and internally. Externally, the identity of a region comprises the image that a region fosters vis-à-vis others and the expectations others have of the region. This is an instrumental process, where specific narratives are employed depending on the recipient or perceiver. The promotion of a certain type of tourism as well as the image of a region as a conflict zone are both elements of external identity. Internally, the identity of a region serves the purpose of providing a reference point to the inhabitants, defining the region they belong to and delineating exclusionary features. Internal identity is thus a means of exercising social control.

Although the fourth stage does not conclusively have to lead an administrative status, Paasi considers the latter to be the culminating condition. If the region becomes a public administration, institutionalization and formalization reach a point from which it is difficult to fall back to previous stages.

Although the fourth stage cannot be properly appreciated in the Triple Border region, there are some elements that point to the limitations that prevent the region to further institutionalize. Institutionalization in terms of providing the region with an independent status has evidently not occurred in the Iguazu case. The involved central nation governments and the formal intergovernmental regionalisms such as the Common Market of the South (MERCOSUR) and the Union of South American Nations (UNASUR) have not shown any particular awareness for the specific regional-building surrounding the Triple Border. Rather than directly reacting to it, either to appropriate or to counter the cross-border dynamics, the dominant mode is to operate in an isolated fashion vis-à-vis the region. Yet, as a somewhat unintended consequence, the region-building of the Triple Border is directly impacted on by formal initiatives. UNASUR's Initiative for the Integration of the Regional Infrastructure of South America (IIRSA) as well as formal regional agreements conducted in the framework of the intergovernmental regional organizations MERCOSUR provide both physical and legal conditions that facilitate cross-border economic activities. Organized crime groups and other regional economic actors already engaged in the Triple Border were thus well-placed to take advantage of new infrastructures or free movement of goods. Although the creation a common market also reduces the opportunities to engage in smuggling, sufficient differences in taxation and availability exist between the different countries of the region, and in any case this caveat does not apply to illicit goods [32]. The economic activities in the Triple Border might thus have been facilitated by lax control of some state actors but at the same time they also benefit from formal agreements promoting open markets. Yet, the economic agreements and infrastructures do not occur in a fashion to strengthen the regional shape. Rather they dilute its delineation and aim at producing a region that does not correspond to the Iguazu.

Conclusion

The four-stage model exhibits limitations with respect to its external dimension. It is primarily geared towards the inside, focusing on the relations between inhabitants and institutions of the region. Beel et al.[33] point out that external actors can take part in the process of territorially and socially demarcating a region, but this does not become a central concern. In this regard, insights on regionalism in the field of international relations become relevant on two accounts. Firstly, they highlight that external actors do not only take part in region-building but can even be key drivers of it. The institutionalization of regions can be supported and steered by external actors. Mechanisms can include external funding, formal recognition and manipulation of identity. They can be supportive of an ongoing process or

---

32. Aguiar, J. C. G. "Cities on edge: Smuggling and neoliberal policies at the Iguazú triangle". In *Singapore Journal of Tropical Geography*. Vol. 33. No. 2, 2012, 171-183.
33. Beel, D., Jones, M., & Jones, I. R. "City-Region Building and Geohistorical Matters". In *Reanimating Regions: Culture, Politics, and Performance*. Abingdon: Routledge, 2017. 194-2004.

transform an existing but frail region into a dominant structure. The name struggle between Iguazu and Triple Border does not take place between elites and organized communities within the region but rather between external and internal perceptions. As region-building is a long-standing process, the distinctive feature of external actors can over time fade. This is most evident in an imperial region-building process, where the line between external and internal actors can be rather blurred, as despite the power asymmetries and the control mechanisms, the metropolis acts in the periphery as if it were a part thereof, thus legitimizing its presence and influence. The occurrence of regional diasporas can be similarly blurred, as they constitute a social extension of a region, which is located in a spatially distant environment. Paasi[34] and Beel et al.[35] acknowledge that a region is both created in bottom-up and top-down dynamics, and that it can be both territorially bound and spatially diffuse. A third transcending dimension would be that a region is both internally and externally constructed. This multiplicity does not mean that everything can be a region. Challenging dichotomies entail that a region-building process is not reducible to one dynamic or the monopoly of one actor.

Looking across the Atlantic Basin and beyond, the case of Iguazu, the Africa, Caribbean and Pacific (ACP) group is one of the starkest examples of a region whose evolution has been dependent on an external sponsor and recognizer, in this case the EU. The ACP group has however acquired a certain identity as a group of former colonies with privileged ties to the EU. This has become visible as the ACP resists the EU's shift from seeing the ACP as a historically contiguous group of former colonies towards an economic segmentation according in order to facilitate trade agreements with congruent sub-ACP groupings. The Sahel is another example in the Atlantic space of external-internal competition over regional narratives, as the intergovernmental G5 Sahel group follows a functional security delineation, contrasting with the circular and dynamic understanding the Tuareg have of the Sahel.

Second, the four-stage model does not pay particular attention to the role and status a region gains within the international system. From their beginning regions hold autonomous capacities, most notable in the later

34. Paasi, A. "The institutionalization of regions: a theoretical framework for understanding the emergence of regions and the constitution of regional identity". In *Fennia-International Journal of Geography*. Vol. *164*, No. 1, 1986, 105-146.
35. Beel, D., Jones, M., & Jones, I.R. "City-Region Building and Geohistorical Matters". In *Reanimating Regions: Culture, Politics, and Performance*. Abingdon: Routledge, 2017. 194-2004.

institutionalization stages, when a region gains a certain independence from its constituents. The concept of actorness is particularly insightful in this regard. In international relations, regions are deemed as actors through their visibility, their recognition and their institutionalization. These characteristics resonate with the four-stage model and they add an important external feature. Visibility, recognition and institutionalization are not considered to be inherent attributes but rather come to being through external interaction. A region that is institutionalized has the capacity and power to interact with other socio-spatial entities, speaking on behalf of its regional constituents. Recognition and visibility are also instrumental in an extra-regional outreach, facilitating the expansion or at least influence of the region in interaction with other regions. The capacity of the region to act beyond its self-defined boundaries would thus be an integral element of the advanced stages in process of regional institutionalization.

A critical application four-stage model also requires more attention to a reversal or stalling of the process. The Iguazu region is largely stuck in stage 2 with little sign of further institutionalizing. Following the diminishing of tension between two regional narratives, the region seems to stagnate. This suggests that the stage model needs to be read in a circular rather than linear fashion. Further research would be required to explain why certain regional ideas institutionalize while others don't, and to understand the process of de-regionalization.

The nuances of Paasi's stage 2 can further be enhanced by not considering it a linear evolution but rather account for a conflictive process. Rather than being reducible to one symbol and one name, stage two is a competitive region-building process. Different names and different shapes are developed by different actors and compete against each other.

A region institutionalizes as a combination of physical features, communitarian sense, as well as internal and external imaginations. Yet, the relative weight of these different aspects can shift over time, as for instance a region can loosen its identification with a certain topography in favor of a value system. The delineation of a region thus reflects a deliberate choice between various available regional rationales each with a different sense of exclusion and inclusion. A region can reflect a certain economic system or paradigm, a history, a language or a dialect. In all cases, a region is negotiated between different constructed and intentional shapes and purposes. Regionalization consequently continuously generates resistance, from within the region against the Triple Border frame and across the region against the Iguazu frame.

The dynamics of the Iguazu region are not singular and there are several other instances in other border settings in around the Atlantic space where at least some characteristics are echoed. Relevant examples include the regions around the border between Colombia, Peru and Ecuador or surrounding Lake Chad. In these two instances, the presence of national state actors is relatively limited and limited intergovernmental agreements are in place, facilitating both licit cross-border activities and organized crime. At the same time, external perceptions of the region do not necessarily coincide with local self-identification. These patterns underline the necessity to understand region-building across the Atlantic space in terms that acknowledge their plurality and their spatial notion. The regional level emerges as a dimension in addition to socio-spatial structures whereas full replacement seldom takes place. As such they become targets of de- and re-territorializing dynamics. Different actors not only create spatial regional formats, but they also reject them, appropriate them and reinterpret them. Actors negotiate with each other but also with the regionalism at stake.

As an impulse for international relations in general and studying the Atlantic space in particular, regionalisms that are not stemming from intergovernmental regional organizations should not only constitute an isolated niche. Taking into account the different stages of region-building also enriches the study of regional organizations to uncover the mutual relationship, even if it occurs on an indirect level or ends in an impasse, as in the case of the Triple Border.

References

Agnew, J. "Sovereignty regimes: territoriality and state authority in contemporary world politics". In *Annals of the association of American geographers*. Vol. 95, No. 2, 2005, 437-461.

Aguiar, J. C. G. "Cities on edge: Smuggling and neoliberal policies at the Iguazú triangle". In *Singapore Journal of Tropical Geography*. Vol. 33. No. 2, 2012, 171-183.

Beel, D., Jones, M., & Jones, I.R. "City-Region Building and Geohistorical Matters". In *Reanimating Regions: Culture, Politics, and Performance*. Abingdon: Routledge, 2017, 194-204.

Brenner, N., Jessop, B., Jones, M., & MacLeod, G. (Eds.) *State/space: a reader*. Malden: Blackwell, 2003.

Costa, T.G., & Schulmeister, G.H. "The puzzle of the Iguazu tri-border area: many questions and few answers regarding organized crime and terrorism links". In *Global Crime*. Vol. 8, No. 1, 2007, 26-39.

Engel, U., & Nugent, P. (Eds.) *Respacing Africa*. Leiden: Brill, 2010.

Engel, U., Zinecker, H., Matheis, F., Dietze, A., & Plötze, T. (Eds.). *The New Politics of Regionalism: Perspectives from Africa, Latin America and Asia-Pacific*. London: Routledge, 2016.

Fogel, R. "La región de la triple frontera: territorios de integración y desintegración". In *Sociologias*. Vol. 10, No. 20, 2008.

Hettne, B., & Söderbaum, F. "Theorizing the rise of regionness". In *New political economy*. Vol. 5, No. 3, 2000, 457-472.

Hudson, R. *Terrorist and organized crime groups in the Tri-Border Area (TBA) of South America*. Federal Research Division, Library of Congress: Washington, DC, 2003.

Jusionyte, I. "On and off the record: The production of legitimacy in an Argentine border town". In *PoLAR: Political and Legal Anthropology Review*. Vol. 36, No. 2, 2013, 231-248.

Karam, J. T. "Crossing the Americas: The US War on Terror and Arab Cross-Border Mobilizations in a South American Frontier Region". In *Comparative Studies of South Asia, Africa and the Middle East*. Vol. *31*, No. 2, 2011, 251-266.

Lyman, M., & Potter, G. *Organized Crime*. Boston: Pearson, 2015.

MacLeod, G., & Jones, M. "Renewing the geography of regions". In *Environment and planning D: society and space*. Vol. 19, No. 6, 2001, 669-695.

Maruschke, M. "Special economic zones and transregional state spatiality". In *The Routledge Handbook of Transregional Studies*. Abingdon: Routledge, 2019. 221-227.

Matheis, F. *New regionalism in the South–Mercosur and SADC in a comparative and interregional perspective*. Leipzig: Leipziger Universitätsverlag, 2014.

Matheis, F., Raineri, L., & Russo, A. *Fringe Regionalism*. Palgrave Pivot: Cham, 2019.

Middell, M. (Ed.). *The Routledge Handbook of Transregional Studies*. Abingdon: Routledge, 2019.

Montenegro, S., & Béliveau, V. G. *La Triple Frontera: Globalización y construcción social del espacio*. Buenos Aires: Miño y Dávila editors, 2006.

Paasi, A. "The institutionalization of regions: a theoretical framework for understanding the emergence of regions and the constitution of regional identity". In *Fennia-International Journal of Geography*. Vol. *164*, No. 1, 1986, 105-146.

Paasi, A. "The resurgence of the 'region' and 'regional identity': Theoretical perspectives and empirical observations on regional dynamics in Europe". In *Review of international studies*. Vol. 35, No. S1, 2009, 121-146.

Paasi, A. "Geography, space and the re-emergence of topological thinking". In *Dialogues in Human Geography*. Vol. 1, No. 3, 2011, 299-303.

Rabossi, F. "En las calles de Ciudad del Este: una etnografía del comercio en la frontera". In *Suplemento antropológico*. No. 43, 2008, 1-282.

Revel, J. *Jeux d'échelles: la micro-analyze à l'expérience*. Paris: Le Seuil, 1996.

Rhi Sausi, J.L., & and Oddone N. "MERCOSUR: El Caso de la Triple Frontera Argentina-Brasil-Paraguay". In *Gobernanza y Prevención Transversal en la Frontera Norte de México*. Mexico: Centro de Alta Dirección Pública, 2013. 157–204.

Ribereio Nogueira, B.F., & Clemente, C. C. "Etnografia da Tríplice Fronteira: Primeiras aproximações". In *Horizonte Científico*. Vol. 5, No. 2, 2011.

Söderbaum, F., & Taylor, I. "Transmission belt for transnational capital or facilitator for development? Problematising the role of the state in the Maputo Development Corridor". In *The Journal of Modern African Studies*. Vol. 39, No. 4, 2001, 675-695.

Zinno, M. J. *Expeditionary Border Security Operations: Eliminating the Seams*. Fort Leavenworth: KS School of Advanced Military Studies, 2008.

Chapter 9

Transatlantic Tensions, Cooperation and the Africa Policies of the United States and the European Union

Gorm Rye Olsen

Donald Trump's entry into the White House in January 2017 led to the launch of a new foreign policy of the United States. Dan Hamilton describes it as 'Jacksonian'[1] with its strong emphasis on American interests and priorities under the headline 'America First'. Jacksonian foreign policy has a highly skeptical attitude towards the European Union and towards transatlantic cooperation. The Jacksonian- inspired foreign policy of Donald Trump also manifested itself in a remarkably limited interest in Africa. The lack of attention to the continent was clearly emphasized by the postponement of the appointment of an Assistant Secretary of State for Africa until September 2018, as well as the lack of filling of important ambassador positions like South Africa after two years in office.

This is not the first time the transatlantic relationship has been severely strained, as it has been under President Trump. Relations between Washington and Brussels, as well as with individual European capitals, were characterized by deep divisions and disagreements under George W. Bush, not least in the wake of the invasion of Iraq in 2003. This chapter asks if the strong disagreements across the Atlantic have affected the Africa policies of the two actors and if it has affected their inclination to cooperate on Africa. The 'Africa policies' of the US and the EU mainly refer to security interventions. Only to a limited degree, it refers to their development aid policies, leaving humanitarian aid out for the analysis.

I argue that the Africa policies of the two Western powers and the cooperation on Africa are not affected by the policies of the shifting administrations in Washington, nor by the possible straining of the transatlantic relationship. The determinants of the policies and of the cooperation on Africa-related issues have very little to do with the ups and downs in the relationship between the US and the EU. Using the terminology of historical institutionalism, the Africa polices of the US and the EU, including

---

1. Hamilton, D. S. *Trump's Jacksonian Foreign Policy and its Implications for European Security*. Stockholm: The Swedish Institute of International Affairs, 2018.

their cooperation on African issues, are assumed to be "path dependent", implying they are basically determined by domestic circumstances and not by changing transatlantic relations.

This chapter is structured as follows. The next section presents the analytical framework. It is followed by a brief presentation of the Africa policies of the United States and the European Union during the period covered by the presidencies of George W. Bush (2001-2008), Barack Obama (2009-2016) and Donald Trump (2017ff). After the overview of the Africa policies, a section follows that looks into the potential impact of leadership perceptions and into the possible impact of the strategic culture on policies and cooperation between the US and the EU. The last two sections deal with state-society relations and with the role and impact of government institutions on policy-making and implementation of policies on Africa in Washington and Brussels.

The analytical framework

The chapter focuses on the possible consequences of the changeable relations between the United States and the EU on their Africa policies and on the possible consequences for the cooperation between the two powers on Africa related issues. The analysis focuses on the domestic determinants of the Africa policies of the US and the EU. The explanatory variables related to the Africa polices of the United States and the European Union as well as to their possible cooperation on Africa related issues are the following. First, the perceptions among leading decision-makers of the transatlantic relationship and of Africa's position in international politics are assumed to be of importance. Closely linked to the question of perceptions, it is assumed that the position of Africa in the strategic cultures of the US and the European Union may have an impact on the Africa policies. Second, the relations between state and society are assumed to have an impact when it comes to African issues and to transatlantic relations. Third, domestic government institutions involved in decision-making and in policy implementation are important explanatory variables.

Briefly, the Africa policies and the cooperation between Washington and Brussels are the dependent variables, whereas perceptions, state-society relations and domestic institutions are the independent variables. The research focuses on identifying indicators that can help explaining the Africa policies and/or cooperation or lack of cooperation between the US and the

EU. In the following analysis, a number of explanatory hypotheses are attached to the independent variables.

The Africa policies of the United States and the European Union

The terrorist attacks on New York in 2001 radically changed the strategic perception of Africa among decision-makers in Washington and increasingly, they emphasized that the US had national security interests in Africa. In particular, it was argued there was a need to fight Islamist radicalization and terrorism on the continent.[2] The priority to fighting terrorism and radicalization led to the launch of a number of anti-terrorism programs covering both the Horn of Africa/East Africa and West Africa/the Sahel. Military training programs and funding of African armed forces became important components in the Africa policy following September 2001.[3]

With the growing priority of Africa followed significant increases in the American military infrastructure on the continent. The establishment of a permanent base in Djibouti in 2002 was followed by a number of outposts such as camps, port facilities and fuel bunkers in no less than 34 African countries. In addition to the establishment of such more or less permanent bases, US Special Operations Command launched two military training programs for the region: 'Operation Enduring Freedom-Trans Sahara' aimed at training African forces and 'Operation Flintlock' to jointly exercise US troops with African forces.[4] Not only have the US and states in West Africa participated in these exercises, France and other European countries have also joined the training.[5]

When Donald Trump assumed office in January 2017, it soon became clear that not only Africa in general but specifically development aid to the continent had low priority for the new administration. The Trump administration did not appoint ambassadors to a number of African countries

---

2. White House *The National Security Strategy of the United States of America*. Washington: White House, 2002; Schraeder, P.J. *The Africa Dimension in US Foreign Policy in the Post 9/11 Era*. Paper prepared for the IV Flad-IPRI International Conference on 'Strategy and Security in Southern Africa', October 12-13, 2006.
3. Olsen, G. Rye "Fighting terrorism in Africa by proxy: the USA and the European Union in Somalia and Mali". In *European Security*. Vol. 23, No. 3, 2014, 290-306.
4. Burgess, S.F. "Comparative challenges in securing the Horn of Africa and Sahara". In *Comparative Strategy*. Vol. 34, No. 2, 2015, 211.
5. Cochi, M. "AFRICOM kick-off Operation Flintlock to counter Jihadism in Africa". 2016. [Consulted at: March, 12, 2019]. Available at: http://www.estonline.eu/en/opinion/sub-saharan-monitor/africom-kicks-off-operation

and the request for foreign aid from Congress for the fiscal year 2018 reflected a 35% decrease from the 2015 aid levels. The reduced aid was to be focused on countries that had the strongest strategic significance to the United States, amplifying the ongoing militarization of American foreign aid policy.[6] In the wake of the killings of four American soldiers in Niger in late 2017, it was estimated that 6,000-7,000 military personnel were assigned to Africa.[7]

The launch of the Trump administration's Africa Strategy in December 2018 signaled a change from the strong focus on fighting terrorism towards a focus on countering Chinese and Russian influence on the continent. The Africa Strategy also indicated a more unobtrusive approach to Africa violent conflicts as well as to the development challenges of the continent. Most importantly, the Pentagon stated it planned to reduce the number of US troops in Africa by 10% by the end of 2020.[8] The Africa policy of the Trump administration seemed to send a signal that the US would reduce its involvement on the continent. Nevertheless, during 2018 and the first months of 2019, the US armed forces stepped up their attacks on terrorists in Somalia alongside it strengthened American focus on the alleged rise in piracy in the waters around the Horn of Africa.[9]

As far as the European Union and Africa is concerned, until the end of the 1990s relations between the two continents were mainly conceived in development terms within the framework of the EU-ACP relations. Maurizio Carbone argues that the close relationship based on development assistance can be interpreted in two different ways. Either, it can be seen as an example of successful cooperation between the two parties based on mutual cooperation and equality. Or it may be perceived as a system maintaining the inequality between the two parties where Africa supplies raw materials and Africa is a market for manufactured products from Europe.[10]

---

6. Signé, L. & Allen, N.D.F. "Trump's Africa policy takes form with focus on security (and China)". In *The Hill*, March 19, 2018.
7. Savitsky, A. "US military presence in Africa: All over the continent and still expanding". 2018. [Consulted at: March, 12, 2019]. Available at: https://www.strategic-culture.org/news/2018/08/30/us-military-presence-in-africa-all-over-continent-still-expanding.html)
8. Schmitt, E. "Where terrorism is rising in Africa and the US is leaving". In *The New York Times*, March 1, 2019.
9. Schmitt, E. & SAVAGE, C. "Trump administration steps up air war in Somalia". In *The New York Times*, 10 March, 2019.
10. Carbone, M. "EU-Africa relations in the twenty-first century: evolution and explanations". In *The European Union in Africa. Incoherent policies, asymmetrical partnership, declining relevance?*. Manchester: Manchester University Press, 2013. 8.

In the current century, the European Union's development aid policy towards Africa has been framed by the Contonou agreement signed in 2000. The new agreement led to comprehensive reforms of the collaboration arrangement.[11] Among the new areas of cooperation were peace, security, migration and good governance.[12] The adoption of these new policy areas reflected the strong European focus on violent conflicts in Africa that started to influence the EU's Africa policy in the 1990s. The terrorist attacks on the United States in September 2001 made a huge impact on decision-makers in Europe and in the European Union and contributed to prioritizing security issues.

The strong attention to security promotion and to fighting terrorism reflected the European Union was increasingly preoccupied with defending the interests of 'Europe'.[13] The European Union's 'Global Strategy' launched in 2016 stressed the importance of the security linkages between Africa and the European Union. It was stated, "we will continue to support peace and security efforts in African Organizations' work on conflict prevention, counterterrorism and organized crime, migration and border management".[14]

The attention to security promotion in Africa manifested itself most clearly in the EU's military involvement on the continent and in the launch of a number of military training missions starting with Somalia and following by Mali and the Central African Republic (CAR). The take-over of power in Northern Mali by radical Islamist groups in 2012 led to a comprehensive European Union involvement together with bilateral European engagements in the country. The deployment in January 2013 of 4,000 French soldiers to fight the Islamists opened the way for an extended EU involvement in Mali within the framework of the EU's comprehensive approach to crisis management.[15]

When a violent crisis broke out in the Central African Republic (CAR) in late 2012, the EU gave high priority to solving the crisis. The EU became the largest donor of humanitarian emergency assistance and together

---

11. Carbone, M. "The European Union and International development". In *International Relations and the European Union*. Oxford: Oxford University Press, 2017, 293.
12. *Ibid*: 300.
13. *Ibid*: 312; 308.
14. EU *Shared Vision, Common Action: A Stronger Europe. A Global Strategy for the European Union's Common Foreign and Security Policy*. Brussels, 2016, 36.
15. Furness, M. & Olsen, G. M. "Europeanisation and the EU's comprehensive approach to crisis management in Africa". In *European Politics and Society*. Vol. 17, No. 1, 2016, 5-6.

with the member states, the EU supported financially an African led UN peace mission aimed at restoring security in the CAR. The most conspicuous EU initiative was the commitment to deploy a significant number of European troops in a mission (EUFOR-RCA) aimed at contributing to the stability in the country.[16]

With the increased military involvement by the European Union, the 'migration crisis' in 2015 turned the EU's attention to migration and to migration from Africa to Europe in particular. The EU launched a number of initiatives aimed at significantly reducing the flow of people from Africa seeking to enter the European Union. By July 2016, the EU had established a permanent mission in Agadez in Niger which should assist building Niger's capacity to prevent migration. The changes in the EU's policy in Niger were in line with the EU's broader responses to the migration crisis which gave increasing emphasis to security and capacity building to prevent the movement of people.[17]

In sum, the above description showed an increasing American military involvement in Africa in the years following September 2001. The continent was important as a component in the United States' global war on terror and for Washington training and cooperation with local security forces was crucial policy instrument. In the same period, the European Union became increasingly involved militarily on the continent. In spite both the United States and the European Union shared the same security goals in Africa apparently, it only led to limited cooperation between the two actors. Interestingly, the cooperation between the US and the EU was most pronounced when it came to fighting piracy around the Horn of Africa and in the Gulf of Guinea.

On the other hand, it is not to be overlooked that the violent crises in the Sahel led to cooperation between the armed forces of the United States and the French military.[18]

---

16. *Ibib*: 10-12.
17. Lebovich, A. *Halting Ambition: EU Migration and Security Policy in the Sahel*. Brussels: ECFR, 2018. 5-10.
18. Olsen, G. Rye "Transatlantic cooperation on terrorism and Islamist radicalization in Africa: The Franco-American axis". In *European Security*. Vol. 27, No. 1, 2018, 41-57.

Perceptions of Africa among foreign policy makers and the strategic culture in the US and the EU

Perceptions of core foreign policy decision-makers are important. It is the hypothesis that such perceptions may lead to decisions that may or may not be implemented. Perceptions are reflected in public statements, speeches and declarations by relevant decision-makers and are important for understanding policy decisions. When it comes to foreign policy decisions, the strategic culture of a country is assumed to contribute to framing and influencing decisions on foreign and security politics. In particular, the strategic culture is expected to constrain a state's foreign policy behavior.[19] As far as Africa is concerned, the continent has never been central to American security and thereby to American strategic culture.[20] In comparison, Richard Whitman and Toni Haastrup argue that within the strategic culture of the EU, Africa is much more important in relation to impacting European Union decisions towards Africa. The impact is indicated by three factors namely the security-development nexus, the human security imperative and the preference for local enforcement i.e. a preference for using African troops to perform military operations.[21]

Donald Trump's idea of 'America First' reflects a strongly isolationist vision for US foreign policy. The vision is against the United States committing itself to obligations abroad like in Africa, the Paris Climate Accord or giving development aid etc.[22] When Donald Trump entered the White House as the 45th US president, it was clear from the beginning that Africa was not among the top priorities of the new administration. Not only did the new president refer to Africa as 'shithole countries'.[23] It took more than a year and a half year to appoint a new Assistant Secretary for Africa

19. Ripsman, N.M., Taliafarro, J.W., Lobell, S.E. (eds.) *Neoclassical Realist Theory of International Politics*. Oxford: Oxford University Press, 2016, 67.
20. Keller, E.J. "US-Africa Relations and AFRICOM: Possibility, Problem and Limitation". In *US-Africa Relations from Clinton to Obama*. Lanham: Lexington Books, 2014, 62.; Schraeder, P.J. *United States foreign policy towards Africa. Incrementalism, crisis and change*. Cambridge: Cambridge University Press, 1995, 12-13; Woodward, P. *US foreign policy and the Horn of Africa*. Abingdon: Ashgate, 2015.
21. Whitman, R. & Haastrup, T. "Locating the EU's strategic behavior in sub-Saharan Arica: an emerging strategic culture?". In *The European Union in Africa. Incoherent policies, asymmetrical partnerships, declining relevance?* Manchester: Manchester University Press, 2013, 61.
22. Hamilton, D. S. *Trump's Jacksonian Foreign Policy and its Implications for European Security*. Stockholm: The Swedish Institute of International Affairs, 2018, 3-4.
23. Vitali, A. et al. "White house/ President Trump". 2018. [Consulted at: March, 12, 2019]. Available at: https://nbcnews.com/politics/white-house/trump-referred-haiti-african-countries-shithole-nations-n836946

(Gavin 2018). Likewise, it took almost two years to appoint ambassadors to important African countries like South Africa.

After two years in office, the Trump administration in December 2018 issued its Africa Strategy that emphasized the importance of countering the rapidly expanding financial and political influence of China and Russia on the continent.[24] Instead of prioritizing the war on terror and Islamist radicalization, great power competition became a core focus of the Trump administration's Africa policy. In spite of the announcement of a 10% cut in the number of US military forces on the ground in Africa, the administration maintained that the fight against terrorism was crucial and cooperation with African armed forces was still important to Washington.[25]

In this context, it is important that the new President did not believe in maintaining old alliances or friendships,[26] implying that the US should not bother about other nations, their interests or their points of view. As far as the transatlantic relationship and in particular the relationship between the US and the European Union is concerned, the EU was hardly mentioned in the 2018 'National Security Strategy'.[27] If the signals from the National Security Strategy concerning the transatlantic relationship can be characterized as mixed, the policy signals sent by Donald Trump were much clearer as far as he described the European Union a 'foe' of the United States.

Since the 2000 Africa-EU Cairo summit, there has been the 'Africa-EU process' where the two regions have met on a regular basis to discuss issues of common interest. The perceptions of the policy-makers in Brussels are reflected in a number of official EU documents and strategies following the start of the process. At the second Africa-EU summit held in Lisbon in 2007, it was decided to launch the 'Joint Africa-EU Strategy' (JAES) stressing the importance of Security. The priorities in the JAES were specified in two regional strategies, one for the Horn of Africa and one for the Sahel respectively. The Horn of Africa strategy identified migration, terrorism

---

24. White House *President Donald J. Trump's Africa Strategy Advances Prosperity, Security and Stability*. Washington: White House, 2018.2018/17

25. Bolton, J. *Remarks by National Security Advisor Ambassador John R. Bolton on the Trump Administration's New Africa Strategy*. Washington: National Security Council, 2018.

26. Brands, H. 'The Unexceptional Superpower: American Grand Strategy in the Age of Trump'. In *Survival*. Vol. 59, No 6, 2017-18, 16.

27. Smith, J. & Rizzo, R. 'Trump's War on Europe Is Revving Up'. In *Foreign Policy*, March 9, 2018, 1-2.

and criminalization including piracy as threats to European security [28]. The Sahel Strategy stated its aim was to improve "security and development (which) has an obvious and direct impact on protecting European citizens and interests…".[29] In 2016 the 'EU Global Strategy" was launched, which underscored the EU's preoccupation with conflict prevention, counterterrorism and organized crime, migration and border management.[30]

Summing up, the Trump administration did not consider Africa important to the interests of the United States and therefore, cooperation with the European Union on African issues was not important to American Africa policy. The low priority was illustrated by the lack of appointments of persons to important policy-making positions related to Africa. In contrast to these perceptions, Africa was perceived a major challenge to the European Union. In recent years the continent had not been considered a development issue. Rather, violent conflicts, migration and terrorism had become main concerns that called for action by the Europeans. In principle, these issues called for cooperation with the Americans as could have been the case in relation to the crises in Mali and the CAR. On the other hand, it is not to be neglected that there was some kind of cooperation between the US and the EU when it came to fighting piracy off the coasts of Africa.

Africa and state-society relations in the US and in the EU

The character of the relationship between the government and the surrounding society is supposed to be important because it may influence decision-making as well as implementation of government policy decisions. Harmony or polarization are two keywords for understanding the relationship between government and society. As a start, there has not been much public debate on American's policies towards Africa and therefore not much disagreement. To the contrary, Africa policy has been a bipartisan issue. It has been helped along because there has not been a big constituency for Africa in the US, which has set clear limits for the constituency to influence American policy-making on the continent. The so-called black voice has historically been very weak and non-influential largely to be explained

---

28. EU COUNCIL *A EU Policy on the Horn of Africa Towards a Comprehensive EU Strategy*. Brussels, 2009.

29. EEAS *Strategy for security and development in the Sahel*. Brussels: EEAS, 2011.

30. EU *Shared Vision, Common Action: A Stronger Europe. A Global Strategy for the European Union's Common Foreign and Security Policy*. Brussels, 2016.

by the absence of an organized constituency capable of working within the American policy-making establishment.[31]

In the wake of 9/11, evangelical Christians showed a growing interest in the foreign affairs of the USA leading to attempts to launch initiatives aimed at fighting global poverty especially in Africa.[32] From the start of his presidency, George W. Bush was under great influence from religious groups that were well represented in and around Washington DC.[33] It is one thing that the President was committed to evangelical Christianity, but approximately 40% of the Republican Presidential vote in 2000 came from white evangelical Christians,[34] stressing that there was a domestic constituency for an active American policy towards Africa including violent conflicts like for example Southern Sudan and Darfur in Sudan.[35]

A number of evangelical non-governmental organizations were putting pressure on the White House often in alliance with Catholics and the Congressional Black Caucus. These different groups came together in a loose grouping known as the 'Freedom House Coalition'.[36] The advocacy groups were successful in influencing Congress on issues related to Africa. The increase in the development aid budget under George W. Bush was partly a response to evangelist demands and the content in the US program on AIDS was heavily influenced by the President's evangelical backers.[37] Also, many members of Congress were open to act on issues based on moral values and therefore, they were willing to react to African topics and issues based on a sense of "we can make a difference". [38] Apparently, the influence of faith-based groups did not weaken during the years of the Obama administration; on the contrary, these groups and their attitudes were gaining influence "increasingly within the US foreign policy apparatus".[39]

31. Schraeder, P.J. *United States foreign policy towards Africa. Incrementalism, crisis and change*. Cambridge: Cambridge University Press, 1995, 45.
32. Huliaras, A. "The evangelical roots of US Africa policy". In *Survival*. Vol. 50. No. 6, 2008-09, 163.
33. Woodward, P. *US foreign policy and the Horn of Africa*. Abingdon: Ashgate, 2015, 114.
34. Ibid, 113.
35. Budabin, A.C. "Diasporas as Development Partners for Peace? The Alliance between the Darfuri Diaspora and the Save Darfur Coalition". In *Third World Quarterly*. Vol. 35, No 1, 2014, 170.
36. Woodward, P. *US foreign policy and the Horn of Africa*. Abingdon: Ashgate, 2015, 144.
37. Huliaras, A. "The evangelical roots of US Africa policy". In *Survival*. Vol. 50. No. 6, 2008-09, 165.
38. Ibid, 174.; personal interview Washington 19 March 2015.
39. Marsden "Bush, Obama and a faith-based US foreign policy". In *International Affairs*. Vol. 88, No. 5, 2012, 953, 955.

In contrast to the Africa policy field, the US political system in general has been characterized by polarization, which has for several decades affected foreign policy-making as legislators in the center have disappeared, leading to the elimination of any overlap between liberal republicans and conservative democrats. According to Nathaniel Persily, the most important consequence of the polarization of the American political system is that it has led to 'gridlock', which refers to "the inability of the system to perform basic policy-making functions and that the political polarization discourages compromise and fosters mistrust.[40] As indicated, the gridlock has not hit US Africa policy, probably due to its bipartisan nature, but also due to the remarkable influence of the evangelical groups. The lack of policy initiatives towards Africa under President Trump is thus not an expression of gridlock or that the evangelical groups did not support Donald Trump at the election in 2016. Rather, it is a reflection of remarkably limited presidential interest in the continent.

As far as state-society relations within the European Union are concerned, in a number of European countries there has been some political attention to Africa and to development issues and thus to development assistance in Africa. It has been particularly clear in France, the UK and in a limited number of countries in North and North-Western Europe.[41] With the increasing merger of policy-making on development assistance and general foreign policy and security issues, it became clear that the common European policy initiatives towards Africa were largely elite-driven.[42] Moreover, the split between the member states and Brussels and the two-level institutional decision-making structure within the European Union have complicated and inhibited the influence of civil society organizations on EU decision-making. The separation between the two levels and the general political polarization within the European Union known as 'Euro-skepticism' directed towards policy-making in Brussels makes it difficult to demonstrate the kind and degree of influence from the civil society.

40. Persily, N. "Introduction". In *Solutions to Political Polarization in America*. Cambridge: Cambridge University Press, 2015, 4.; Thurber, J.A. & A. Yoshinaka "Introduction". In *American gridlock: The Sources, Character and Impact of Political Polarization*. New York: Cambridge University Press, 2015, 1.
41. Hoebink, P. & Stokke, O. "Introduction: European Development Co-operations at the Beginning of a New Millennium". In *Perspectives on European Development Co-operation*. London: Routledge, 2005, 1-31.
42. Olsen, G.R. "The European Union's Development Policy: Shifting Priorities in a Rapidly Changing World". In *Perspectives on European Development Cooperation. Policy and performance of individual donor countries and the EU*. Abingdon: Routledge, 2005, 603-405, 577.

Summing up, it appears quite clear that faith-based organizations have influenced American Africa policy. Apparently, these organizations did not pay attention to the European Union or to the prospects of cooperation between the US and the EU. As far as the European Union and its Africa policy is concerned, decision-making is largely elite-driven. In these processes, there are no indications that the participants paid special attention to the United States or to the possibility of cooperating with Washington on African issues.

Africa and domestic government institutions

Government institutions are important, as they may affect both decision-making and implementation of policy decisions. Inspired by the theory of 'bureaucratic politics', it is the hypothesis that decision-making processes and implementation in Washington as well as in Brussels may be influenced by institutional interests and not only by general policy directives. In the case of the United States, the Pentagon tended to argue in favor of initiatives that relied heavily on military instruments whereas the Department of State has preferred soft and diplomatic means in its policy advice.[43] Historically, US Africa policy has been characterized by limited input from the President and from the White House[44] and therefore much policy input has had to come from government bureaucracies, illustrating the possible relevance of the hypothesis that bureaucratic and institutional interests may influence decision-making in Washington. In particular, the State Department and the Pentagon have been prominent in policy-making and for that reason, US Africa policy has been described as the result of 'bureaucratic incrementalism'.[45]

When Donald Trump came into power in January 2017, his first Secretary of State Rex Tillerson started making dramatic cuts in the number of employees leading to significant reductions in the number of experienced insightful experts and advisors. Data from the American Foreign Service Association showed that 60% of the State Department's highest-ranking career officers quit during Trump's first year. Fewer than half of all top-level positions that require confirmation by the US Senate were filled by April

43. Schraeder, P.J. *United States foreign policy towards Africa. Incrementalism, crisis and change*. Cambridge: Cambridge University Press, 1995.
44. *Ibid*, pp. 12-15.; Woodward, P. *US foreign policy and the Horn of Africa*. Abingdon: Ashgate, 2015.
45. Schraeder, P.J. *United States foreign policy towards Africa. Incrementalism, crisis and change*. Cambridge: Cambridge University Press, 1995.

2018. Vital posts such as ambassadors in Egypt and South Africa were not filled. The State Department was in a situation where it was described as "dysfunctional" and "brought to the brink of ruin by Trump and Tillerson in equal parts".[46]

The appointment of Mike Pompeo in March 2018 did nothing to change the situation, rather to the contrary. By the time, Pompeo came into the State Department, Ronan Farrow concluded "the State Department is simply wiped out.......".[47] The result of the dramatic reductions in the State Department was that it was increasingly difficult for its staff to access the President and in general to influence the policy processes in this case towards Africa. The Trump administration's general lack of interest in Africa left the Pentagon in a position where it was forced to take responsibility for policy-making. The pressure on the Pentagon to lead policy-making on Africa was supported by the increasing funding the Department received under Trump.[48]

Apparently, bureaucratic policy-making continued during the first two years of the Trump administration, but importantly without the traditional input from the State Department. This demonstration was backed by the sudden increase in the US air war in Somalia during the last four months of 2018 and continuing into 2019. On the face of it, it seems difficult to explain the surge considering the signal of the Africa Strategy to change of focus of the American Africa policy from fighting terrorism in Africa towards countering China and Russia.[49] On the other hand, the increase in attacks on terrorists in Somalia indicated the independent decision-making influence of the Pentagon continued under the leadership of James Mattis. The strong praise of the G5 Sahel alliance by National Security Advisor John Bolton as "a great example of the enormous potential of African joint security cooperation". Bolton also had a remarkable influence on the funding of the G5 Sahel force when the US blocked the Security Council resolution that would have given the force a mandate under the UN Charter's

46. Beaucamp, Z. 'The State Department's collapse as explained by Rex Tillerson'. In *Vox. Com.* April 19, 2018.; Farrow, R. *War on Peace. The End of Diplomacy and the Decline of American Influence.* London: William Collins, 2018, 295.
47. Ibid; Pesca, M. 'The Trump administration is decimating the State Department'. In *Slate.* April 24, 2018.
48. Ward, A. 'Why does the Pentagon keep getting surprised by Trump?'. In *Vox.com,* 25 June, 2018.
49. Schmitt, E. & Savage, C. "Trump administration steps up air war in Somalia". In *The New York Times,* 10 March, 2019.

Chapter VII. Such a mandate would have shifted the financial burden from France and the EU onto the United States.[50]

The European foreign policy policy-making system appears complex in comparison to the American one. On the one hand, there are the Brussels-based institutions -- the Council of Ministers, the European Commission and the European External Action Service (EEAS), each with its specific institutional interests. No doubt, the Commission and the EEAS try to promote common 'European' notions and interests, whereas the Council of Ministers due to its nature pays more attention to the concerns of the member states. As far as the member states are concerned, they generally prefer decisions on foreign and security policy to remain the prerogative of national capitals. In recent years, there has been dramatic changes and developments in these configurations involving not only individual and prominent member states like France. The European Commission has also increasingly been involved in European Union decision-making on Africa. The same has been the case for the Secretariat in the Council of Ministers and the EEAS in relation to foreign policy-making on African issues.[51]

The involvement of these institutional actors may contribute to explain the EU decision to get involved in Somalia in 2006-07. The support to AMISOM on land and the launch of the naval operation 'Atalanta' suggested that a number of EU member states and increasingly the Commission[52] shared the ambition of enhancing the visibility of the European Union as a niche security provider in Africa.[53] On the other hand, the extended EU involvement in Mali following the unilateral French intervention in January 2013 illustrates that not only the institutions located in Brussels but a number of prominent member states like France and Germany articulated common European security concerns in Africa.

---

50. Fernandez, M. *West Africa: Bolton's risky bet in the Sahel*. Atlantic Council Africa Center: Washington DC, 2019.
51. Riddervold, M. & Trondal, J. "Integrating nascent organisations. On the settlement of the European External Action Service". In *Journal of European Integration*. Vol. 39, No. 1, 2017; Riddervold, M. "(Not) in the Hands of the member States: How the European Commission Influences EU Security and Defense Policies". In *Journal of Common Market Studies*. Vol. 54, No. 2, 2016, 353-369.; Riddervold, M. "New threats different response: EU and NATO and Somali piracy". In *European Security*. Vol. 23, No. 4, 2014, 546-564.
52. Riddervold, M. "New threats different response: EU and NATO and Somali piracy". In *European Security*. Vol. 23, No. 4, 2014, 546-564.
53. Oksamytna, K. *The European Union Training mission in Somalia. Lessons learnt for EU security sector reform*. Roma: Instituto Affari Internazionali, 2011, 12.

The ambition of the EU to take responsibility as a security provider in Africa was emphasized by the launch of an EU military training mission in Mali and another one in Niger, clearly reflecting the depth of the concerns over the growing threat from Islamic militancy in the Sahel. This new and proactive role manifested itself in relation to solving the crisis in the Central African Republic (CAR) that broke out in late 2012. The protracted EU decision-making process related to the crisis in the CAR illustrates the challenges involved in the two-level decision-making system of the EU. It is worth noting that the decision to deploy European troops in the CAR was different from the situation in Mali. In the CAR case, the decision only came after the involvement of some member states and in particular after heavy political pressure from France supported by Germany.[54]

Summing up, the statement of Peter Schraeder that US Africa policy generally is the result of 'bureaucratic incrementalism' seems to be confirmed by developments in the current century, not least the heavy military involvement on the continent that lasted until the Trump administration came into power. On the other hand, the lack of interest in and priority of Africa from the Presidency of Donald Trump has resulted in a general lack of policy initiatives towards the continent, including absence of cooperation with the European Union. The Africa policy of the European Union can also (but to a lesser extent than American policy) be explained with reference to bureaucratic and institutional interests as well as political interests in establishing international visibility for the European Union. Neither the bureaucratic interests in the US nor the mix of 'European', bureaucratic and national interests in European Union seem to have argued in favor of cooperation with the United States on Africa-related issues.

Conclusion

This chapter asked if the recurring conflicts and crises in the transatlantic relationship have affected the Africa policies of the United States and the European Union. It also asked if these tensions in the transatlantic relationship affected the cooperation between the US and the EU on African issues. The conclusion to both questions is identical, namely that the transatlantic relationship has not affected either the Africa policies of the two Western powers or the cooperation between them. The analysis

---

54. Furness, M. & Olsen, G. M. "Europeanisation and the EU's comprehensive approach to crisis management in Africa". In *European Politics and Society*. Vol. 17, No. 1, 2016, 115.

indicated that the absence of an impact from the changeable transatlantic relationship in both respects has to be explained with reference to domestic circumstances.

Among these circumstances, it has to be emphasized that the perceptions of Africa in Washington and in Brussels have been that the continent is of limited importance and therefore, the perception of the value of cooperation between the actors is that it is equally limited. Looking at state-society relations in the US and within the European Union as possible explanations to the Africa policies and to the lack of cooperation between the two actors, the analysis suggests that this element only contributes somewhat to answering the two questions. Finally, the domestic government institutions and their institutional interests do not supply the explanations asked for. In brief, all three explanatory elements points towards domestic circumstances as explanations to the Africa policies as well as to the limited cooperation between the United States and the EU on Africa. Thereby, the three elements buttress the conclusion that the transatlantic relationship has had no strong impact on the two issues discussed here.

References

Beaucamp, Z. 'The State Department's collapse as explained by Rex Tillerson'. In *Vox. Com*. April 19, 2018.

Bolton, J. *Remarks by National Security Advisor Ambassador John R. Bolton on the Trump Administration's New Africa Strategy*. Washington: National Security Council, 2018.

Brands, H. 'The Unexceptional Superpower: American Grand Strategy in the Age of Trump'. In *Survival*. Vol. 59, No 6, 2017-18, 7-40.

Budabin, A.C. "Diasporas as Development Partners for Peace? The Alliance between the Darfuri Diaspora and the Save Darfur Coalition". In *Third World Quarterly*. Vol. 35, No 1, 2014, 163-180.

Burgess, S.F. "Comparative challenges in securing the Horn of Africa and Sahara". In *Comparative Strategy*. Vol. 34, No. 2, 2015, 202-217.

Carbone, M. "EU-Africa relations in the twenty-first century: evolution and explanations". In *The European Union in Africa. Incoherent policies, asymmetrical partnership, declining relevance?*. Manchester: Manchester University Press, 2013. 3-21.

Carbone, M. "The European Union and International development". In *International Relations and the European Union*. Oxford: Oxford University Press, 2017. 292-315.

Cochi, M. "AFRICOM kick-off Operation Flintlock to counter Jihadism in Africa". 2016. [Consulted at: 21 January 2019]. Available at: http://www.eston-line.eu/en/opinion/sub-saharan-monitor/africom-kicks-off-operation

EEAS *Strategy for security and development in the Sahel*. Brussels: EEAS, 2011.

EU *Shared Vision, Common Action: A Stronger Europe. A Global Strategy for the European Union's Common Foreign and Security Policy*. Brussels, 2016.

EU COUNCIL *A EU Policy on the Horn of Africa Towards a Comprehensive EU Strategy*. Brussels, 2009.

Farrow, R. *War on Peace. The End of Diplomacy and the Decline of American Influence*. London: William Collins, 2018.

Fernandez, M. *West Africa: Bolton's risky bet in the Sahel*. Atlantic Council Africa Center: Washington DC, 2019.

Furness, M. & Olsen, G. M. "Europeanisation and the EU's comprehensive approach to crisis management in Africa". In *European Politics and Society*. Vol. 17, No. 1, 2016, 105-119.

Hamilton, D. S. *Trump's Jacksonian Foreign Policy and its Implications for European Security*. Stockholm: The Swedish Institute of International Affairs, 2018.

Hoebink, P. & Stokke, O. "Introduction: European Development Co-operations at the Beginning of a New Millennium". In *Perspectives on European Development Co-operation*. London: Routledge, 2005, 1-31.

Huliaras, A. "The evangelical roots of US Africa policy". In *Survival*. Vol. 50. No. 6, 2008-09, 161-182.

Keller, E.J. "US-Africa Relations and AFRICOM: Possibility, Problem and Limitation". In *US-Africa Relations from Clinton to Obama*. Lanham: Lexington Books, 2014.

Lebovich, A. *Halting Ambition: EU Migration and Security Policy in the Sahel*. Brussels: ECFR, 2018.

Marsden "Bush, Obama and a faith-based US foreign policy". In *International Affairs*. Vol. 88, No. 5, 2012, 953-947.

NNS *National Security Strategy of the United States of America*. Washington: The White House, 2017.

Oksamytna, K. *The European Union Training mission in Somalia. Lessons learnt for EU security sector reform*. Roma: Instituto Affari Internazionali, 2011

Olsen, G. Rye "Fighting terrorism in Africa by proxy: the USA and the European Union in Somalia and Mali". In *European Security*. Vol. 23, No. 3, 2014, 290-306.

Olsen, G. Rye "Transatlantic cooperation on terrorism and Islamist radicalization in Africa: The Franco-American axis". In *European Security*. Vol. 27, No. 1, 2018, 41-57.

Olsen, G.R. "The European Union's Development Policy: Shifting Priorities in a Rapidly Changing World". In *Perspectives on European Development Cooperation. Policy and performance of individual donor countries and the EU*. Abingdon: Routledge, 2005. 573-608.

Persily, N. "Introduction". In *Solutions to Political Polarization in America*. Cambridge: Cambridge University Press, 2015. 3-14.

Pesca, M. 'The Trump administration is decimating the State Department'. In *Slate*. April 24, 2018.

Riddervold, M. "(Not) in the Hands of the member States: How the European Commission Influences EU Security and Defense Policies". In *Journal of Common Market Studies*. Vol. 54, No. 2, 2016, 353-369.

Riddervold, M. "New threats different response: EU and NATO and Somali piracy". In *European Security*. Vol. 23, No. 4, 2014, 546-564.

Riddervold, M. & Trondal, J. "Integrating nascent organisations. On the settlement of the European External Action Service". In *Journal of European Integration*. Vol. 39, No. 1, 2017, 33-47.

Ripsman, N.M., Taliafarro, J.W., Lobell, S.E. (eds.) *Neoclassical Realist Theory of International Politics*. Oxford: Oxford University Press, 2016.

Savitsky, A. "US military presence in Africa: All over the continent and still expanding". 2018. [Consulted at: 21 January 2019]. Available at: https://www.strategic-culture.org/news/2018/08/30/us-military-presence-in-africa-all-over-continent-still-expanding.html)

Schmitt, E. "Where terrorism is rising in Africa and the US is leaving". In *The New York Times*, March 1, 2019.

Schmitt, E. & Savage, C. "Trump administration steps up air war in Somalia". In *The New York Times*, 10 March, 2019.

Schraeder, P.J. *The Africa Dimension in US Foreign Policy in the Post 9/11 Era*. Paper prepared for the IV Flad-IPRI International Conference on 'Strategy and Security in Southern Africa', October 12-13, 2006.

Schraeder, P.J. *United States foreign policy towards Africa. Incrementalism, crisis and change*. Cambridge: Cambridge University Press, 1995.

Signé, L. & Allen, N.D.F. "Trump's Africa policy takes form with focus on security (and China)". In *The Hill*, March 19, 2018.

Smith, J. & Rizzo, R. 'Trump's War on Europe Is Revving Up'. In *Foreign Policy*, March 9, 2018.

Thurber, J.A. & A. Yoshinaka "Introduction". In *American gridlock: The Sources, Character and Impact of Political Polarization*. New York: Cambridge University Press, 2015. 1-16.

Vitali, A. et al. "White house/ President Trump". 2018. [Consulted at: 21 January 2019]. Available at: https://nbcnews.com/politics/white-house/trump-referred-haiti-african-countries-shithole-nations-n836946

Ward, A. 'Why does the Pentagon keep getting surprised by Trump?'. In *Vox.com*, 25 June, 2018.

White House *President Donald J. Trump's Africa Strategy Advances Prosperity, Security and Stability*. Washington: White House, 2018.

White House *The National Security Strategy of the United States of America*. Washington: White House, 2002

Whitman, R. & Haastrup, T. "Locating the EU's strategic behavior in sub-Saharan Arica: an emerging strategic culture?". In *The European Union in Africa. Incoherent policies, asymmetrical partnerships, declining relevance?*. Manchester: Manchester University Press, 2013. 77-97.

Woodward, P. *US foreign policy and the Horn of Africa*. Abingdon: Ashgate, 2015.

Chapter 10

Climate Change Governance in the Atlantic Basin: The Cases of the United States, the European Union, and Brazil

Joana Castro Pereira

Emerging from the scale and speed of human interferences on the Earth system, climate change is potentially the most pressing dimension of the global environmental crisis facing the planet. The magnitude of the threat—and recognition of humanity's dominant role in destabilizing the global climate—poses profound questions about the current human development paradigm and widely accepted values and beliefs.[1]

Climate change is a "super wicked" problem, involving virtually all aspects of a country's domestic policy—water, energy, food, land use, development, transportation, trade, investment, housing, security, etc. In addition, solving the climate crisis requires massive, unparalleled collective action and global cooperation by actors with highly heterogeneous circumstances, interests, and priorities,[2] where powerful actors resisting major changes to the conventional carbon-intensive development paradigm challenge the path towards deep decarbonization of the economy.[3]

The Atlantic Basin holds some of the world's largest greenhouse gas (GHG) emitters, namely the US, the EU, Brazil, Canada, Mexico, and South Africa. Ambitious cooperation among these actors could trigger a low carbon revolution in the Atlantic[4] and encourage global climate action

1. Pereira, Joana C. "Environmental Security in the Anthropocene." In *Security at a Crossroad: New Tools for New Challenges*. New York: Nova Science Publishers, 2019, 35-54.
2. Bodansky, Daniel. "The Paris Climate Change Agreement: A New Hope?" In *American Journal of International Law*. Vol. 110, No. 2, 2016, 288-239. DOI: 10.5305/amerjintelaw.110.2.0288.
3. Viola, Eduardo; Franchini, Matías. *Brazil and Climate Change: Beyond the Amazon*. Abingdon and New York: Routledge, 2018.
4. Hamilton, Daniel. *A New Atlantic Community: Generating Growth, Human Development and Security in the Atlantic Hemisphere*. Washington, DC: Center for Transatlantic Studies, 2014.; Pelegry, Eloy A.; Isbell, Paul (Eds.). *The Future of Energy in the Atlantic Basin*. Washington, DC: The German Marshall Fund of the United States, 2012.; Kotschwar, Barbara. *North-South Rebalancing. The Role of Innovation, Technology Transfer, and Sharing of Best Practices*. Washington, DC: The German Marshall Fund of the United States.

towards stabilization of the Earth's climate. Nevertheless, all these actors face challenges that hinder their capacity to implement truly ambitious climate policies and act as effective leaders in this domain.

This chapter sheds light on the political constraints hindering deep decarbonization and climate leadership in the US, the EU, and Brazil, the world's current second, third, and seventh largest emitters,[5] respectively, together accounting for approximately 25% of the global GHG emissions. The chapter is divided into two sections. The first offers a brief description and analysis of global efforts to mitigate climate change from the signing of the United Nations Framework Convention on Climate Change (UNF-CCC) in 1992 to the adoption of the Paris Agreement in 2015. This review provides the necessary background for situating the US, the EU, and Brazil in the context of global climate negotiations. The second section presents and analyzes the domestic and foreign climate policies of the three Atlantic actors from 1992 to the present day.

The Global Governance of Climate Change

Global efforts to fight the threat of climate change began in 1992, at the United Nations Conference on Environment and Development, held in Rio de Janeiro, Brazil, where 154 states signed the UNFCCC, committing to pursue efforts to stabilize GHG concentrations in the atmosphere at a level that would prevent dangerous climate change. The convention recognized the historical responsibility of the developed world in causing the problem as well as the needs and special circumstances of developing countries. Under the principle of "common but differentiated responsibilities and respective capabilities" (CBDRRC), parties to the UNFCCC were divided into annexes: Annex I comprising the developed states that were members of the Organization for Economic Co-operation and Development (OECD) in 1992, plus countries with economies in transition (Europe's post-communist states), whose responsibilities include a non-binding commitment to reduce emissions; Annex II consisting only of the OECD members of Annex I, parties required to provide financial and technological resources to enable and support mitigation actions in developing countries and economies in transition; and non-Annex I including mostly developing countries,

---

5.   China is the world's largest emitter; India is the fourth; Russia and Japan are the fifth and sixth.

parties with fewer commitments. Accordingly, the North was expected to assume leadership and responsibility, making room for the South to grow.[6]

In 1997, parties to the convention adopted the Kyoto Protocol, an international climate treaty binding Annex I country parties to a global emission reduction target of 5% below 1990 levels for the 2008-2012 period. Individual emissions targets were internationally negotiated. Parties were allowed to trade emissions and establish emissions-abatement projects in other countries to reach their targets. Under the protocol, developed states were also obliged to provide new and additional financial resources to assist developing countries in their mitigation efforts.[7] The protocol entered into force in 2005. After adoption of decisions agreed in previous meetings on implementing the protocol, discussions under the climate convention focused on the post-Kyoto era.

In 2007, parties initiated negotiations either to revise the Kyoto Protocol or secure a new climate treaty in the near future. The Bali Action Plan was adopted. It recognized that avoiding dangerous anthropogenic interference with the climate system would require deeper emissions cuts at the global level, and called for enhanced mitigation commitments by developed states as well as nationally appropriate mitigation actions by developing countries.[8] Developed states argued for a new agreement binding all major emitters, including fast-growing developing countries such as China, India, and Brazil, whose emissions were increasing at a rapid pace.[9] These, however, committed to avoid legally binding emissions reduction targets that could jeopardize their economic growth and development, strongly supported continuation of the Kyoto Protocol and its rigid interpretation of the CDBRRC principle, stressing the North's historical responsibility in creating the problem.[10]

In 2009, parties signed the Copenhagen Accord, adopting a long-term goal of limiting global warming to 2 °C and establishing a system of vol-

6. United Nations. *United Nations Framework Convention on Climate Change.* FCCC/ INFORMAL/84, 1992.
7. United Nations. *Kyoto Protocol to the United Nations Framework Convention on Climate Change.* 11 December 1997.
8. UNFCCC. *Report of the Conference of the Parties on its Thirteenth Session*, held in Bali from 3 to 15 December 2007. FCCC/CP/2007/6/Add.1 of 14 March 2008.
9. Bodansky, Daniel. "The Copenhagen Climate Change Conference: A Postmortem." In *American Journal of International Law.* Vol. 104, No. 2, 2010, 230-240. DOI: 10.5305/ amerjintelaw.104.2.0230.
10. Hochstetler, Kathryn; Milkoreit, Manjana. "Emerging Powers in the Climate Negotiations: Shifting Identity Conceptions." In *Political Research Quarterly.* Vol. 67, No. 1, 2014, 224-235. DOI: 10.1177/1065912913510609.

untary pledges to fight climate change[11] that would break the "top-down" model of targets and timetables of Kyoto. Although the accord fit the view and concerns of all major emitters, its formal adoption was blocked by a small group of states including Sudan, Venezuela, and Bolivia.

In 2011, parties agreed on a second commitment period (2013-2020) to the Kyoto Protocol—fulfilling the fast-growing developing states' demand—as well as on a roadmap towards a new global climate treaty including all parties to be signed in 2015 and concluded by 2020—in line with the preferences of developed states, particularly the EU.[12]

In 2012, the Doha Amendment to the Kyoto Protocol was signed, establishing the treaty's second commitment period.[13] In 2015, parties adopted the Paris Agreement, a new universal climate treaty binding its signatories to "holding the increase in global average temperature to well below 2 °C" and "pursuing efforts to limit the temperature increase to 1.5 °C above pre-industrial levels."[14] The agreement cemented the system of voluntary pledges of the Copenhagen Accord. It entered into force in November 2016.

Despite almost three decades of global efforts to mitigate climate change, the concentration of GHGs in the atmosphere has increased significantly and at a rapid pace. In 2017, global GHG emissions were 55% higher than in 1990.[15] Extreme weather events (e.g., heatwaves, droughts, floods, hurricane activity) have intensified in all continents,[16] and global temperatures have risen beyond projections. The years between 2015 and 2018 were the warmest since 1880.[17] The Earth has already warmed by nearly 1.0 °C beyond pre-industrial levels. At current emissions rates, the global carbon

11. UNFCCC. *Report of the Conference of the Parties on its Fifteenth Session*, held in Copenhagen from 7 to 19 December 2009. FCCC/CP/2009/11/Add.1 of 30 March 2010.
12. Backstränd, Karin; Elgström, Ole. "The EU's Role in Climate Change Negotiations: From Leader to 'Leadiator'." In *Journal of European Public Policy*. Vol. 20, No. 10, 2013, 1369-1386. DOI: 10.1080/13501763.2013.781781.
13. UNFCCC. *Doha Amendment to the Kyoto Protocol*. 8 December 2012.
14. United Nations. *Paris Agreement*. 12 December 2015. (Art. 2.a).
15. Olivier, Jos G. J.; Peters, Jeroen A. H. W. *Trends in Global CO2 and Total Greenhouse Gas Emissions: 2018 Report*. The Hague: PBL Netherlands Environmental Assessment Agency.
16. AMS. Explaining Extreme Events of 2017 from a Climate Perspective. In *Bulletin of the American Meteorological Society*. Vol. 99, No. 12, 2018.
17. WMO. *"The State of the Global Climate in 2018."* 2018 [Consulted at: 19 February 2019]. Available at: https://public.wmo.int/en/our-mandate/climate/wmo-statement-state-of-global-climate.

budget to stand a reasonable chance (66%) of limiting warming to 1.5 °C and avoid dangerous climate change can be depleted by 2030.[18]

Several flaws in the design of the UNFCCC and the Kyoto Protocol hindered efforts to address climate change. First, decisions under the convention are taken by consensus. As a result, the outcomes of negotiations reflect the lowest-common-denominator.[19] Second, the UNFCCC did not set a timeframe for considering stronger commitments for non-Annex I parties, which collectively became the world's largest emitters.[20] Third, the convention's rigid annex division discouraged the formation of ambitious coalitions between developed and developing country parties sharing similar interests and concerns.[21] Fourth, the Kyoto Protocol hardened the UNFCCC's approach to differentiation and bound very few parties to mitigate climate change by exempting developing countries from cutting emissions. The protocol imposed obligations on wealthy states while not putting any constraints on their trade competitors.[22] Fifth, Kyoto's top-down imposition of absolute targets and timetables was politically unsustainable for the world's largest emitter at the time, the US—as shall be seen in the next section—and unacceptable for other major emitters such as China, India, and Brazil.[23] Sixth, by providing a very short time frame for action, the protocol did not encourage the design and implementation of ambitious climate change mitigation policies.[24]

18. IPCC. *Global Warming of 1.5 °C: An IPCC Special Report on the impacts of global warming of 1.5 °C above pre-industrial levels and related global greenhouse gas emission pathways, in the context of strengthening the global response to the threat of climate change, sustainable development, and efforts to eradicate poverty.* Geneva: WMO, 2018.
19. Keohane, Robert. O; Oppenheimer, Michael. "Paris: Beyond the Climate Dead End Through Pledge and Review?" In *Politics and Governance*. Vol. 4, No. 3, 2016, 142-151. DOI: 10.17645/pag.v4i3.634.
20. Gupta, Joyeeta. *The History of Global Climate Governance.* Cambridge and New York: Cambridge University Press, 2014.
21. Depledge, Joanna; Yamin, Farhana. "The Global Climate-change Regime: A Defence." In *The Economics and Politics of Climate Change*. Oxford and New York: Oxford University Press, 2009, 433-453.
22. Victor, David G. *Global Warming Gridlock: Creating More Effective Strategies for Protecting the Planet.* Cambridge and New York: Cambridge University Press, 2011.
23. Bodansky, Daniel. "Targets and Timetables: Good Policy but Bad Politics?" In *Architectures for Agreement: Addressing Global Climate Change in the Post-Kyoto World.* Cambridge and New York: Cambridge University Press, 2007, 57-66.
24. Rosen, Amanda M. "The Wrong Solution at the Right Time: The Failure of the Kyoto Protocol on Climate Change." In *Politics & Policy*. Vol. 43, No. 1, 2015, 30-58. DOI: 10.1111/polp.12105.

The Paris Agreement inaugurated a new era in global climate governance. The treaty does not allocate parties to annexes and is based on a new approach to differentiation, the modified principle of "common but differentiated responsibilities and respective capabilities in light of different national circumstances" (CBDRRC-NC). It recognizes the primacy of national politics. The parties' nationally determined contributions (NDCs) to fight climate change, the core of the treaty, are voluntary. Parties are allowed to define their own mitigation efforts and timings. These will take stock of collective action every five years and submit new NDCs—which are expected to represent a progression beyond current pledges and reflect each party's highest possible ambition—within two years of each global stocktaking.[25] The agreement's pledge and review system provides a more solid foundation for incremental progress than the Kyoto Protocol did. However, incremental efforts can now hardly avoid dangerous climate change. Solving the climate crisis demands immediate, radical action. In addition, the Paris Agreement suffers from severe limitations to its effectiveness. First, it avoids the fundamental issues of the allocation of responsibilities for avoiding dangerous climate change and fairness of each party's mitigation efforts.[26] Second, it fails to include legal obligations determining specific mitigation actions, means for coordinating individual contributions, and dates by which parties must achieve their emissions peaks.[27] Third, it lacks robust mechanisms for monitoring the implementation of the parties' pledges and helping developing countries leapfrog into the renewable energy transition as well as tools to punish those that do not comply with its provisions. The agreement also fails to include any reference to the end of fossil fuel subsidies. Reaching the 1.5 °C and 2 °C targets of the Paris Agreement requires parties to raise their current level of ambition by five and three times, respectively,[28] and even full implementation of all unconditional pledges and targets made under the agreement would limit warming to nearly 3 °C by the end of the century,[29] placing the planet at

25. United Nations. *Paris Agreement*. 12 December 2015.
26. Keohane, Robert. O; Oppenheimer, Michael. "Paris: Beyond the Climate Dead End Through Pledge and Review?" In *Politics and Governance*. Vol. 4, No. 3, 2016, 142-151. DOI: 10.17645/pag.v4i3.634.
27. Christoff, Peter. "The Promissory Note: COP 21 and the Paris Climate Agreement." In *Environmental Politics*. Vol. 25, No. 5, 2016, 765-787. DOI: 10.1080/09644016.2016.1191818.
28. UNEP. *The Emissions Gap Report 2018*. Nairobi, 2018.
29. CAT. *"The CAT Thermometer."* 2018 [Consulted at: 19 February 2019]. Available at: https://climateactiontracker.org/global/cat-thermometer/.

a potentially catastrophic level of climate change.[30] Two-thirds of major emitting parties are currently not even on track to meet their NDCs.[31] It is worth noting that successful pledge and review relies on peer and public pressure. Consequently, transparency is essential.[32] Nevertheless, the agreement's transparency framework is weak.[33] In light of all limitations, it seems highly unlikely that the Paris Agreement can provide an adequate response to the global climate crisis.

Climate Change Politics and Policies in the Atlantic

The US, the EU, and Brazil are among the world's seven largest emitters, accounting for 13.1%, 9.0%, and 2.4%, respectively, of the global GHG emissions in 2017.[34] A high level of commitment to low carbon development by these Atlantic actors is a *sine qua non* condition for any successful response to the climate crisis. Nevertheless, the US and Brazil have predominantly been laggards in global climate governance, while the EU, although by far the most reformist climate power in negotiations, is under growing pressure to relinquish its long-standing commitment to sustainable development.

The US

Climate change mitigation has long been a contentious issue in the US. As a result, the country has no comprehensive climate legislation at the

30. Xu, Yangyang; Veerabhadran, Ramanathan. "Well Below 2 °C: Mitigation Strategies for Avoiding Dangerous to Catastrophic Climate Changes." In *Proceedings of the National Academy of Sciences*. Vol. 114, No. 39, 2017, 10315-10323. DOI: 10.1073/pnas.1618481114.
31. Kuramochi, Takeshi [et al.]. *Greenhouse Gas Mitigation Scenarios for Major Emitting Countries. Analysis of Current Climate Policies and Mitigation Commitments: 2018 Update*. Cologne: New Climate Institute, 2018.
32. Bodansky, Daniel. "The Paris Climate Change Agreement: A New Hope?" In *American Journal of International Law*. Vol. 110, No. 2, 2016, 288-239. DOI: 10.5305/amerjintelaw.110.2.0288.
33. Keohane, Robert. O; Oppenheimer, Michael. "Paris: Beyond the Climate Dead End Through Pledge and Review?" In *Politics and Governance*. Vol. 4, No. 3, 2016, 142-151. DOI: 10.17645/pag.v4i3.634.
34. Olivier, Jos G. J.; Peters, Jeroen A. H. W. *Trends in Global CO2 and Total Greenhouse Gas Emissions: 2018 Report*. The Hague: PBL Netherlands Environmental Assessment Agency.

federal level, "but rather a patchwork of different policies spread unevenly across states, sectors, and levels of governance."[35]

In the 1990s, although the Bill Clinton-Al Gore administration was committed to make climate change mitigation a policy priority and has largely influenced the design of the Kyoto Protocol—in particular with regard to the flexibility mechanisms, an American demand for joining the protocol—strong domestic opposition led the president to sign the treaty but not send it to the Senate for ratification.[36] The oil, coal, gas, automotive, and manufacturing industries, powerful interest groups, feared the potentially harmful effects of climate change mitigation policies, and their concerns were supported by legislators. In July 1997, the American Senate passed the Byrd-Hagel resolution, refusing ratification of any climate treaty that did not contain emissions reduction obligations for fast-growing developing countries, or that could damage the US economy.[37] In March 2001, the new president, George W. Bush, whose intentions of increasing fossil fuel supply were inconsistent with the protocol's provisions, withdrew the US from the Kyoto agreement, evoking the Byrd-Hagel resolution and the California energy crisis to support his decision.[38]

President Barack Obama, elected in 2008, although determined to break with the legacy of his predecessor and make the US a leader in global climate governance, was limited by the American domestic institutions and circumstances. During his first term, Obama had to face not only resistance by the hydrocarbon lobbies and the Senate, but also the financial crisis affecting the country, which exacerbated political neglect of climate issues and weakened public support for climate action. At the Copenhagen meetings of 2009, the new president was forced to continue the main lines of the Bush-era climate policy, i.e., opposition to any treaty imposing targets and timetables on the US and exempting major developing country emitters

35. European Parliament. *U.S. Climate Change Policy*. IP/A/ENVI/2015-02, April 2015, p 15.
36. Depledge, Joanna. "Against the Grain: The United States and the Global Climate Change Regime." In *Global Change, Peace & Security*. Vol. 17, No. 1, 2005, 11-27. DOI: 10.1080=0951274052000319337.
37. Hovi, Jon; Sprinz, Detlef F.; Bang, Guri. "Why the United States Did Not Become a Party to the Kyoto Protocol: German, Norwegian, and US Perspectives." In *European Journal of International Relations*. Vol. 18, No. 1, 2010, 129-150. DOI: 10.1177/1354066110380964.
38. Lisowski, Michael. "Playing the Two-level Game: US President Bush's Decision to Repudiate the Kyoto Protocol." In *Environmental Politics*. Vol. 11, No. 4, 2002, 101-119. DOI: 10.1080/714000641.

from emissions cuts.[39] The system of voluntary pledges that emerged with the Copenhagen Accord was in part a reflection of the domestic constraints facing Obama. During his second term, climate change was knocked off the political agenda by more imminent issues like the federal budget, gun control, and immigration, and external challenges such as terrorism and North Korea's nuclear threat.[40]

However, the Obama administration was, despite all challenges, able to pursue a large set of climate initiatives. These included new investments in renewable energy and energy efficiency, regulations to cut air pollution and mitigate climate change, as well as stable flows of climate finance to support the mitigation and adaptation efforts of developing countries. To implement their climate agenda, Obama and his cabinet members shifted from "climate change" rhetoric to a clean energy and energy independence discourse,[41] made extensive use of executive power, partnered with climate-friendly state governments,[42] and took advantage of existing laws,[43] a strategy that proved key to initiate regulation of GHG emissions in the US.

"Behind the administration's silent front on climate change, the EPA [the country's Environmental Protection Agency] quietly developed a regulatory system."[44] In 2009, following a 2007 Supreme Court decision (*Massachusetts v. Environmental Protection Agency*) declaring that GHGs fit within the 1970 Clean Air Act definition of air pollutants, and that the EPA has the authority and obligation to determine whether GHGs represent a danger to public health and welfare as well as to proceed with regulation if it concludes that they do, the agency published an endangerment finding

39. Christoff, Peter. "Cold Climate in Copenhagen: China and the United States at COP15." In *Environmental Politics*. Vol. 19, No. 4, 2010, 637-656. DOI: 10.1080/09644016.2010.489718.
40. European Parliament. *U.S. Climate Change Policy*. IP/A/ENVI/2015-02, April 2015.
41. Kincaid, Graciela; Roberts, J. Timmons. "No Talk, Some Walk: Obama Administration First-Term Rhetoric on Climate Change and US International Climate Budget Commitments." In *Global Environmental Politics*. Vol. 13, No. 4, 2013, 41-60. DOI: 10.1162/GLEP_a_00197.
42. Konisky, David M.; Woods, Neal D. "Environmental Policy, Federalism, and the Obama Presidency." In *Publius: The Journal of Federalism*. Vol. 46, No. 3, 2016, 366-391. DOI: 10.1093/publius/pjw004.
43. Farber, Daniel A. "U.S. Climate Policy. Obama, Trump, and Beyond." In *Revista de Estudos Constitucionais, Hermenêutica e Teoria do Direito*. Vol. 10, No. 2, 2018, 95-108. DOI: 10.4013/rechtd.2018.102.01.
44. Kincaid, Graciela; Roberts, J. Timmons. "No Talk, Some Walk: Obama Administration First-Term Rhetoric on Climate Change and US International Climate Budget Commitments." In *Global Environmental Politics*. Vol. 13, No. 4, 2013, 41-60. DOI: 10.1162/GLEP_a_00197, 47.

on GHGs.[45] EPA started by setting GHG standards in the transportation sector.[46] Using the Clean Air Act to regulate GHG emissions "was a relatively straightforward issue legally in terms of vehicle emissions."[47] In 2015, the agency released the Clean Power Plan, a regulation aiming to limit carbon dioxide emissions from coal-fired power plants by 32% below 2005 levels by 2030.[48] Opponents have, nevertheless, worked to weaken the plan's content and delay its implementation. The plan would be repealed by Obama's successor.[49]

In the months preceding the Paris meetings, Obama worked to improve cooperation with Chinese president, Xi Jinping.[50] In November 2014, both presidents announced a bilateral climate accord. In Paris, the US assumed a leadership role. Obama personally lobbied the Chinese and Indian leaders, and partnered with the EU and its allies.[51] However, to avoid congressional gridlock, the American president was forced to shape the Paris Agreement in such a way that it would not require ratification at home, thus contributing to weaken the treaty's final text.[52]

Under the Paris agreement, the US pledged to cut emissions by 26-28% below 2005 levels by 2025, including land use, land-use change, and forestry (LULUCF). However, in June 2017, Obama's successor, Donald Trump, announced that the US would withdraw from the treaty, describing

45. Duffy, Philip B. [et al.]. "Strengthened Scientific Support for the Endangerment Finding for Atmospheric Greenhouse Gases." In *Science*. Vol. 363, No. 6427, 2019. DOI: 10.1126/science.aat5982.
46. Freeman, Jody. "Climate and Energy Policy in the Obama Administration." In *Pace Environmental Law Review*. Vol. 30, No. 1, 2012, 375-390.
47. Farber, Daniel A. "U.S. Climate Policy. Obama, Trump, and Beyond." In *Revista de Estudos Constitucionais, Hermenêutica e Teoria do Direito*. Vol. 10, No. 2, 2018, 95-108. DOI: 10.4013/rechtd.2018.102.01., 99.
48. Konisky, David M.; Woods, Neal D. "Environmental Policy, Federalism, and the Obama Presidency." In *Publius: The Journal of Federalism*. Vol. 46, No. 3, 2016, 366-391. DOI: 10.1093/publius/pjw004.
49. Union of Concerned Scientists. *"The Clean Power Plan."* 2018 [Consulted at: 1 March 2019]. Available at: https://www.ucsusa.org/our-work/global-warming/reduce-emissions/what-is-the-clean-power-plan#bf-toc-3.
50. Parker, Charles F.; Karlsson, Christer. "The UN Climate Change Negotiations and the Role of the United States: Assessing American Leadership from Copenhagen to Paris." In *Environmental Politics*. Vol. 27, No. 3, 2018, 519-540. DOI: 10.1080/09644016.2018.1442388.
51. Dimitrov, Radoslav S. "The Paris Agreement on Climate Change: Behind Closed Doors." In *Global Environmental Politics*. Vol. 16, No. 3, 2016, 1-11. DOI: 10.1162/GLEP_a_00361.
52. Schreurs, Miranda A. "The Paris Climate Agreement and the Three Largest Emitters: China, the United States, and the European Union." In *Politics and Governance*. Vol. 4. No. 3, 2016, 219-223. DOI: 10.17645/pag.v4i3.666.

it as "an agreement that disadvantages the United States to the exclusive benefit of other countries."[53] The new administration has halted all implementation of the climate deal; dismantled national climate policies and institutions; adopted a pro-fossil fuel energy policy; cut the federal budget on climate change research; and reneged on a \$2 billion pledge to assist developing countries in their mitigation and adaptation efforts.[54] EPA has proposed to replace the Clean Power Plan with the Affordable Clean Energy rule, whose impact may be worse than having no climate plan at all.[55] The Obama administration's NDC was inconsistent with holding warming to < 2 °C—if all parties followed this level of ambition, the planet would potentially warm between 2 °C and 3 °C by the end of the century. US current policies, if taken as a benchmark by all parties, could lead to warming of > 4 °C by 2100.[56]

If a new president committed to climate change mitigation takes office in 2021, the impact of Trump's policies is probably manageable and may be partially reversed. Several state governments and cities as well as businesses and investors are taking climate action, and the courts have already slowed down the Trump administration's efforts to undo climate regulations.[57] Moreover, the shale gas revolution that began in 2007 in the country is building a new energy economy. It lowered energy costs and is driving a shift from coal in the power sector.[58] In the low-carbon field, technological progress has been such that the economic case for green en-

---

53. White House. "*Statement by President Trump on the Paris Climate Accord.*" 2017 [Consulted at: 1 March 2019]. Available at: https://www.whitehouse.gov/briefings-statements/statement-president-trump-paris-climate-accord/.

54. Hongyuan, Yu. "The U.S. Withdrawal from the Paris Agreement." In *China Quarterly of International Strategic Studies*. Vol. 4, No. 2, 2018, 281-300. DOI: 10.1142/S2377740018500100.; Jotzo, Frank; Depledge, Joanna; Winkler, Harald. "US and International Climate Policy under President Trump." In *Climate Policy*. Vol. 18, No. 7, 2018, 813-817. DOI: 10.1080/14693062.2018.1490051.; Curtin, Joseph. "*Trump Has Officially Ruined Climate Change Diplomacy for Everyone.*" In Foreign Policy. 2018 [Consulted at: 19 February 2019]. Available at: https://foreignpolicy.com/2018/12/12/trump-has-officially-ruined-climate-change-diplomacy-for-everyone/.

55. See Keyes, Amelia T. [et al.]. "The Affordable Clean Energy Rule and the Impact of Emissions Rebound on Carbon Dioxide and Criteria Air Pollutant Emissions." In *Environmental Research Letters*. 2019. DOI: 10.1088/1748-9326/aafe25.

56. CAT. "*Country Summary: USA.*" 2018 [Consulted at: 19 February 2019]. Available at: https://climateactiontracker.org/countries/usa/.

57. Aldy, Joseph E. "Real World Headwinds for Trump Climate Change Policy." In *Bulletin of the Atomic Scientists*. Vol. 73, No. 6, 2017, 376-381. DOI: 10.1080/00963402.2017.1388673.

58. Weiss, Barbara; Obi, Michiyo. *Environmental Risk Mitigation: Coaxing a Market in the Battery and Energy Supply and Storage Industry.* Cham: Palgrave Macmillan, 2016.

ergy is becoming ever stronger.[59] Within this context, projections suggest that the country's emissions will most likely remain flat in the near-term. Nevertheless, if the president is reelected in 2020, the consequences will be far more damaging.[60]

Trump's withdrawal from the Paris Agreement has triggered a global wave of criticism. Many world leaders have expressed their intention to continue their own climate commitments.[61] However, considering the urgency in decarbonizing the global economy, non-participation of a major emitter is problematic. It is also worth noting that US non-cooperation in raising climate finance may severely compromise multilateral efforts to address climate change,[62] and that reluctant parties may reduce their levels of ambition and compliance as a reaction to the country's withdrawal.[63]

The EU

The EU has been the most active and committed actor in global climate governance, firmly advocating binding international agreements and establishing its own binding emissions reduction targets.[64] The bloc's climate activism is driven by: a) its belief in multilateralism and international law; b) early adoption of the precautionary principle[65] and commitment to sustainable development; c) conviction in the propositions of ecological modernization;[66] d) economic interest in obtaining a competitive advantage

---

59. Jotzo, Frank; Depledge, Joanna; Winkler, Harald. "US and International Climate Policy under President Trump." In *Climate Policy*. Vol. 18, No. 7, 2018, 813-817. DOI: 10.1080/14693062.2018.1490051.

60. Galik, Christopher S.; Decarolis, Joseph F.; Fell, Harrison. "Evaluating the US Mid-Century Strategy for Deep Decarbonization Amidst Early Century Uncertainty." In *Climate Policy*. Vol. 17, No. 8, 2017, 1046-1056. DOI: doi.org/10.1080/14693062.2017.1340257.

61. Betsill, Michele M. "Trump's Paris Withdrawal and the Reconfiguration of Global Climate Change Governance." In *Chinese Journal of Population Resources and Environment*. Vol. 15, No. 3, 2017, 189-191. DOI: 10.1080/10042857.2017.1343908.

62. Urpelainen, Johannes; Van De Graaf, Thijs. "United States Non-cooperation and the Paris Agreement." In *Climate Policy*. Vol. 18. No. 7, 2018, 839-851. DOI: 10.1080/14693062.2017.1406843.

63. Pickering, Jonathan [et al.]. "The Impact of the US Retreat from the Paris Agreement: Kyoto Revisited?" In *Climate Policy*. Vol. 18, No. 7, 2018, 818-827. DOI: 10.1080/14693062.2017.1412934.

64. Schreurs, Miranda A. "The Paris Climate Agreement and the Three Largest Emitters: China, the United States, and the European Union." In *Politics and Governance*. Vol. 4. No. 3, 2016, 219-223. DOI: 10.17645/pag.v4i3.666.

65. The precautionary principle enables decision makers to take preventive action against possible risk of severe and irreversible damage.

66. The ecological modernization theory suggests that economic and ecological concerns are complementary. The concept "implies that it is possible, through the development

on renewable energy technologies and becoming less dependent on fossil fuels, and need to improve energy security; e) concern with "threat multiplier" climate change;[67] and (f) citizens wide support for climate action.[68]

The early members of the bloc soon demonstrated their commitment to solving the problem. In 1989, at a high level meeting on the issue, most European countries agreed that climate change should be addressed by setting emissions reduction targets and timetables.[69] In 1990, the European Community announced its intention of pursing efforts to stabilize carbon emissions by 2000 with respect to 1990 levels.[70] During negotiations of the Kyoto Protocol, the EU proposed emissions cuts of 15% below 1990 levels for Annex I parties, and opposed flexibility mechanisms, arguing, unsuccessfully, that emissions reductions should be achieved mostly though domestic action.[71] In the post-Kyoto years, it adopted an inflexible bargaining approach, refusing the unlimited use of flexibility mechanisms under the protocol—a demand by the Umbrella Group (a coalition including Australia, Canada, Japan, New Zealand, Norway, the Russian Federation, Ukraine, and the US).[72] In 2000, agreement on how to operationalize the Kyoto Protocol's mechanisms failed mainly due to a severe rift between the US and the EU.[73]

---

of new and integrated technologies, to reduce the consumption of raw materials, as well as the emissions of various pollutants, while at the same time creating innovative and competitive products." See Andersen, Mikael S.; Massa, Ilmo. "Ecological Modernization. Origins, Dilemmas and Future Directions." In *Journal of Environmental Policy & Planning*. Vol. 2, No. 4, 2000, 337-345. DOI: doi.org/10.1080/714852820, 337.

67. The effects of climate change exacerbate existing frailties and sources of conflict (e.g., poverty, food and water scarcity, political instability, and social tensions), and may induce mass migration, thus destabilizing entire regions of the world.

68. Van Schaik, Louise G.; Schunz, Simon. "Explaining EU Activism and Impact in Global Climate Politics: Is the Union a Norm- or Interest-Driven Actor?" In *JCMS: Journal of Common Market Studies*. Vol. 50, No. 1, 2012, 169-186. DOI: 10.1111/j.1468-5965.2011.02214.x.

69. Bodansky, Daniel. "The History of the Global Climate Change Regime." In *International Relations and Global Climate Change*. London and Cambridge: The MIT Press, 2001, 23-40.

70. Gupta, Joyeeta. *The History of Global Climate Governance*. Cambridge and New York: Cambridge University Press, 2014.

71. Bodansky, Daniel. "The History of the Global Climate Change Regime." In *International Relations and Global Climate Change*. London and Cambridge: The MIT Press, 2001, 23-40.

72. Afionis, Stavros. *The European Union in International Climate Change Negotiations*. London and New York: Routledge, 2017.

73. Grubb, Michael; Farhana, Yamin. "Climatic Collapse at The Hague: What Happened, Why, and Where Do We Go From Here?" In *International Affairs*. Vol. 77, No. 2, 2001, 261-276. DOI: doi.org/10.1111/1468-2346.00191.

After the US withdrawal from the protocol, the EU made substantial efforts outside the climate change regime to ensure that Kyoto would enter into force. To guarantee ratification by the remaining Annex I country parties, it had to make several concessions, including no limits on the use of flexible mechanisms and watered-down accounting rules. In 2004, the EU secured Russian ratification of the protocol by agreeing on supporting the country's entrance into the World Trade Organization.[74]

Under the protocol, the EU committed to reduce its emissions by 8%. A "burden sharing" agreement among its then-15 members was negotiated, allowing less developed members states to grow economically and increase their emissions, while the richer, more environmentally progressive members states made quite significant reductions. Nevertheless, the European leaders soon acknowledged that national efforts combined would be insufficient to achieve the emissions reduction targets required under Kyoto, and developed an internal emissions trading system (ETS),[75] which was adopted in 2003. Its first (pilot) phase began in 2005.[76]

When international negotiations for the post-Kyoto era started in 2007, the EU, based on the latest scientific findings on climate change and aiming to persuade parties to adopt emissions targets compatible with the goal of limiting global warming to 2 °C,[77] pressed for emissions reductions of 25-40% by 2020 for the developed world, and argued in favor of a new agreement including all countries in its mitigation effort, particularly fast-growing developing economies, namely China, India, Brazil, and South Africa.[78] The European leaders also set their climate and energy targets for 2020: a 20% cut in GHG emissions from 1990 levels, excluding LULUCF (a target that the block is very close to achieve); a 20% improve-

---

74. Van Schaik, Louise G.; Schunz, Simon. "Explaining EU Activism and Impact in Global Climate Politics: Is the Union a Norm- or Interest-Driven Actor?" In *JCMS: Journal of Common Market Studies*. Vol. 50, No. 1, 2012, 169-186. DOI: 10.1111/j.1468-5965.2011.02214.x.

75. See https://ec.europa.eu/clima/policies/ets_en.

76. Rayner, Tim; Jordan, Andrew. "Climate Change Policy in the European Union." In *Oxford Research Encyclopedia of Climate Science*. Oxford University Press. DOI: 10.1093/acrefore/9780190228620.013.47.

77. Gippner, Olivia. "The 2 °C Target: A European Norm Enters the International Stage. Following the Process to Adoption in China." In *International Environmental Agreements: Politics, Law and Economics*. Vol. 16, No. 1, 2016, 49-65. DOI: 10.1007/s10784-014-9246-5.

78. Walker, Hayley; Biedenkopf, Katja. "The Historical Evolution of EU Climate Leadership and Four Scenarios for its Future." In *EU Climate Diplomacy: Politics, Law and Negotiations*. Abingdon and New York: Routledge, 2018, 33-45.

ment in energy efficiency; and a 20% of total energy consumption coming from renewables. These would be enacted in legislation in 2009.[79]

At the Copenhagen meetings, the EU, pursuing a heavily normative agenda and urging for a single-top down binding global agreement containing highly ambitious emissions reduction targets and rigid timetables, would find itself isolated[80] — the Copenhagen Accord's final text was discussed behind closed doors by the US, China, India, Brazil, and South Africa. After the meetings, the European diplomacy recognized its failure and improved its strategy, significantly moderating its climate policy objectives. The EU abandoned its argument for a new climate treaty modelled on Kyoto; engaged in dialogue with the US and China; partnered with developing country parties that also wished for a legally binding agreement including all major emitters; and accepted a second commitment period for the Kyoto Protocol in exchange for the adoption of a roadmap towards a new global climate treaty including all parties to be adopted in 2015.[81]

In 2014, the EU set a new goal of building an Energy Union[82] and approved the "2030 framework for climate change and energy policies", putting forward a binding target of reducing GHG emissions by at least 40% below 1990 levels by 2030 (including LULUCF); a binding target of generating no less than 27% of energy from renewable resources; a non-binding target of improving energy efficiency by at least 27%; and an electricity connection target of 10% among member states.[83] The goals for renewables and energy efficiency were revised upwards in 2018 to 32%

79. https://ec.europa.eu/clima/policies/strategies/2020_en.
80. Oberthür, Sebastian. "The European Union's Performance in the International Climate Change Regime." In *Journal of European Integration*. Vol. 33, No. 6, 2011, 667-682. DOI: 10.1080/07036337.2011.606690.
81. Backstränd, Karin; Elgström, Ole. "The EU's Role in Climate Change Negotiations: From Leader to 'Leadiator'." In *Journal of European Public Policy*. Vol. 20, No. 10, 2013, 1369-1386. DOI: 10.1080/13501763.2013.781781.
82. See https://ec.europa.eu/energy/en/topics/energy-strategy-and-energy-union/building-energy-union and Delbeke, Jos; Klaaseen, Ger; Zapfel, Peter. "Climate-related Energy Policies." In *EU Climate Policy Explained*. Abingdon and New York: Routledge. Many energy issues are still decided at the domestic level, in contrast to environmental policy. The Lisbon Treaty explicitly asserts that the EU's energy policy shall not affect its member states' right to define the conditions for exploiting their energy resources; choice between different energy sources; and the general structure of their energy supply.
83. Averchenkova, Alina [et al.]. *Climate Policy in China, the European Union and the United States: Main Drivers and Prospects for the Future*. Grantham Research Institute on Climate Change and the Environment, Centre for Climate Change Economics and Policy, and Bruegel, 2019.

and 32.5%, respectively.[84] The emissions reduction target became the basis for the EU's NDC under the Paris Agreement.

At the Paris climate meetings of 2015, the EU, having learned the lesson from Copenhagen, continued to pursue moderate policy objectives:

> instead of insisting on emission reduction commitments by all countries in line with the 2 °C target, the EU moved to demand firm provisions on transparency and accountability as well as an 'ambitious mechanism'. (…) It also eventually gave up on agreeing detailed rules for transparency and accountability already in Paris.[85]

As the world's largest provider of official development assistance and climate finance to developing countries, and having downscaled its demands, the EU was able to encourage and lead an influential coalition (the "High Ambition Coalition") of small island states, developing countries, and like-minded parties,[86] which was critical in helping to ensure China and India's support for the new climate agreement.[87]

Continued EU leadership will be essential to raise the global level of climate change mitigation ambition. "Effective leadership demands credibility and the ability to convince prospective followers that one is acting on behalf of the common good."[88] More ambition by the European leaders is needed. The EU's pledge under the Paris Agreement is inconsistent with holding warming to < 2 °C—if all parties followed this level of ambition, the planet would potentially warm between 2 °C and 3 °C by the end of the century. In 2018, the European Parliament called for the adoption of a new emissions reduction target of 55% below 1990 levels by 2030. This would, however, still be insufficient to achieve the temperature goal of the

---

84. https://ec.europa.eu/clima/policies/strategies/2030_en
85. Oberthür, Sebastian; Groen, Lisanne. "Explaining Goal Achievement in International Negotiations: The EU and the Paris Agreement on Climate Change." In *Journal of European Public Policy*. Vol. 25, No. 5, 2018, 708-727. DOI: 10.1080/13501763.2017.1291708, 719.
86. Rayner, Tim; Jordan, Andrew. "Climate Change Policy in the European Union." In *Oxford Research Encyclopedia of Climate Science*. Oxford University Press. DOI: 10.1093/acrefore/9780190228620.013.47.
87. Dimitrov, Radoslav S. "The Paris Agreement on Climate Change: Behind Closed Doors." In *Global Environmental Politics*. Vol. 16, No. 3, 2016, 1-11. DOI: 10.1162/GLEP_a_00361.
88. Parker, Charles F.; Karlsson, Christer. *"EU Climate Leadership in Katowice Helped Deliver the Deal on the Paris Agreement Rulebook."* 2018 [Consulted at: 19 February 2019]. Available at: https://blogs.lse.ac.uk/europpblog/2018/12/20/eu-climate-leadership-in-katowice-helped-deliver-the-deal-on-the-paris-agreement-rulebook/.

agreement.[89] In addition, it is uncertain whether the block is on track to meet its NDC.[90] The EU has been under growing pressure to abandon its commitment to low carbon development and leadership role in climate negotiations. Among the challenges to ambitious and assertive action by the EU in this domain are resistance by the coal-dependent Eastern EU members; the rise of populism as a result of public discontent with socio-economic inequalities, security fears, and sharp reactions against African and Middle Eastern immigrants; Germany's struggle to phase out coal; and the unsolved Brexit negotiations.[91] Nevertheless, despite all challenges the EU "remains the only actor that can realistically be expected to provide leadership on global environmental problems for the coming decade or two."[92]

Brazil

Brazil is an "underachieving environmental power"—despite its vast natural capital (forests, biodiversity, water, and low carbon energy potential), as an environmental power the country remains underdeveloped due to its low socioeconomic capital, i.e., an economic and political system overly focused on narrow, short-term goals of vested interests that repeatedly collide with the needs of sustainability.[93]

In 1992, as host of the United Nations Conference on Environment and Development, and led by President Fernando Collor de Mello, who saw the event as an opportunity to project his government internationally and

89. CAT. *"Country Summary: EU."* 2019 [Consulted 19 February 2019]. Available at: https://climateactiontracker.org/countries/eu/.
90. Kuramochi, Takeshi [et al.]. *Greenhouse Gas Mitigation Scenarios for Major Emitting Countries. Analysis of Current Climate Policies and Mitigation Commitments: 2018 Update.* Cologne: New Climate Institute, 2018.
91. Clémençon, Raymond. "The Two Sides of the Paris Climate Agreement: Dismal Failure or Historic Breakthrough?" In *Journal of Environment & Development.* Vol. 25, No. 1, 2016, 3-24. DOI: 10.1177/1070496516631362.; Parker, Charles F.; Karlsson, Christer. *"EU Climate Leadership in Katowice Helped Deliver the Deal on the Paris Agreement Rulebook."* 2018 [Consulted at: 19 February 2019]. Available at: https://blogs.lse.ac.uk/europpblog/2018/12/20/eu-climate-leadership-in-katowice-helped-deliver-the-deal-on-the-paris-agreement-rulebook/; Schreurs, Miranda A. "The Paris Climate Agreement and the Three Largest Emitters: China, the United States, and the European Union." In *Politics and Governance.* Vol. 4. No. 3, 2016, 219-223. DOI: 10.17645/pag.v4i3.666.
92. Clémençon, Raymond. "Sustainable Development, Climate Politics and EU-Leadership: A Historical-Comparative Analysis." In *European Journal of Sustainable Development.* Vol. 5, No. 1, 2016, 125-144. DOI: 10.14207/ejsd.2016.v5n1p125., 139.
93. Viola, Eduardo; Franchini, Matías. *Brazil and Climate Change: Beyond the Amazon.* Abingdon and New York: Routledge, 2018.

attract foreign funding and investment, Brazil facilitated agreements on the UNFCCC.[94]

During negotiations of the Kyoto Protocol, the Brazilian diplomacy, grounded on a radical interpretation of the CBDRRC principle, firmly rejected any possibility of non-Annex I parties assuming emissions reduction obligations, even if voluntary, and stressed the historical responsibility of the developed world in creating the problem; advocated the right to development; and strongly refused the inclusion of LULUCF, particularly avoided deforestation, in the protocol's flexibility mechanisms.[95] The country's standing in negotiations stemmed from its emissions and climate policy profiles: very high emissions growing on an average of almost 10% per year, a trend mostly driven by very high rates of deforestation in the Amazon, and setbacks in the hydroelectricity and ethanol sectors leading to increased reliance on thermoelectric power plants.[96]

In the second half of the 2000s, Brazil progressively moderated its rigid interpretation of the CBDRRC principle and began to shift away from its historical international positions regarding forests under the climate change regime.[97] Considerably reducing deforestation between 2005 and 2012, the country's overall emissions fell by more than 40%.[98] In fact, in the 2005-2009 period—mainly due to the vigorous action of the two ministers of the environment of the governments of President Lula da Silva, Marina Silva (2003-2008) and Carlos Minc (2008-2010), renowned Brazilian environmentalists—reducing deforestation in the Amazon was a political priority for the Brazilian government.[99] Between 2010 and 2012, the federal government's main goal was to avoid a new increase in deforestation rates.

94. Viola, Eduardo. "O Regime Internacional de Mudança Climática e o Brasil." In *Revista Brasileira de Ciências Sociais*. Vol. 17, No. 50, 2002, 25-46. DOI: 10.1590/S0102-69092002000300003.
95. Viola, Eduardo; Franchini, Matías. "Climate Policy in Brazil: Public Awareness, Social Transformation and Emission Reductions." In *Feeling the Heat: The Politics of Climate Policy in Rapidly Industrializing Countries*. Hampshire: Palgrave Macmillan, 2012, 175-201. DOI: 10.1057/9780230374973.
96. Viola, Eduardo; Franchini, Matías. *Brazil and Climate Change: Beyond the Amazon*. Abingdon and New York: Routledge, 2018.
97. Pereira, Joana C. "Reducing Catastrophic Climate Risk by Revolutionizing the Amazon: Novel Pathways for Brazilian Diplomacy." In *Global Development and Climate Change: Market, Global Players and Empirical Evidence*. Cham: Springer, 2019, 189-218. DOI: 10.1007/978-3-030-02662-2_10.
98. Data from the Brazilian Greenhouse Gas Emissions Estimate System (SEEG), available at http://plataforma.seeg.eco.br/total_emission.
99. Viola, Eduardo. "Transformations in Brazilian Deforestation and Climate Policy Since 2005." In *Theoretical Inquiries in Law*. Vol. 14, No. 1, 2013, 109-124.

Indeed, the 2012 deforestation rate was nearly 84% lower than the 2004 peak.[100] This abrupt fall was the result of various factors: law enforcement and enhanced institutional capacity; substantial cooperation between the Amazon state governments and the national government; the creation of new and extensive national parks and conservation units; the emergence of coalitions among several stakeholders against the consumption of soy beans and beef produced in deforested areas; and greater influence by NGOs and the scientific community on the media.[101]

Encouraged by domestic success in deforestation control and pressured by the Ministry of Environment (MMA), environmental NGOs, and the business sector, Brazil began to assume a more active and committed role in climate change negotiations. In 2006, the Brazilian diplomacy proposed the creation of a global deforestation fund within the UNFCCC; over the following years, Brazil became a key supporter of the REDD+ mechanism.[102] The Amazon became an asset for attracting international climate financing. In 2008, the country released its National Climate Plan containing quantitative targets. At the Copenhagen climate meetings, Brazil submitted a relatively ambitious voluntary emissions reduction commitment (36-39% below the business-as-usual scenario for 2020, including LULUCF).[103] Nevertheless, the Brazilian diplomacy continued to stress the right to development and joined with countries such as China and India in opposing a legally binding climate treaty including emissions reduction obligations for Non-Annex I parties.[104]

In 2011, in a clear demonstration of the organizational robustness of the rural caucus representing the interests of the agribusiness sector, the Brazilian Congress approved a reform to the Forest Code, largely reducing environmental protections. The positive trend of deforestation reduction

---

100. Data from the Brazilian State Institute for Space Research (INPE), available at http://www.obt.inpe.br/prodes/dashboard/prodes-rates.html.
101. Pereira, Joana C. "Reducing Catastrophic Climate Risk by Revolutionizing the Amazon: Novel Pathways for Brazilian Diplomacy." In *Global Development and Climate Change: Market, Global Players and Empirical Evidence*. Cham: Springer, 2019, 189-218. DOI: 10.1007/978-3-030-02662-2_10.
102. Reducing emissions from deforestation and forest degradation and the role of conservation, sustainable management of forests and enhancement of forest carbon stocks in developing countries, a mechanism that emerged within the UNFCCC in 2005.
103. Viola, Eduardo; Franchini, Matías; Ribeiro, Thais Lemos. *Sistema Internacional de Hegemonia Conservadora: Governança Global e Democracia na Era da Crise Climática*. São Paulo: Annablume, 2013.
104. Viola, Eduardo; Franchini, Matías. "Brazilian Climate Politics 2005-2012: Ambivalence and Paradox." In *WIREs Climate Change*. Vol. 5, No. 5, 2014, 677-688. DOI: 10.1002/wcc.289.

would start to reverse in 2013.[105] The intensity of fossil fuel usage in the energy sector would also increase as a result of public investment in the oil sector, subsidies to gasoline and electricity prices, and tax exemptions conceded to the manufacturing sector.[106]

The political priority of the new president, Dilma Rousseff, was short-term GDP growth. Environmental conservation was overlooked by the new administration.[107] Environmental neglect was aggravated by economic and political turmoil: a profound economic recession and huge corruption scandals involving politicians, the country's oil and gas company, and several infrastructure firms have turned public and political attention away from sustainability matters, further reinforcing the capacity of the Agribusiness Parliamentary Force (APF) in the Congress to reverse environmental progress.[108]

Between 2016 and 2018, Rousseff's successor, Michel Temer, supported by a coalition of conservative/particularistic interests (among them, those of the agribusiness sector), took major measures against environmental protection in general and the Amazon in particular. The new president

> signed provisional acts, decrees, and laws that reduced the size of pro-
> tected areas in the [Amazon] forest, suspended the ratification of in-
> digenous lands, enabled land grabbers to legalize their holdings in the
> [Amazonian] region, and forgave billions of dollars in environmental
> fines and debts that farmers and ranchers owed the government. (…)
> [He also] released vast sums in pork-barrel allocations ("*emendas*") to
> selected federal deputies (…) as well as other expensive concessions.
> (…) The cost of Temer's *emendas* exacerbated cutbacks in science
> and environmental spending in Brazil (…)[,] affecting a key basis of
> public policies for nature conservation and sustainable development,

105. Pereira, Joana C. "Reducing Catastrophic Climate Risk by Revolutionizing the Amazon: Novel Pathways for Brazilian Diplomacy." In *Global Development and Climate
Change: Market, Global Players and Empirical Evidence*. Cham: Springer, 2019, 189-
218. DOI: 10.1007/978-3-030-02662-2_10.
106. Viola, Eduardo; Basso, Larissa. "Low Carbon Green Economy: Brazilian Policies
and Politics of Energy, 2003-2014." In *Handbook on Sustainability Transition and
Sustainable Peace*. Zurich: Springer International Publishing, 2016, 811-830. DOI:
10.1007/978-3-319-43884-9_38.
107. Viola, Eduardo; Franchini, Matías. *Brazil and Climate Change: Beyond the Amazon*.
Abingdon and New York: Routledge, 2018.
108. Pereira, Joana C. "Reducing Catastrophic Climate Risk by Revolutionizing the Amazon: Novel Pathways for Brazilian Diplomacy." In *Global Development and Climate
Change: Market, Global Players and Empirical Evidence*. Cham: Springer, 2019, 189-
218. DOI: 10.1007/978-3-030-02662-2_10.

that is, research on biodiversity (...) [and] critically weakening the (...) [MMA's] capacity to promote effective policies and to ensure the rule of law in the Amazonian region.[109]

Unsurprisingly, deforestation is increasing at an alarming pace—Amazonian deforestation rates in the 2016-2018 period were approximately 66% higher than the 2012 minimum of 4500 km^2.[110]

In international climate negotiations, Brazilian diplomacy has returned to its historical standing, adding that "the country has already done its part in terms of mitigation because of the decreasing path of emissions that began in the mid-2000s."[111]

Under the Paris Agreement, Brazil pledged to reduce its overall GHG emissions by 37% on 2005 levels by 2025, including LULUCF.[112] If taken as a benchmark by all parties, the country's NDC would potentially lead to warming between 2 °C and 3 °C by 2100.[113] Brazil is not even on track to meet its NDC.[114]

The future looks unpromising. Jair Bolsonaro, the country's new president in office since January 2019, has promise to open parts of the Amazon to mining and has already dismantled governmental divisions dedicated to climate change. The APF, which will continue to be very powerful during the 2019-2022 legislature, has already formalized its support to the president. Other reasons for concern include the fact that the MMA is now headed by Ricardo Salles, a lawyer with strong ties to the ruralists, and who was recently convicted for environmental fraud, as well as the fact that the

109. Pereira, Joana C.; Viola, Eduardo. "Catastrophic Climate Risk and Brazilian Amazonian Politics and Policies: A New Research Agenda." In *Global Environmental Politics*. Vol. 19, No. 2, 2019, 98-99. DOI: 10.1162/glep_a_00499.
110. Data from INPE, available at http://www.obt.inpe.br/prodes/dashboard/prodes-rates. html.
111. Viola, Eduardo; Franchini, Matías. *Brazil and Climate Change: Beyond the Amazon*. Abingdon and New York: Routledge, 2018, p. 156.
112. It is worth noting that "when assessing progress towards decarbonisation, the inclusion of LULUCF into an emissions reduction target has the potential to disguise increasing trends of energy and industrial emissions in the country concerned. For example, if LULUCF emissions have a strong decrease over a period of time, (...) the country's total net emissions may show decreasing trends even if its energy and industrial emissions are still increasing." See https://climateactiontracker.org/methodology/indc-ratings-and-lulucf/. Brazil is a noteworthy example of this issue.
113. CAT. *"Country Summary: Brazil."* 2018 [Consulted 19 February 2019]. Available at https://climateactiontracker.org/countries/brazil/.
114. Kuramochi, Takeshi [et al.]. *Greenhouse Gas Mitigation Scenarios for Major Emitting Countries*. Analysis of Current Climate Policies and Mitigation Commitments: 2018 Update. Cologne: New Climate Institute, 2018.

new Minister of Foreign Affairs is Ernesto Araújo, a climate change denier. Consequently, Brazil will most likely remain a laggard in global climate negotiations over the next few years.[115] However, if the anti-corruption and economic policies of Bolsonaro's government are successful, public attention to climate and forest issues might increase. If this is the case, it could be possible to retake the goals of the Brazilian NDC after 2022.

Conclusion

Climate change skepticism and denial in the US and Brazil and political constraints to assertive climate action and leadership by the EU are a threat to all humanity. The US, as the world's largest economy and second largest emitter, is a de facto veto player to any effective solution to the problem. Brazil accounts for almost 70% of the Amazon rainforest, a global carbon stock and tipping point of the Earth's climate system whose dieback may trigger a global climate catastrophe. Current Amazonian politics and policies put the ecological resilience of the forest in jeopardy.[116] The EU, although struggling to maintain is commitment to sustainable development, will most likely continue to be the most active actor in global climate governance. However, more ambition is needed. Leadership of Northern Europe is critical for a successful decarbonization coalition capable of galvanizing global climate action to emerge. It remains to be seen whether the EU's environmentally progressive member states have the strength to overcome resistance by the most conservative ones.

References

Afionis, Stavros. *The European Union in International Climate Change Negotiations*. London and New York: Routledge, 2017.

---

115. Pereira, Joana C.; Viola, Eduardo. "Catastrophic Climate Risk and Brazilian Amazonian Politics and Policies: A New Research Agenda." In *Global Environmental Politics*. Vol. 19, No. 2, 2019, 93-103. DOI: 10.1162/glep_a_00499.
116. See Pereira, Joana C. "Reducing Catastrophic Climate Risk by Revolutionizing the Amazon: Novel Pathways for Brazilian Diplomacy." In *Global Development and Climate Change: Market, Global Players and Empirical Evidence*. Cham: Springer, 2019, 189-218. DOI: 10.1007/978-3-030-02662-2_10; Pereira, Joana C.; Viola, Eduardo. "Catastrophic Climate Risk and Brazilian Amazonian Politics and Policies: A New Research Agenda." In *Global Environmental Politics*. Vol. 19, No. 2, 2019, 93-103. DOI: 10.1162/glep_a_00499.

Aldy, Joseph E. "Real World Headwinds for Trump Climate Change Policy." In *Bulletin of the Atomic Scientists*. Vol. 73, No. 6, 2017, 376-381. DOI: 10.1080/00963402.2017.1388673.

AMS. Explaining Extreme Events of 2017 from a Climate Perspective. In *Bulletin of the American Meteorological Society*. Vol. 99, No. 12, 2018.

Andersen, Mikael S.; Massa, Ilmo. "Ecological Modernization. Origins, Dilemmas and Future Directions." In *Journal of Environmental Policy & Planning*. Vol. 2, No. 4, 2000, 337-345. DOI: doi.org/10.1080/714852820.

Averchenkova, Alina [et al.]. *Climate Policy in China, the European Union and the United States: Main Drivers and Prospects for the Future*. Grantham Research Institute on Climate Change and the Environment, Centre for Climate Change Economics and Policy, and Bruegel, 2019.

Backstränd, Karin; Elgström, Ole. "The EU's Role in Climate Change Negotiations: From Leader to 'Leadiator'." In *Journal of European Public Policy*. Vol. 20, No. 10, 2013, 1369-1386. DOI: 10.1080/13501763.2013.781781.

Betsill, Michele M. "Trump's Paris Withdrawal and the Reconfiguration of Global Climate Change Governance." In *Chinese Journal of Population Resources and Environment*. Vol. 15, No. 3, 2017, 189-191. DOI: 10.1080/10042857.2017.1343908.

Bodansky, Daniel. "Targets and Timetables: Good Policy but Bad Politics?" In *Architectures for Agreement: Addressing Global Climate Change in the Post-Kyoto World*. Cambridge and New York: Cambridge University Press, 2007, 57-66.

Bodansky, Daniel. "The Copenhagen Climate Change Conference: A Postmortem." In *American Journal of International Law*. Vol. 104, No. 2, 2010, 230-240. DOI: 10.5305/amerjintelaw.104.2.0230.

Bodansky, Daniel. "The History of the Global Climate Change Regime." In *International Relations and Global Climate Change*. London and Cambridge: The MIT Press, 2001, 23-40.

Bodansky, Daniel. "The Paris Climate Change Agreement: A New Hope?" In *American Journal of International Law*. Vol. 110, No. 2, 2016, 288-239. DOI: 10.5305/amerjintelaw.110.2.0288.

CAT. *"Country Summary: Brazil."* 2018 [Consulted 19 February 2019]. Available at https://climateactiontracker.org/countries/brazil/.

CAT. *"Country Summary: EU."* 2019 [Consulted 19 February 2019]. Available at: https://climateactiontracker.org/countries/eu/.

CAT. *"Country Summary: USA."* 2018 [Consulted at: 19 February 2019]. Available at: https://climateactiontracker.org/countries/usa/.

CAT. *"The CAT Thermometer."* 2018 [Consulted at: 19 February 2019]. Available at: https://climateactiontracker.org/global/cat-thermometer/.

Christoff, Peter. "Cold Climate in Copenhagen: China and the United States at COP15." In *Environmental Politics*. Vol. 19, No. 4, 2010, 637-656. DOI: 10.1080/09644016.2010.489718.

Christoff, Peter. "The Promissory Note: COP 21 and the Paris Climate Agreement." In *Environmental Politics*. Vol. 25, No. 5, 2016, 765-787. DOI: 10.1080/09644016.2016.1191818.

Clémençon, Raymond. "Sustainable Development, Climate Politics and EU-Leadership: A Historical-Comparative Analysis." In *European Journal of Sustainable Development*. Vol. 5, No. 1, 2016, 125-144. DOI: 10.14207/ejsd.2016.v5n1p125.

Clémençon, Raymond. "The Two Sides of the Paris Climate Agreement: Dismal Failure or Historic Breakthrough?" In *Journal of Environment & Development*. Vol. 25, No. 1, 2016, 3-24. DOI: 10.1177/1070496516631362.

Curtin, Joseph. "Trump Has Officially Ruined Climate Change Diplomacy for Everyone." In *Foreign Policy*. 2018 [Consulted at: 19 February 2019]. Available at: https://foreignpolicy.com/2018/12/12/trump-has-officially-ruined-climate-change-diplomacy-for-everyone/.

Delbeke, Jos; Klaaseen, Ger; Zapfel, Peter. "Climate-related Energy Policies." In *EU Climate Policy Explained*. Abingdon and New York: Routledge, 2016.

Depledge, Joanna. "Against the Grain: The United States and the Global Climate Change Regime." In *Global Change, Peace & Security*. Vol. 17, No. 1, 2005, 11-27. DOI: 10.1080=0951274052000319337.

Depledge, Joanna; Yamin, Farhana. "The Global Climate-change Regime: A Defence." In *The Economics and Politics of Climate Change*. Oxford and New York: Oxford University Press, 2009, 433-453.

Dimitrov, Radoslav S. "The Paris Agreement on Climate Change: Behind Closed Doors." In *Global Environmental Politics*. Vol. 16, No. 3, 2016, 1-11. DOI: 10.1162/GLEP_a_00361.

Duffy, Philip B. [et al.]. "Strengthened Scientific Support for the Endangerment Finding for Atmospheric Greenhouse Gases." In *Science*. Vol. 363, No. 6427, 2019. DOI: 10.1126/science.aat5982.

European Parliament. *U.S. Climate Change Policy*. IP/A/ENVI/2015-02, April 2015.

Farber, Daniel A. "U.S. Climate Policy. Obama, Trump, and Beyond." In *Revista de Estudos Constitucionais, Hermenêutica e Teoria do Direito*. Vol. 10, No. 2, 2018, 95-108. DOI: 10.4013/rechtd.2018.102.01.

Freeman, Jody. "Climate and Energy Policy in the Obama Administration." In *Pace Environmental Law Review*. Vol. 30, No. 1, 2012, 375-390.

Galik, Christopher S.; Decarolis, Joseph F.; Fell, Harrison. "Evaluating the US Mid-Century Strategy for Deep Decarbonization Amidst Early Century Uncertainty." In *Climate Policy*. Vol. 17, No. 8, 2017, 1046-1056. DOI: doi.org/10.1080/14693062.2017.1340257.

Gippner, Olivia. "The 2 °C Target: A European Norm Enters the International Stage. Following the Process to Adoption in China." In *International Environmental Agreements: Politics, Law and Economics*. Vol. 16, No. 1, 2016, 49-65. DOI: 10.1007/s10784-014-9246-5.

Grubb, Michael; Farhana, Yamin. "Climatic Collapse at The Hague: What Happened, Why, and Where Do We Go From Here?" In *International Affairs*. Vol. 77, No. 2, 2001, 261-276. DOI: doi.org/10.1111/1468-2346.00191.

Gupta, Joyeeta. "Climate Change Governance: History, Future, and Triple loop Learning?" In *WIREs Climate Change*. Vol. 7, No. 2, 2016, 192-210. DOI: 10.1002/wcc.388.

Gupta, Joyeeta. *The History of Global Climate Governance*. Cambridge and New York: Cambridge University Press, 2014.

Hamilton, Daniel. *A New Atlantic Community: Generating Growth, Human Development and Security in the Atlantic Hemisphere*. Washington, DC: Center for Transatlantic Studies, 2014.

Hochstetler, Kathryn; Milkoreit, Manjana. "Emerging Powers in the Climate Negotiations: Shifting Identity Conceptions." In *Political Research Quarterly*. Vol. 67, No. 1, 2014, 224-235. DOI: 10.1177/1065912913510609.

Hongyuan, Yu. "The U.S. Withdrawal from the Paris Agreement." In *China Quarterly of International Strategic Studies*. Vol. 4, No. 2, 2018, 281-300. DOI: 10.1142/S2377740018500100.

Hovi, Jon; Sprinz, Detlef F.; Bang, Guri. "Why the United States Did Not Become a Party to the Kyoto Protocol: German, Norwegian, and US Perspectives." In *European Journal of International Relations*. Vol. 18, No. 1, 2010, 129-150. DOI: 10.1177/1354066110380964.

IPCC. *Global Warming of 1.5 °C: An IPCC Special Report on the impacts of global warming of 1.5 °C above pre-industrial levels and related global greenhouse gas emission pathways, in the context of strengthening the global response to the threat of climate change, sustainable development, and efforts to eradicate poverty*. Geneva: WMO, 2018.

Jotzo, Frank; Depledge, Joanna; Winkler, Harald. "US and International Climate Policy under President Trump." In *Climate Policy*. Vol. 18, No. 7, 2018, 813-817. DOI: 10.1080/14693062.2018.1490051.

Keohane, Robert. O; Oppenheimer, Michael. "Paris: Beyond the Climate Dead End Through Pledge and Review?" In *Politics and Governance*. Vol. 4, No. 3, 2016, 142-151. DOI: 10.17645/pag.v4i3.634.

Keyes, Amelia T. [et al.]. "The Affordable Clean Energy Rule and the Impact of Emissions Rebound on Carbon Dioxide and Criteria Air Pollutant Emissions." In *Environmental Research Letters*. 2019. DOI: 10.1088/1748-9326/aafe25.

Kincaid, Graciela; Roberts, J. Timmons. "No Talk, Some Walk: Obama Administration First-Term Rhetoric on Climate Change and US International Climate Budget Commitments." In *Global Environmental Politics*. Vol. 13, No. 4, 2013, 41-60. DOI: 10.1162/GLEP_a_00197.

Konisky, David M.; Woods, Neal D. "Environmental Policy, Federalism, and the Obama Presidency." In *Publius: The Journal of Federalism*. Vol. 46, No. 3, 2016, 366-391. DOI: 10.1093/publius/pjw004.

Kotschwar, Barbara. *North-South Rebalancing. The Role of Innovation, Technology Transfer, and Sharing of Best Practices*. Washington, DC: The German Marshall Fund of the United States.

Kuramochi, Takeshi [et al.]. *Greenhouse Gas Mitigation Scenarios for Major Emitting Countries*. Analysis of Current Climate Policies and Mitigation Commitments: 2018 Update. Cologne: New Climate Institute, 2018.

Lisowski, Michael. "Playing the Two-level Game: US President Bush's Decision to Repudiate the Kyoto Protocol." In *Environmental Politics*. Vol. 11, No. 4, 2002, 101-119. DOI: 10.1080/714000641.

Oberthür, Sebastian. "The European Union's Performance in the International Climate Change Regime." In *Journal of European Integration*. Vol. 33, No. 6, 2011, 667-682. DOI: 10.1080/07036337.2011.606690.

Oberthür, Sebastian; GROEN, Lisanne. "Explaining Goal Achievement in International Negotiations: The EU and the Paris Agreement on Climate Change." In *Journal of European Public Policy*. Vol. 25, No. 5, 2018, 708-727. DOI: 10.1080/13501763.2017.1291708.

Olivier, Jos G. J.; Peters, Jeroen A. H. W. *Trends in Global CO2 and Total Greenhouse Gas Emissions: 2018 Report*. The Hague: PBL Netherlands Environmental Assessment Agency, 2018.

Parker, Charles F.; Karlsson, Christer. "*EU Climate Leadership in Katowice Helped Deliver the Deal on the Paris Agreement Rulebook.*" 2018 [Consulted at: 19 February 2019]. Available at: https://blogs.lse.ac.uk/europpblog/2018/12/20/eu-climate-leadership-in-katowice-helped-deliver-the-deal-on-the-paris-agreement-rulebook/.

Parker, Charles F.; Karlsson, Christer. "The UN Climate Change Negotiations and the Role of the United States: Assessing American Leadership from Copenhagen to Paris." In *Environmental Politics*. Vol. 27, No. 3, 2018, 519-540. DOI: 10.1080/09644016.2018.1442388.

Parker, Charles F.; Karlsson, Christer; HJERPE, Mattias. "Assessing the European Union's Global Climate Change Leadership: From Copenhagen to the Paris Agreement." In *Journal of European Integration*. Vol. 39, No. 2, 2017, 239-252. DOI: 10.1080/07036337.2016.1275608.

Pelegry, Eloy A.; Isbell, Paul (Eds.). *The Future of Energy in the Atlantic Basin*. Washington, DC: The German Marshall Fund of the United States, 2012.

Pereira, Joana C. "Environmental Security in the Anthropocene." In *Security at a Crossroad: New Tools for New Challenges*. Nova Science Publishers, 2019, 35-54.

Pereira, Joana C. "Reducing Catastrophic Climate Risk by Revolutionizing the Amazon: Novel Pathways for Brazilian Diplomacy." In *Global Development and Climate Change: Market, Global Players and Empirical Evidence*. Cham: Springer, 2019, 189-218. DOI: 10.1007/978-3-030-02662-2_10.

Pereira, Joana C.; Viola, Eduardo. "Catastrophic Climate Change and Forest Tipping Points: Blind Spots in International Politics and Policy." In *Global Policy*. Vol. 9, No. 4, 2018, 513-524. DOI: 10.1111/1758-5899.12578.

Pereira, Joana C.; Viola, Eduardo. "Catastrophic Climate Risk and Brazilian Amazonian Politics and Policies: A New Research Agenda." In *Global Environmental Politics*. Vol. 19, No. 2, 2019, 93-103. DOI: 10.1162/glep_a_00499.

Pickering, Jonathan [et al.]. "The Impact of the US Retreat from the Paris Agreement: Kyoto Revisited?" In *Climate Policy*. Vol. 18, No. 7, 2018, 818-827. DOI: 10.1080/14693062.2017.1412934.

Rayner, Tim; Jordan, Andrew. "Climate Change Policy in the European Union." In *Oxford Research Encyclopedia of Climate Science*. Oxford University Press, 2016. DOI: 10.1093/acrefore/9780190228620.013.47.

Rosen, Amanda M. "The Wrong Solution at the Right Time: The Failure of the Kyoto Protocol on Climate Change." In *Politics & Policy*. Vol. 43, No. 1, 2015, 30-58. DOI: 10.1111/polp.12105.

Schreurs, Miranda A. "The Paris Climate Agreement and the Three Largest Emitters: China, the United States, and the European Union." In *Politics and Governance*. Vol. 4. No. 3, 2016, 219-223. DOI: 10.17645/pag.v4i3.666.

Unep. *The Emissions Gap Report 2018*. Nairobi, 2018.

UNFCCC. *Doha Amendment to the Kyoto Protocol*. 8 December 2012.

UNFCCC. *Report of the Conference of the Parties on its Fifteenth Session, held in Copenhagen from 7 to 19 December 2009*. FCCC/CP/2009/11/Add.1 of 30 March 2010.

UNFCCC. *Report of the Conference of the Parties on its Thirteenth Session, held in Bali from 3 to 15 December 2007*. FCCC/CP/2007/6/Add.1 of 14 March 2008.

Union Of Concerned Scientists. *"The Clean Power Plan."* 2018 [Consulted at: 1 March 2019]. Available at: https://www.ucsusa.org/our-work/global-warming/reduce-emissions/what-is-the-clean-power-plan#bf-toc-3.

United Nations. *Kyoto Protocol to the United Nations Framework Convention on Climate Change*. 11 December 1997.

United Nations. *Paris Agreement*. 12 December 2015.

United Nations. *United Nations Framework Convention on Climate Change*. FCCC/INFORMAL/84, 1992.

Urpelainen, Johannes; Van De Graaf, Thijs. "United States Non-cooperation and the Paris Agreement." In *Climate Policy*. Vol. 18. No. 7, 2018, 839-851. DOI: 10.1080/14693062.2017.1406843.

Van Schaik, Louise G.; Schunz, Simon. "Explaining EU Activism and Impact in Global Climate Politics: Is the Union a Norm- or Interest-Driven Actor?" In *JCMS: Journal of Common Market Studies*. Vol. 50, No. 1, 2012, 169-186. DOI: 10.1111/j.1468-5965.2011.02214.x.

Victor, David G. *Global Warming Gridlock: Creating More Effective Strategies for Protecting the Planet*. Cambridge and New York: Cambridge University Press, 2011.

Viola, Eduardo. "O Regime Internacional de Mudança Climática e o Brasil." In *Revista Brasileira de Ciências Sociais*. Vol. 17, No. 50, 2002, pp. 25-46. DOI: 10.1590/S0102-69092002000300003.

Viola, Eduardo. "Transformations in Brazilian Deforestation and Climate Policy Since 2005." In *Theoretical Inquiries in Law*. Vol. 14, No. 1, 2013, 109-124.

Viola, Eduardo; Basso, Larissa. "Low Carbon Green Economy: Brazilian Policies and Politics of Energy, 2003-2014." In *Handbook on Sustainability Transition and Sustainable Peace*. Zurich: Springer, 2016, 811-830. DOI: 10.1007/978-3-319-43884-9_38.

Viola, Eduardo; Franchini, Matías. "Brazilian Climate Politics 2005-2012: Ambivalence and Paradox." In *WIREs Climate Change*. Vol. 5, No. 5, 2014, 677-688. DOI: 10.1002/wcc.289.

Viola, Eduardo; Franchini, Matías. "Climate Policy in Brazil: Public Awareness, Social Transformation and Emission Reductions." In *Feeling the Heat: The Politics of Climate Policy in Rapidly Industrializing Countries*. Hampshire: Palgrave Macmillan, 2012, 175-201. DOI: 10.1057/9780230374973.

Viola, Eduardo; Franchini, Matías. *Brazil and Climate Change: Beyond the Amazon*. Abingdon and New York: Routledge, 2018.

Viola, Eduardo; Franchini, Matías; Ribeiro, Thais Lemos. *Sistema Internacional de Hegemonia Conservadora: Governança Global e Democracia na Era da Crise Climática*. São Paulo: Annablume, 2013.

Walker, Hayley; Biedenkopf, Katja. "The Historical Evolution of EU Climate Leadership and Four Scenarios for its Future." In *EU Climate Diplomacy: Politics, Law and Negotiations*. Abingdon and New York: Routledge, 2018, 33-45.

Weiss, Barbara; OBI, Michiyo. *Environmental Risk Mitigation: Coaxing a Market in the Battery and Energy Supply and Storage Industry*. Cham: Palgrave Macmillan, 2016.

WHITE HOUSE. *"Statement by President Trump on the Paris Climate Accord."* 2017 [Consulted at: 1 March 2019]. Available at: https://www.whitehouse.gov/briefings-statements/statement-president-trump-paris-climate-accord/.

WMO. *"The State of the Global Climate in 2018."* 2018 [Consulted at: 19 February 2019]. Available at: https://public.wmo.int/en/our-mandate/climate/wmo-statement-state-of-global-climate.

Xu, Yangyang; Veerabhadran, Ramanathan. "Well Below 2 °C: Mitigation Strategies for Avoiding Dangerous to Catastrophic Climate Changes." In *Proceedings of the National Academy of Sciences*. Vol. 114, No. 39, 2017, 10315-10323. DOI: 10.1073/pnas.1618481114.